SPONTANEOUS COMBUSTION

GRASS-ROOTS CHRISTIANITY, LATIN AMERICAN STYLE

Clayton L. ("Mike") Berg, Jr.
& Paul Pretiz

William Carey Library

PASADENA, CALIFORNIA

Published by
William Carey Library
P.O. Box 40129
Pasadena, California 91114
(818) 798-0819

In Cooperation With
Latin America Mission
Post Office Box 52-7900
Miami, Florida 33152-7900

Library of Congress Cataloging-in-Publication Data

Berg, Clayton L., 1928-
    Spontaneous combustion : grass roots Christianity, Latin American
Style / Clayton L. ("Mike") berg, Jr. & Paul E. Pretiz.
        p.   cm.
    Includes bibliographical references and index.
    ISBN 0-87808-265-4
    1. Protestant churches--Latin America--History--20th century.
2. Latin America--Church history--20th century. I. Pretiz, Paul E., 1926-
    II. Title.

BX4832.5.B47   1996   95-49639
278' . 082--dc20   CIP

Cover Art by Maryola Hylek

PRINTED IN THE UNITED STATES OF AMERICA

This book is dedicated with great gratitude to

EUGENE A. NIDA

whose noteworthy linguistic and cultural contributions,
as well as his early writings about the "grass-roots movements"
in Latin America,
kindled our desire to do the research and writing for this work.

Contents

Preface

Seldom do we see things for which we have no categories. This has been particularly true with regard to our knowledge of the rapid growth of local, indigenous churches around the world. Clayton ("Mike") Berg and Paul Pretiz have done us a great service by tracing the growth of these "grass-roots" churches in Latin America, and by giving us categories with which to understand their diversity, vitality, and problems. Traditionally, we think of missions as the West bringing the gospel to the "non-West," and planting western style churches. It takes us by surprise to see that God is at work raising up indigenous churches outside the sphere of Western missions.

In this book, the authors survey the key grass-roots church movements in Latin America. Their findings are exciting and, at times, disturbing. Certainly, God is at work in Latin America calling people to faith in Jesus Christ through His Word and His Spirit. Moreover, many of the grass-roots churches base their teachings on the Bible. But lacking Biblical training, some of the leaders pursue theological tangents that lead them far from the gospel. We also see conversions, revivals, and the correcting work of God's Word and fellowship with other believers bringing many of them back towards a Biblically balanced message.

What accounts for the apparently spontaneous expansion of these churches, when Western missions and churches have worked so hard for often meager results? The authors make it clear that one reason is the indigenous nature of these grass-roots churches. Their worship styles, church ministries, and community orientation fit the Latin American cultures, and newcomers feel at home in them. By contrast, many of the practices of churches planted by missionaries look foreign and strange.

A second reason is the grass-roots nature of these churches. They emerge out of the local context and belong to the people. While many of them are run by authoritarian leaders, their growth occurs through the outreach of ordinary members seeking to win their relatives and friends. In a very real sense, they feel that the church belongs to them. This mobilization of the laity in the church in ministry leads to spontaneous growth that has a powerful effect on the life of the churches, producing enthusiasm and commitment.

The authors note that another reason for their growth is that these churches take spiritual realities seriously in everyday life. In Latin America, with the rapid rise of Umbanda, Xango, Kardecism and other forms of spiritism, the Church cannot ignore the question of spirits. This concern is one of the strengths of the grass-roots churches. It is also potentially one of their weaknesses. In responding to spiritism and reacting to the everyday secularism of North American preaching, some end up with a syncretistic Christian spiritism built on traditional animistic assumptions of power and gods. Many, however, seem to be aware of this danger and preach a message of submission to God and resistance of Satan and his demons.

Finally, these churches proclaim a message of hope, often in desperate settings. Some will fault them for failing to challenge the oppressive social structures that create poverty and oppression. Others will accuse them of offering a gospel of prosperity. Both are true in many cases. But many of these churches do provide a sense of hope in God that is a beacon to many caught in seemingly hopeless situations. And from this hope springs sharing and love, and the first steps to meaningful lives in Christian faith.

The authors trace the response of Catholic and Protestant churches to the grass-roots churches and lead us through theological reflections on their place in Christ's Church. Their study helps keep us from relying on anecdotes and making premature judgments. They remind us that our task is not to try to take control of these churches, but to learn from them, and to share with them our understandings of the Scriptures, pastoral ministries, and missionary outreach. We need to reexamine our own mission methods so that the people hear the gospel not from the tongue of foreigners, but from God in their own languages. We need to see with discernment what God is doing in our day, and to worship Him with all who truly are His children.

Paul G. Hiebert
Chairman of the Department and
Professor of Mission and Anthropology
Trinity Evangelical Divinity School

Introduction

When the musicians strode to the church platform with their guitars, violins and trumpets, a dozen enthusiasts rushed to the front with their cassette recorders, eager to capture every note of the expected musical offering. Playing their typically unique blend of fast rhythms and soulful melodies, this Christian *mariachi* band was the high point of the afternoon. The silver buckles on their black uniforms added sparkle to the scene.

Musical groups and preaching alternated to provide day-long inspiration to the hundreds gathered for this annual church convention in Pachuca, Mexico. Downstairs, huge sides of beef hung from the ceiling, and on the fire were enormous pots of *mole*--a rich traditional Mexican hot sauce--to feed the participants who took time out from the continuous services to enjoy a meal.

The flavors, the kitchen smells, the rhythms, the preaching style and the happy confusion made the gathering unmistakably Mexican. And indeed, this was a gathering of Christians from churches that had grown out of the soil of Mexico. Foreign missionaries had never been involved in the beginnings or the development of the congregations represented at this convention.

In tents, storefronts, former cinemas, factories, homes and in church buildings, too, churches are arising by spontaneous combustion in every Latin American country. Outside of the congregations that have sprung up through missionary efforts, Latins are coming to know Christ, entering into fellowship and sharing the Good News through the ministries of churches independent of the traditional mission structures.

11

What's in a Name?

How do we recognize these churches? Our first problem is a name for them. Names have a way of revealing prejudices or communicating approval.   In fact, the non-existence of an adequate name for a phenomenon may indicate a blind spot in the perception of it.

As we consider the phenomenon of congregations or networks of congregations by the people from their own country or culture, we discover that we do not even have a name for such churches in North America. Perhaps we are already so accustomed to them that it is like trying to describe the air we breathe. Not all our North American churches are Anglican, Presbyterian or Lutheran, direct descendants of the Reformation in Europe. We have churches founded by U.S. nationals, so to speak, ranging from the very evangelical Christian and Missionary Alliance churches to the non-Biblical Latter Day Saints. Not having a name for such U.S.-originated movements, we hardly know what to call locally-originated ones elsewhere.

We considered a number of terms, any of which might have been used--"indigenous," "nativistic," "independent," "second generation churches," "new religious movements," and "autochthonous." Consult the Glossary for a definition of each.

We chose, however, the phrase: *"Grass-Roots (GR) Churches"* which suggests something that is unimported, which springs up naturally from the soil. *We are dealing with those churches whose origin cannot be immediately traced to an intentional foreign missionary action or which have broken sufficiently from established groups to display a distinctly local flavor.*

Although Latin America is increasingly urban, the term "grass-roots" may conjure up a barefoot, rural image on the part of some.

Nevertheless, we will adopt "grass-roots" as the most precise term to describe these churches.

These are the churches, some of which are the result of the seed of the gospel having been scattered, that have taken root and developed on their own, taking on the characteristics that result from that particular soil, climate and other elements of its environment. Others become truly grass-roots in their style, even though their origins may have come from roots elsewhere.

There are probably few 100% truly GR churches in the world. In the U.S., the Church of the Nazarene, a "GR" denomination if you please, can trace its "holiness" roots to the Wesleyan movement. Likewise, in Latin America there is hardly a leader of a new GR movement that did not have contact with some Christian group, either abroad or in his or her own country.

More precisely for our purposes, we consider as "grass-roots" those churches in the following categories:

1. Group A - the "purest" GR groups

Whatever the initial contact a founder may have had, these are churches that have no history of being a product of a missionary organization or of an established foreign denomination.

2. Group B - those formerly related to a foreign mission

Many groups, perhaps because their break from a parent church was conflictive, have become decidedly free of foreign influence. These have adopted authentic national characteristics and are, in our opinion, GR churches.

Many churches, once related to a foreign organization, have been given their independence. They have been "indigenized." Some of these autonomous churches maintain strong links to the parent organization. Missionaries may still be present, teaching their pastors or otherwise influencing them. They may receive project money from outside sources, funds almost always conditioned to the interest of the donor organization. Such "indigenized" churches are not what we are discussing in this work.

Time is also a factor. The Methodist Pentecostal Church in Chile, for example, broke from the Methodists in 1909. Even though some Methodist patterns persist (e.g. infant baptism) and even though former Methodist missionary Willis Hoover continued to influence the group for many years, this denomination is unquestionably a church with its own unique characteristics, very independent and highly contextualized.

How long must it be since the break occurred, or what degree of contextualization must be achieved, before we include a church in this category? We cannot avoid some subjective opinion. Charles Kraft (1979) attempted to measure the contextualization of some churches, but objective measures are difficult to establish. So, his method eventually ended up utilizing a combined score of a panel of people who expressed their personal opinions regarding various dimensions of contextualization of these churches. For our chapter on statistics, we too solicit the opinion of people locally as to whether breakaway churches in their area have indeed become sufficiently GR in their style to be included in this category of churches.

Some missions or denominations have granted much autonomy to their churches in Latin America. In fact, these Latin American church groups may have become so large that they may overshadow the mother church in size. The few U.S. missionaries still attached to the group wield no significant influence. This is the case of the Assemblies of God in Brazil with its estimated 6 million members.

While a case could be built for classifying such groups as GR, our study will concentrate on those that have no ties with sister denominations outside of Latin America except those which they themselves have initiated.

3. Group C - Latin American, though not local

A third category is that of churches planted by foreign missionaries from another Latin American country. For example, Guatemalan missionaries plant churches in Honduras and Puerto Ricans plant churches in Costa Rica. While such churches may not, in the strictest sense, be GR Honduran or Costa Rican churches, nevertheless the influence, though foreign, was Latin American.

Some More Defining

Rome's Dissenters. In addition, there have been some interesting movements that are breakaways from the Roman Catholic Church in Mexico, Brazil and Puerto Rico which have resulted in Catholic Church bodies independent of Rome. While we will also mention a group of former Roman Catholics in Costa Rica that has now become part of the Evangelical stream, for the purposes of our consideration, groups that continue with typically Catholic practices will receive only incidental attention in this study.

Latin America. For our purposes, Spanish and Portuguese-speaking countries in the Western Hemisphere are our subject. Haiti, though sometimes classified as part of Latin America, presents a unique scenario with its mix of Christian and African religions and use of the French language, and so must be considered separately. The same applies in varying degrees to the Caribbean former colonies which reflect British, Dutch and French/Creole cultures.

Evangélico. "Evangelical" in Latin America is generally equivalent to "Protestant," regardless of theological persuasion, although Latin America's *evangélicos* are generally theologically evangelical too. *Protestante* may be used in more formal sociological or official government classifications, and when employed in this way may often include other non-Roman Catholic groups such as Mormons or Jehovah's Witnesses.

Catholic Communities. A Roman Catholic Bible study and Christian action movement of "Basic Ecclesial Communities" or "Basic Church Communities" is sometimes referred to as the "grass-roots Christian communities" movement. Our study does not encompass this movement.

Not Every GR Movement. We will be looking at some of the larger movements and others that may be representative of GR churches of various types, without attempting to make an exhaustive listing of all of them.

Who has Studied Latin America's Grass-Roots Churches?

Much has been written about African independent churches. By way of contrast, current literature on evangelical churches in Latin America is just beginning to recognize the GR churches (e.g. Deiros 1992 and Berg/Pretiz 1992). But the only study focusing exclusively on GR churches in Latin America is a little-known 16-page book containing an address by Eugene Nida, *The Indigenous Church in Latin America* (1962).

Some works on Latin American GR churches do not identify them as such. With the explosive Protestant growth in Latin America, secular observers studying the phenomenon now focus more on GR churches. Even though they are growing most rapidly, often the authors superficially label all they see as "Protestant."

More common is the classification made by observers between "historic" and "pentecostal" groups (or in Roman Catholic literature, between historic groups and the "sects"). But again, in some studies of the latter, the analysis is more accurately applied to GR pentecostal churches, and not to such groups of U.S. origin.

Some authors, however, have differentiated the GR churches from the foreign churches. Ignacio Vergara (1962), in his study of Chilean Protestants, separated out the *iglesias populares* (churches of the masses) from the others. Likewise, David Barrett, editor of the *World Christian Encyclopedia* (1982), considers the "non-white indigenous churches" as something quite apart from Protestant, Roman Catholic, Orthodox or other streams of Christianity.

A Burning Issue for Mission Leaders

Can the gospel take root in the soul of a people so deeply that it becomes a folk religion? Can such grass-roots Christianity entirely displace an old folk religion? What shape will the Church take in such situations?

"There is a growing awareness among mission leaders that these issues arising out of the folk religions will be central in missiology in the twenty-first century," says Paul Hiebert (1993, 254). He clearly indicates that this is a two-pronged issue: (1) the study of old folk religions, and (2) the study of new structures of Christian churches around the world.

It is to the latter point, as well as theological views, church life, and outreach strategies, that the authors of this work address themselves, as it pertains to Latin America, with "fear and trembling."

By way of the authors' experience, Paul Pretiz, native of Boston, Massachusetts, is of American Baptist church background and a part of the pastoral team of a church associated with the Fraternity of Costa Rican Evangelical Churches. Mike Berg was ordained by a council of independent churches in California, for over twenty years was a ruling elder in a Presbyterian church, and more recently is an active member of an Episcopal church. With a combined Latin America Mission service record of eighty years, the authors have had contact and involvement with the widest spectrum of Protestant churches--conciliar, evangelical, pentecostal, grass-roots.

Our Road Map

Part I (Chapters 1-8) of this book is generally descriptive. We will look at two typical GR churches, then examine the GR phenomenon from a worldwide perspective, make estimates of the numbers of GR churches and their faithful, review some of their early history, and look more closely at some of the major movements.

Part II (Chapters 9-15) of the book is generally analytical, briefly viewing GR churches from the perspectives of social scientists, Roman Catholics and Protestants. We will then attempt to make some non-exhaustive generalizations about their doctrinal views, church life and outreach, concluding with a review of the implications of Latin American GR movements for the rest of the Church.

Some Well-Deserved Acknowledgments

We are grateful indeed for the great encouragement given to us by former Latin America Mission president, J. Paul Landrey, and other LAM colleagues to persevere once again and follow up our first book--*The Gospel People of Latin America*, and in Spanish, *Mensajeros de esperanza: los evangélicos*--with this effort.

We especially appreciate the many pastors and leaders in Latin America who gave so much in time-consuming interviews to provide us with invaluable information and insight.

Profound thanksgiving is expressed to a host of good friends who kindly and graciously consented to critique our manuscript. These are, besides Paul Landrey and then LAM board chair, Paul E. Pierson, other authors W. Dayton Roberts, Robert B. Reekie, David M. Howard and John D. Maust, as well as distinguished missionaries or missiologists related to Latin America, Guillermo Cook, Samuel Escobar, Roger Greenway, Elisabeth F. Isáis, Kenneth B. Mulholland, C. René Padilla, Rubén ("Tito") Paredes, Dorothy F. Quijada, John E. Stam, and C. Peter Wagner. To each--*mil gracias!*

We are particularly indebted for the fine service of Kathleen Clark in the editing and pre-printing process, and to Mariola Chylek for the cover design.

Finally, to our long-suffering wives of so many years, Ruth in Costa Rica and Jo in northern Florida, thanks for the memories... for your understanding, encouragement, and prayers.

The authors
Penney Farms, Florida
San José, Costa Rica

PART I
VISITING THE BARRIOS

Prologue: Two Churches in
Santafé de Bogotá, Colombia

Behind the facades of former factories and warehouses on a narrow street in Santafé de Bogotá, Colombia, the inside floors and walls have been gutted and a vast space created. Here some 3,000 people are singing "The Joy of the Lord is my Strength." Their exuberant song is punctuated by shouts. At the verse reading "If you have this joy, you too can jump," many are jumping. A period of prayer follows and the shirt-sleeved leader on the platform in the center encourages the congregation to rebuke the devil. A roar of prayer fills the place, each person crying to God and rebuking the evil one, sometimes throwing punches at an invisible enemy. Signaling the close of prayer time, Enrique Gómez, the leader, cries *"A Su nombre!"* (to His name), and the crowd replies *"Gloria!"*

Gómez' message depicts Christ as just, holy, loving, the Head of the Church. Politicians *never* help God's people. Hitler betrayed the Church; Castro did, too. Who gives people jobs? Only God.

This is the Bethesda Missionary Center in the capital of Colombia, traditionally Latin America's most Roman Catholic country. Whenever the clouds lift, the Monserrate shrine can be seen overlooking Santafé de Bogotá from a range of the Andes that rises abruptly to the east. In the past, a treaty ("concordat") with the Vatican put religious education exclusively in the hands of local Catholic clergy. For years vast areas of the country were off-limits to Protestant missions. Now the capital city, Santafé de Bogotá, boasts several large Evangelical congregations.

A simple invitation is given for people to come forward to accept Christ. Little explanation is given, but a large number leave the crude angle-iron and wooden-plank benches and bleachers to come from the four corners of the auditorium to the blue-skirted platform in the center. "Renounce your sin!" Gómez shouts. "Repeat this prayer after me."

An appeal for funds follows--to make 150 benches to seat a thousand more people. People come forward, handing the preacher their offerings. The money is counted and reported to the congregation as it is received, and the process continues until the total is raised.

The God of the Impossible

Aside from the pastor, the only participants on the palm-decked platform are the musicians who perform with electric guitars, a keyboard and a drum-set. The sections of the roof overhead, remnants of the buildings that had been removed to create this space, follow odd angles and various heights. Exposed brick walls of neighboring properties have been whitewashed and graced with banners: "The impossible does not exist. Believe in the Lord Jesus Christ and all will become possible." Another: "Welcome. Jesus Christ saves, heals, baptizes and gives us power."

Trusting in a Christ who performs the impossible, who heals and empowers, these working-class *Bogotanos* stop traffic as they spill out into the narrow streets after the Sunday morning or afternoon service.

At home, the faithful can continue listening to a message of hope. Seven radio stations carry the Center's message. A 16-page newspaper proclaims its message along with news of other evangelical denominations mixed with local and international news. A day school and a Bible institute prepare its leaders. Founded in 1975, this growing movement has already spread to five other Colombian cities.

A Hidden Surge

Travelers making missionary visits to Latin America are usually taken to churches of their own denominations. Usually they remain unaware of churches like Bethesda. Often those who know of their existence see only disorder, authoritarianism, superficiality or escapism from social responsibility that is said to characterize many of them. But the enthusiasm and growth of these mass movements cannot be ignored. These grass-roots (GR) churches, founded by national Christians without missionary involvement, are winning the masses in almost every Latin American country. They are growing at a faster rate than most mission-related churches. In Chile, numerically they leave all mission-related groups in the dust.

Behind the Facades

Our next visit is to the "Church on the Rock" in a middle class *barrio*.

Leaving the grimy south side of Santafé de Bogotá, one finds the north to be middle-class suburbia. It is marked by modern shopping malls, homes and apartment buildings topped by bright orange-tile roofs. Many homes are single-storey townhouses, abutting each other. The Church on the Rock appears to be simply one of these homes. However, upon entering the front door a visitor is surprised to step into a spacious auditorium with a capacity to seat about 2,000 persons. This, like the Bethesda Center, was created by gutting several adjacent structures while leaving the facades intact. Here, unlike Bethesda Missionary Center, the seating is comfortable, the decor tasteful.

A well-trimmed beard highlights the pastor's rugged look. His manner suggests a background of association with professional people and higher levels of society. The blurb on the back cover of Darío Silva's autobiography describes him as a "seminarian [Silva studied briefly at a Roman Catholic seminary], soldier, poet, journalist, bohemian, sorcerer's apprentice, rich man, poor man, frustrated in suicide, and minister of the Gospel" (Silva-Silva 1991). When he directed Colombia's Noticolor and RCN nationwide newscasts, he was known for his caustic commentaries. This created for him loyal friends and bitter enemies among Colombia's political leaders. Darío read widely, delved into the esoteric and consulted with mediums.

During a deep personal financial crisis, his mood became suicidal. In the depths of his desperation a Christian woman, who came to loan him money, read Job 33 to him: "He opens the eyes of men and terrifies them with warnings, that he may turn aside man from his deed, and cut off pride from man; He keeps back his soul from the Pit, and his life from perishing by the sword" (NIV, vs. 16-18). And "Then man prays to God, and he accepts him. . . He has redeemed my soul from going down into the Pit, and my life shall see the light" (*ibid.*, 26, 28). Through her fasting and prayer, God had led Esther Lucía to select the passages with which Darío's poetic spirit could identify.

As in the case of many GR Christian leaders, Darío's encounter with Christ was a deep and revolutionary experience. After committing himself to Christ in 1984, he devoured Berkhof's text,

Systematic Theology, and materials from Campus Crusade. He sought counsel from other Christian leaders. And he married Esther Lucía, the woman who had come to him at his darkest hour.

Contacts with a congregation in Houston called "The Church on the Rock" inspired the name of the Colombian church he founded in 1987. However, there is no dependency on the U.S. group. Silva believes that his pre-conversion contact with the spirit world equipped him uniquely for a ministry to discern the spirits. Although the Church on the Rock is charismatic, he prefers to define himself as "a Baptist with an accelerator and a Pentecostal with brakes." He refers to the Apostle Paul who declared that his preaching of the Gospel was both through the Word and signs of power (*ibid.*).

Timothys, Nehemiahs, Aquilas, Priscillas and Joshuas

A daily telephone prayer chain alerts between 400 and 800 members of the congregation every morning to pray for people in need. A weekly women's group surpassing 500 meets on Thursdays. The Timothys (the church's young people), the Nehemiahs (professional and business people), the Aquila and Priscilla people (couples) and the Joshuas (singles) are other groups. A Bible institute program trains the movement's leadership.

Fifteen percent of the church's gross income goes into a "Mercy, Love and Service Fund." Much of this money goes to operate several homes for Colombia's numerous street children. The one hundred children in these shelters, according to Silva (1992), ". . . will not become *sicarios* (professional killers), nor raw material for the homosexuals, nor *gamines* (street children) to die of cold under the bridges." Over a hundred needy families also receive food.

Other Church on the Rock congregations are starting up in several Colombian cities. An Argentine professional soccer player, converted in Silva's church, returned to plant a Church on the Rock in Buenos Aires.

Silva is not reacting to missions or missionaries. "Every morning I thank the Lord for those who brought us the Gospel," he says. "The pioneers sowed with tears. The irrigation canals were filled with their tears. They turned over the soil with love and with their own hands planted the seed. Now we reap what others have sown" (*ibid.*).

Spontaneous Combustion

Although missionaries continue to plant churches in Latin America, now, without outsiders igniting the tinder, spontaneous combustion is also taking place. National believers are establishing new congregations on their own. It is regrettable that those who know something about the GR churches often harbor stereotyped images about them.

Most are churches filled with the poor. But there are others like Santafé de Bogotá's Church on the Rock.

Most are pentecostal. Some, without question, go to what might be called charismatic extremes. But a few are not pentecostal at all.

Some are one-man movements, highly authoritarian. Others share leadership.

Many are accused of lacking concern about society's needs. But now there is a perceptible shift by many GR leaders to take advantage of the region's increasingly democratic regimes to enter the political arena.

Many are new. New storefront congregations are born daily. But others with a long history reach back to the early 20th century.

Some are isolated movements, exclusive possessors of eternal truth. The Church on the Rock and Pastor Silva, however, work actively with Colombia's confederation of Protestant churches.

Some are large, like the above-mentioned Santafé de Bogotá churches. But there are countless small storefront GR congregations.

Some are in Latin America's vast urban areas. But others are in the smaller cities and rural areas.

Some ought to be labeled aberrations. Others are excellent models for other churches to study and emulate.

ONE

A Worldwide Phenomenon

In 525 AD, European merchants were surprised to find about 100,000 Christians in India, a church allegedly founded by Thomas the Apostle. A visit by Marco Polo and a series of other contacts confirmed the presence of this early GR church. In the 16th century the Thomas Church came into conflict with Roman Catholic missionaries. The Indians had never heard of the Pope, and had "scrupulously avoided the use of images" which the outsiders were introducing. In an early example of de-indigenization, this church was absorbed by Rome. Later, Anglicans and other groups entered (Neil 1970, 17-106) and the original GR church split into five branches (Johnson 1976, 499).

Underdeveloped nations charge that raw materials are extracted from their soil, sold cheaply to the developed nations for transformation into manufactured products, and then returned to them for sale at high prices. There is an analogy here: Early Christianity in its simplicity had been taken from the Mideast by Europeans, then refined, elaborated, restructured and returned to the countries of its origins.

Throughout the history of the West, GR movements, whether the pre-Reformation Waldensians or the Anabaptists of the Reformation period, have been the object of persecution and repeated attempts to force them into the orbit of Christianity's dominant form at that time. Theologians attribute the appearance of such "sects" to theological differences. Sociologists and secular historians observe that during periods of crisis, people look for new sources of stability and authority when their worlds are crumbling about them.

Naisbitt and Aburdene (1990, 272) note that such a crisis occurred in the U.S. in the 19th century ". . .when the country's economy changed from agriculture to industry. That century witnessed the creation of several major made-in-America religions --Mormon, Adventist, Jehovah's Witness, and Christian Scientist. . . ."

Telescoping Revolutions

The revolutions that have shaken most of the Western world-- industrialization, urbanization, the awakening of peoples to their political rights--were spread out over centuries and absorbed gradually. In many parts of the underdeveloped world, however, these revolutions have been telescoped into a single generation. The existing traditional or tribal religions offer little help in adjusting to abrupt change. Therefore, an adequate worldview to withstand these wrenching forces is missing.

Speaking of the most extreme of the GR movements that arise in the underdeveloped world, historian Paul Johnson (1983, 702) says,

> "These syncretistic forms of Christianity have always tended to appear in periods of rapid population growth, racial and cultural mingling, movement and change. In the 1970s, they were particularly marked in Brazil . . . They were a still more important feature of Christianity in Africa itself, a boiling maelstrom of expansionism, revivalism, strange sects, gnosticism, evangelism, Zionism, fervent orthodoxy and fanatic zeal, rather as primitive Christianity had been, in the Balkans and Asia Minor, during the third century AD. While theologians at the Universities of

Tübingen and Utrecht were diminishing the total of
Christian belief, strange charismatics in the slums
of Mexico City and São Paulo, of Recife and Rio,
of Cape Town, Johannesburg, Lagos and Nairobi,
were adding to it. The first group spoke for
thousands; the second for scores of millions."

It is easy to understand why one observer, looking at the
darkest side of the African phenomenon, says that " . . . less than
10% could be considered to have accepted Christ as Savior in the
Biblical sense of the new birth" (Johnstone 1978, 159). We
cannot address the African scene, but Latin American GR
movements, although some are obvious aberrations, are far more
evangelical and in all countries most of them have become a part
of the Protestant stream.

"The big Western Christian communities do not know what
they ought to do about these African churches," says Johnson
(1976, 502). Some belong to the World Council, he says, while
others are "barely Christian" and many, unstable. By 2000, there
may be 350 million professing African Christians, the largest single
block in the global Christian community. And the majority will be
"independents"--GR groups (*ibid.*).

A Third Church?

In general, increasing attention is being given to churches in
the underdeveloped world. In most cases, as mentioned before, no
distinction is made between traditional and GR movements in
these areas.

Walbert Buhlman's *The Coming of the Third Church* (1977, 4)
is an example. "Third" does not refer to the "Third World"
(already an obsolete term), but a Third Church chronologically:
the First Church being the Eastern Church (now a "church of

silence"), the Second, the Western Church, and the Third Church, that of the newer nations. As a Roman Catholic, Buhlman points to the shift in his own communion: in 1960 Roman Catholics in North America and Europe represented 51.5% of world Catholics (Africa, Asia and South America, 48.5%). He estimated that by 2000 AD African, Asian and South American Catholics would represent 70% of world Catholics (*ibid.*, 20).

The Third Church, he says (*ibid.*, 385-386), can teach the West " . . . what conversion really means, and, given the shortage of priests, how few priests can minister to thousands, as lay people take more responsibility." At Rome's last synod (Vatican Council II) the majority of the bishops were from the Third Church, and two-thirds of the addresses were delivered by them (*ibid.*, 393).

Christians of the undeveloped world are the majority. Most of the world's Christians are also non-white. And most of them are poor. In Latin America, among Protestants the majority are pentecostal. And while GR groups are not yet a majority, in many countries they soon will be.

They are under leadership that is less educated, but spiritually vital. These churches experience development that is often disorderly and competitive--but there is growth. And they are composed of people less interested in knowing about doctrine than knowing God experientially.

In all of these churches, and in all of their variety, we find a common denominator: a flame in the hearts of Latin Americans to create their own expressions of the Body of Christ in the churches that they themselves establish.

TWO

Trying to Count Them

The Jotabeche Methodist Pentecostal Cathedral in Santiago, Chile, is on a major thoroughfare. The Light of the World headquarters church in Guadalajara, Mexico, is in the center of a large neighborhood where all the streets lead to the church like spokes of a wheel.

The Protestant churches of the mainline denominations built 75 or 100 years ago when foreign denominations could afford to buy the property in the heart of the city are often visible to a visitor or tourist. In many cases they are suffering the same fate as the "Old First" churches in downtown U.S. cities, trying to minister in areas that have lost residents and become commercial.

In general, however, Latin American GR churches are not in the public eye. So it is easy to remain unaware of the existence and the strength of these churches which are often storefront meeting places in poor *barrios* and in squatter settlements. Or they may be larger GR churches occupying former warehouses, old factories, or abandoned neighborhood cinemas. If they build their own buildings, these are usually simple and functional.

Because of their lesser visibility we often ask, "How many of these churches are there in Latin America, and to how many people do they minister?"

Grass-Roots Churches According to Barrett

David Barrett's *World Christian Encyclopedia*--W.C.E. (1982) is not only the most ambitious statistical study of the

Christian world scene, but by creating a category of "non-white indigenous churches," it also demonstrates the editor's sensitivity to the Church in the developing world. Barrett's years of service as a missionary in Africa unquestionably led him to this categorization.

The encyclopedia's "non-white indigenous churches" are distinguished from the other categories: Roman Catholic, Orthodox, Catholic (Non-Roman and Orthodox), Anglican, Protestant, and Marginal Christians (e.g. Jehovah's Witness). These "non-white indigenous churches" are the " . . . denominations, churches and movements that have been initiated, founded, operated, led, controlled and spread not by caucasian whites or Europeans from today's Western or Communist worlds but by black, non-white or non-European peoples from most of the major geographical races of what is now termed the Third World . . . with no dependence on European or North American white initiative, leadership, control, assistance or ties" (*ibid.*, 60).

Although he refers to non-Western initiative, he recognizes that most began as schisms from the major blocs, mostly from the Protestant sector, although some have broken from Roman Catholic and Anglican bodies as well (*ibid.*). In Latin America in most cases they are perceived by Protestants as well as non-Protestants as variants of Protestantism. In addition, Barrett's nomenclature ("non-white indigenous") does not fit in Latin America. The middle-class GR congregation in Santafé de Bogotá, Colombia (the Church on the Rock) is composed of some very European-looking people.

However clumsy from the viewpoint of our particular terminology, Barrett's definitions of what these "non-white indigenous churches" are, coincides well with our definition of GR churches in Latin America.

The World Scene: Will Most Protestants be
Grass-Roots Christians?

Before studying the numbers of GR churches in Latin America, the world picture according to David Barrett is revealing. He publishes an annual "Status of Global Mission" in the *International Bulletin of Missionary Research,* (IBMR) from which the following table is derived (*ibid.*, January-March 1994, 25).

Global Growth of Non-white Indigenous Christians

1900	7,743,100	1.4%	of total Christian
1970	60,130,000	4.8%	population
mid 1994	167,360,000	8.8%	
2000	204,418,000	9.6%	
2015	425,211,000	13.9%	

Annual growth measured across the 1970 to mid-1994 period: 4.56%.

By 2025, GR churches will represent nearly 14% of all Christians. Incidentally, while GR churches in Latin America are largely pentecostal, on the world scene Pentecostals represent only 36.1% of the total number of GR adherents.

Although these churches with only 8.8% of all Christians (mid-1994) may seem to be small in number, editor Barrett's projections in the IBMR indicate the direction of the trends. The January 1994 projection (IBMR, 24-25) reveals that in the year 2025 these churches will outnumber all churches in the "Protestant" category. Or, if we should consider these churches "Protestant" (as they are in Latin America), they will become a majority among all Protestants.

	Non-white Indigenous	Protestant	Non-white Indigenous as Percent of Total
mid 1994	167,360,000	348,640,000	32.4%
AD 2000	204,418,000	386,602,000	34.6%
2025	425,211,000	420,300,000	50.3%

How Many in Latin America?

The W.C.E. publishes tables listing the Christian denominations in each country and identifies those considered to be "non-white indigenous." Assembling the data from the tables of the Latin American countries, we can construct the following table. The "non-white indigenous" groups that follow Catholic practices (even though they may have broken from Rome) are not included in the table. The last column is constructed from the W.C.E. growth rates of both "indigenous" and traditional Protestant churches, projecting what the percentage of indigenous church members would be in 1993 according to the estimated growth rates.

Mid-1980, Christians affiliated, thousands

	In Indigenous Churches	In Protestant Churches	Total	Percent Indigenous 1980	Percent Indigenous 1993
Argentina	351.8	784.9	1,136.7	30.9	33.1
Bolivia	20.0	265.0	285.0	7.0	7.7
Brazil	7,583.3	11,122.2	18,705.5	40.5	40.6
Chile	1,853.7	230.3	2,084.0	88.9	90.7
Colombia	220.0	430.0	650.0	33.8	41.4
Costa Rica	7.0	70.9	77.9	9.9	8.9
Cuba	84.0	150.0	234.0	35.9	46.5
Dominican Rep.	6.1	151.0	157.1	3.9	3.2
Ecuador	50.0	224.0	274.0	18.2	24.1
El Salvador	39.0	211.8	250.8	15.6	14.5
Guatemala	92.3	426.0	518.3	17.8	22.0
Haiti	104.1	574.9	679.0	15.3	15.7
Honduras	3.0	106.4	109.4	2.7	2.4
Mexico	1,539.2	1,189.4	2,728.6	56.4	57.4
Nicaragua	24.0	230.0	254.0	9.4	11.7
Panama	9.4	100.0	109.4	8.6	8.4
Paraguay	2.1	59.0	61.1	3.4	3.4
Peru	60.0	478.0	538.0	11.2	12.7
Puerto Rico	96.6	261.4	358.0	11.2	29.9
Uruguay	3.3	63.5	66.8	4.9	5.6
Venezuela	156.0	226.1	382.1	40.8	41.9
Latin America, 1985 (W.C.E., 791)	14,949	21,915	36,864	40.6	42.1

Obviously the situation in Latin America is very uneven, with GR churches representing nearly 89% of all Evangelical ("Protestant" + "non-white indigenous") churches in Chile, to a meager 2.7% in Honduras. Even in 1980 there was a higher percentage of Christians in the Latin American GR churches (40.6%) than the world average (32.8%).

PERCENT OF GRASS ROOTS CHURCH MEMBERS WITHIN THE
PROTESTANT MOVEMENT IN LATIN AMERICA

CUBA 46.5   DOMINICAN REPUBLIC 3.2

HAITI 15.7

PUERTO RICO 29.9

HONDURAS 2.4

MEXICO 57.4   NICARAGUA 11.7   VENEZUELA 41.9

GUATEMALA 22.0
EL SALVADOR 14.5
COSTA RICA 8.9
PANAMA 8.4
COLOMBIA 41.4   BRAZIL 40.6

ECUADOR 24.1

PERU 12.7

BOLIVIA 7.7

CHILE 90.7   PARAGUAY 3.4

0 - 10%
10 - 25%
25 - 50%
OVER 50%

URUGUAY 5.6

ARGENTINA 33.1

1993 Estimates based on membership statistics and growth rates of "non-white
indigenous" churches in the *World Christian Encyclopedia*, David Barrett, Ed.

The W.C.E. also estimates yearly growth rates of the two groups. In Colombia, GR churches, for example, are estimated to be growing at 7.21% yearly while the other Protestant churches grow at 4.58%. In a few countries, however, the non-GR churches are growing more rapidly (e.g. Dominican Republic).

Looking at some Selected Cities and Countries

While the W.C.E. gives us some of the best estimates on a country-by-country level in Latin America, recent surveys in certain cities and countries can give us some more sharply focused estimates in selected areas.

In the following tables we will identify the major groups as

Historic denominations (Lutherans, Presbyterians, Friends, Baptists, etc. with connections to groups in the U.S. or in other countries outside of Latin America).

New denominations ("non-historic" groups such as the Christian and Missionary Alliance, Nazarenes, Conservative Baptists, Evangelical Covenant, Evangelical Free, denominations composed of churches which are products of interdenominational missions, the U.S.-related pentecostal denominations, etc.).

GR churches (groups born in the country, contextualized breakaways from the above denominations, groups with relationships with missionary organizations in other Latin American countries).

Unidentified groups (two or more churches in association, for which we have no definite information as to their origins or relationships).

Unidentified single churches
We have selected membership data rather than broader data categories (such as "evangelical community").

Guatemala

The PROCADES (*Proyecto Centroamericano de Estudios Socio-religiosos*, an Evangelical research agency) studies provided some more finely tuned estimates of the number of Evangelical churches and their membership in Central America, including the Guatemala PROCADES survey of 1981. While the PROCADES data upon which the following table is based is somewhat dated, it gives us a base for comparison with more recent data and thus enables us to appreciate the rapid growth of some of the GR groups.

	Churches		Members	
	Number	Percent of Total	Number	Percent of Total
Historic denominations	298	6.4	22,728	6.8
New denominations	3,010	64.4	209,291	62.8
GR churches	888	19.0	66,012	19.8
Unidentified groups	395	8.4	29,848	9.0
Single churches	85	1.8	5,482	1.6

If we apply an adjustment (which has been confirmed by colleagues to be an effective procedure to arrive at a reasonable estimate) that assumes conservatively that 50% of the unidentified groups and 90% of the single churches are GR congregations, we arrive at an estimate that 1,161 churches (24.8% of total) and 85,870 members (25.8% of total) are in this category.

In this analysis, as in the ones that follow, we do not list as GR congregations the various Church of Christ groups, nor the various Plymouth Brethren-type assemblies. While these groups stress their autonomy, their international networks with other groups are very strong.

The largest GR Guatemalan congregation is the Elim Church, considered by Virgilio Zapata in 1982 as probably the largest church in Central America. The pastor, Otoniel Ríos, a medical doctor and former sports announcer, was converted to the gospel in an Evangelism-in-Depth campaign. The church broke from the Cinco Calles Church in 1962. By 1978 it had 3,000 members, and in 1980, 5,800 adults plus 2,500 children. By then, Zapata reports, it had given birth to 69 new churches with a total of 20,000 members (15,290 according to the 1980 PROCADES survey). The present building in the capital, dedicated in 1979, may have attendances of up to 9,000. By 1993, Johnstone (1993, 252) estimated there were 50,000 in this movement, then only 24 years old.

Elim churches have extended into other Central American countries, Mexico and elsewhere. What may be an example of evangelistic overstatement is a report that the Elim Church in San Salvador, pastored by Sergio Solórzano, was reported to have 75,000 adherents in 1992 and a goal of 112,000 for 1993 (MILAMEX, Jan. 31, 1993, 4).

Another major GR Guatemalan group is the Príncipe de Paz movement, founded about 1955, numbering over 29,000 members when the PROCADES survey was conducted. This group had 567 churches in Guatemala and was extending into other Central American republics. By the time of the 1993 edition of *Operation World* (252), Johnstone estimated there were 900 churches and

72,000 members in this movement in Guatemala, a group then only some 38 years old.

Mexico City

The *México, Hoy y Mañana* (Mexico, Today and Tomorrow) directory, based on a 1986 survey, gives us a picture of the Mexican capital's metropolitan area.

	Churches		Members	
	Number	Percent of Total	Number	Percent of Total
Historical denominations	197	19.5	43,790	26.4
New denominations	157	15.6	31,437	18.7
Grass-roots churches	456	45.2	63,614	38.3
Unidentified	196	19.4	26,995	16.3
Single churches	3	0.3	276	0.2
Total	1,009		166,112	

Making the same adjustments to include 50% of the unidentified church groups and 90% of the single churches, we arrive at 557 GR churches (55.2%) with 77,387 members (46.6%).

All the independent churches were combined into two groups in this survey, and these were all listed as GR churches. Furthermore, all small denominations without reference to outside relationships with the word "independent" in their title were also included. In Mexico "independence" suggests more than simple autonomy. It is more often than not a declaration of complete independence from all ties with any denomination or outside organization. Furthermore, since the publication of the directory, a segment of the Mexican Presbyterians has established ties with the Presbyterian Church in America.

The Presbyterian denominations, while appearing in the directory as having no connections with outside groups, are listed as "historic groups" because contextually they conserve many of the organizational patterns and worship styles of the parent groups.

On the other hand, one of the largest and most rapidly growing groups, the Missionary Revival Crusade, which founded the Faith, Hope, and Love Center churches, might well, because of its highly contextual style, be listed as "GR." The largest Evangelical congregation in the city is the Center of Faith Church. This congregation meets in a former winery and has services every day of the week, every hour beginning at 8 a.m. Since the origin of the church in 1974 it has grown to a membership of 8,600 in 1986 (Rengifo in his chapter in a Mexico City directory of 1989, 36). But because of this group's connections with a U.S. parent organization in Texas, as tenuous as they are, this movement is not listed as a GR group.

There are a number of large Mexican congregations, some GR and others not, which are not listed in the directory because, for legal reasons, they decided not to incorporate as churches.

Four Colombian Cities

The Latin America Mission's Christ for the City program has encouraged surveys and the publication of church directories to measure church growth and foment unity which should result from churches and pastors coming to know more about each other and their ministries. The following is the combined data from a survey in Medellín (Vera 1993), and surveys in Cali (1992), Barranquilla (1991) and Cartagena (1990).

| | Churches | | Members | |
	Number	Percent of Total	Number	Percent of Total
Historic denominations	67	15.2	6620	16.2
New denominations	219	49.5	18,333	44.8
GR churches	76	17.2	11,092	27.1
Unidentified	34	7.7	2,131	5.2
Single churches	46	10.4	2,710	6.6
Total	442		40,886	

Applying the same adjustments utilized in aforementioned studies, we estimate that there may be 134 GR churches (30.3%) in these cities, with a membership of 14,596 (35.7%).

The largest congregation in Medellín, the Pan American Church (2,965 members in 1993), and its denomination, was included in the GR category although it has on occasion availed itself of U.S. missionaries. This group was founded by Colombian Ignacio Guevara, and its GR style was defined before the foreigners began to participate in its life. Starting off as a truly indigenous church and then inviting missionaries to cooperate on the local church's already-established terms is worlds apart from foreigners starting a ministry which later adopts a national style.

In Medellín alone, given the existence of the large Pan American Church and other similar groups, GR church members represent 51.1% of all members.

One church expected to grow rapidly is the *"Ekklesia"* Colombian Church Center in Cali. While it has only 250 members now, its leader is Julio César Ruibal, a former Bolivian Roman Catholic evangelist and preacher of faith healing whose evangelical moorings filled many Latin American stadiums with listeners. Ruibal was a medical student who accepted Christ at a meeting conducted by Kathryn Kuhlmann. Having discovered that he, too, had a gift of healing, he interrupted his studies to hold large healing campaigns. Truckloads of crutches and orthopedic devices were said to be discarded as the result of the meetings.

Eventually, Ruibal identified himself with the Protestants, and after creating a large movement in Bolivia, began the GR church in Cali. He finished his medical studies and now specializes in natural medicines, founding the Chiropractic Medical Center and also directing the Latin American Christian University. In addition to preaching, he advocates nutrition and a healthful lifestyle. "It's better to prevent than to cure" is a major element in his message (*Maranatha* ca. 1992--year 11, issue #138, 12).

Lima, Peru

A 1991 survey of churches in metropolitan Lima and its port, Callao, was conducted by the Peruvian National Evangelical Council and published by PROMIES (Proyección Misionera, Estadística y Estudios Socio-religiosos), the Council's research program.

	Churches		Evangelical Community	
	Number	Percent of Total	Number	Percent of Total
Historic denominations	148	12.3	25,841	12.3
New denominations	357	37.2	95,807	45.4
GR churches	248	25.8	39,797	18.9
Unidentified	206	21.5	49,485	23.5
Single churches	1	-0-	6	-0-

Making the same kind of adjustments, we arrive at an estimate of 351 GR churches (36.6%) with 64,540 members (30.6%). Since the Israelites of the New Covenant movement is not recognized by Peruvian Evangelicals, it was not included in the survey.

The large Peruvian Evangelical Church which has 60 churches and 10,518 members in the metropolitan area of Lima, often considered a GR group, was not included in this category, given its origins and continued missionary contacts.

Caracas, Venezuela

Similarly a 1993 survey of Caracas (*El Directorio de Iglesias Evangélicas de Caracas,* published by *La Coalición de Iglesias Evangélicas de Caracas y Amanecer*) gives us numbers of churches, but not membership estimates.

	Churches	Percent
Historic	4	2.1
New denominations	82	42.7
GR churches	31	16.1
Unidentified denominations	9	4.7
Single churches	66	34.4
Total	192	

Making the adjustments (50% of the churches of unidentified denominations and 90% of the single churches considered as GR), we arrive at 64 autochthonous churches, 33% of the total.

The Las Acacias Pentecostal Church, the largest Evangelical congregation in the city, would be considered by most as a GR church. It acquired a former movie theater which seats 2,000 people, occupies an entire city block and attracts a wide range of social classes. Its ministries to people in need include medical, dental and counseling services. It was instrumental in establishing the Evangelical Seminary of Caracas and a drug rehab center, the New Life Home. Although a son of missionary parents, the pastor, Samuel Olson, is fully inserted into the Venezuelan scene, married to a Latin, and the church has no ties with any missionary organization.

Rio de Janeiro, Brazil

Information from the Institute for Religious Studies (Fernandes 1992) gives us numbers of churches and not membership estimates.

	Churches	Percent
Historic	1,355	39.0
New denominations	934	26.9
GR churches	373	10.7
Others	815	23.4
Total	3,477	

The study only identifies the 12 major denominations, hence the large number of "others." We would estimate that 75% of these "others" may be GR churches. Such an adjustment would give us 984 GR churches, 28.3% of the total. The headquarters churches of some of the largest GR movements (Brazil for Christ and God Is Love, for example) are in São Paulo, so the percentage of GR church adherents would be higher there.

São Paulo, Brazil

A 1985 survey conducted personally by Silas Pinto gives us the following data:

	Churches		Members	
	Number	Percent of Total	Number	Percent of Total
Historic	576	13.9	111,128	7.9
New denominations	2,109	50.8	647,247	46.0
GR churches	1,468	35.3	649,649	46.1

The survey did not include smaller denominations and single churches, which are mostly GR movements. Being an older survey, it did not include the newer movements, such as the Universal Church of the Kingdom of God, which have appeared subsequently. The charismatic break-offs from the historic denominations (e.g. the Wesleyan Church, a break-off from the Methodist Church) are treated as GR churches. A description of the major GR movements is in the chapter on Brazilian churches.

Buenos Aires, Argentina

A 1992 directory of the churches in Buenos Aires by Norberto Saracco (*Fundación Argentina de Educación y Acción Comunitaria*) is the basis for this data:

	Churches		Members	
	Number	Percent of Total	Number	Percent of Total
Historic	91	29.4	14,384	23.8
New denominations	85	27.6	11,703	19.4
GR churches	42	13.6	23,368	38.7
Unidentified denominations	29	9.4	2,181	3.6
Single churches	62	20.1	8,738	14.5

Making the usual adjustments, we arrive at 112 GR churches (36.2% of the total) with 32,322 members (53.5% of the total). This survey covers the inner city (*Capital Federal*), not the suburban areas. The many Brethren Assemblies are considered as congregations of the "new denominations" category. Inexplicably the survey did not include the large downtown Vision of the Future Church, a G.R. congregation that will be described later. This would add several thousand more to the GR total.

Churches identified as Christian Communities, the product of the Argentinian renewal movement, are considered GR congregations. While they do have some missionary participation, the development of style and organization of these groups was strictly Argentine.

A Summary

The adjusted data on GR churches in the above cities and countries permits us to develop the following table:

	Percent of Churches	Percent of Evangelical Church Members
Guatemala (1981)	24.8	25.8
Mexico City (1986)	55.2	46.6
Colombian cities (1990-1993)	30.3	35.7
Lima, Peru (1993)	36.6	30.6
Rio de Janeiro (1992)	28.3	
Caracas (1993)	33.3	
São Paulo, Brazil (1985)	35.3	46.1
Buenos Aires, Argentina(1992)	36.2	53.5

Uneven Growth--Why?

Obviously the cities we have studied show marked differences in the distribution of the various types of churches. About the only generalization that can be made is that the distribution of GR churches in Latin American cities is very uneven. While it may be true that over 40% of Latin America's Evangelicals are in GR churches, this is due primarily to the high percentages of such churches in Chile and Brazil.

Why are there such differences?

-- **Access to the Scriptures.** David Barrett (1968), in studying the rise of the African Independent churches, argues that the availability of the Scriptures in the vernacular is the major factor in the development of such movements. Likewise, in Latin America, the Bible has been accessible in Spanish and Portuguese since the 19th century. But this availability was very relative. The Bible in Spanish or Portuguese was available typically to those taking the initiative to look for one in a dusty cabinet in the back of the small Evangelical church. The Scriptures were largely unavailable to the general Roman Catholic public, which was warned by the clergy not to buy it or read it. However, this did not deter some Protestants from attempting to distribute it.

After Vatican Council II, Bible reading was encouraged in many Catholic circles. The Scriptures became available in easy-to-read versions in general bookstores. There may be a parallel with the African scene. Access to the Bible in Africa led to the desertion from mission-related churches in favor of the independent churches. However, in Latin America the open Bible was a major factor in desertion from the Roman Catholic churches in favor of the Protestant denominations. Nevertheless, it would be difficult to prove that access to the Bible was a major factor in the rise of the GR churches.

-- **Size of a country**. The higher percentage of GR movements in countries like Brazil, Chile, Argentina and Mexico suggests that in larger, more populated countries the stronger sense of national identity and lesser economic, cultural and religious dependence on outside resources may be a factor. The mentality in a small country is less conducive to nationalistic movements than the proud, can-do spirit of people in the larger republics. In larger countries GR movements can develop into such proportions, with the multiplication not only of churches but also of institutions such as radio stations and programs for pastoral education. This contributes to their self-sufficiency. In smaller countries, churches are less likely to break away from missionary ties since they may feel a greater dependence on outside resources.

-- **Distance from foreign resources.** Leadership in Latin America's countries farthest from the U.S. or Europe is more apt to create independent movements than in Central America or the Caribbean. While Mexico is geographically close to the U.S., culturally it may be farther than Central America or Venezuela. Impediments to missionary activity in Mexico have also made it "distant" from the U.S. and a fertile ground for GR movements.

-- **Reaction to missionary constraints.** In areas where dominant Protestant mission groups have been anti-charismatic, people with a pentecostal persuasion will break away. An example of the opposite situation is Cartagena, Colombia. There the largest mission-related groups are two pentecostal denominations (Church of the Foursquare Gospel and the Assemblies of God), and the Caribbean Evangelical Church Association (related to the Latin America Mission). All three groups are open to charismatic expression. These three denominations represent 32 of the city's 71 churches. Pentecostal Colombians find no need to break away. There are only eight clearly-defined GR congregations in the entire metropolitan area.

-- **Other factors.** There are other factors that may account for the uneven distribution of GR movements. According to many social scientists (e.g. Willems 1967) the degree of industrialization and the incidence of anomie (sense of disorientation) in the population are major factors. The recent rise of GR movements in Argentina may be attributable to the despair and frustration of that proud nation as it has suffered economic, political and military disasters (Deiros 1994). And the most significant of all may well be the most unpredictable--the rise of leadership that can capture the hearts and minds of people and create a GR church.

Other Questions that Statistics Raise

Traditionally Evangelicals have accused government census departments of engaging in a coverup in order to minimize the number of Evangelicals. Now, rather than finding that non-church-sponsored data underestimates the Evangelical population, secular studies are finding more Protestants than are reported in the churches.

The 1986 Greater Mexico City survey discovered 244,652 members of the Evangelical community, 1.27% of the estimated 19,305,000 population. Yet, the government census indicated that Protestants comprised over 2% of the population. Why this disparity?

There are several explanations. For example, the government includes groups such as the Jehovah's Witnesses in the "Protestant" category. Also, the Evangelicals' survey simply failed to include all Evangelical churches. But this hardly explains the large difference.

One hypothesis is that there is a growing nominalism in areas where there are already several generations of Protestants. These may be second or third generations of people whose parents were active. They themselves no longer attend, but they will still identify themselves as Protestants.

Similar data is emerging in Costa Rica, Chile and Argentina. Pablo Deiros (1994) of the International Baptist Seminary in Buenos Aires quoted public opinion polls which indicated there

were 6 to 7% Evangelicals in his city while only 2 to 2.5% of the
population was included in the "head-count" in the churches. In
this case, he attributes the difference to the numbers of people
who have been touched by the large GR ministries and who are
not yet incorporated into church life. "This 4% may have been
healed in a campaign, bought a Bible, but they don't attend."

We suspect that in countries marked by an extraordinary surge
of evangelism through GR campaigns and ministries in recent
years, such as Argentina or Brazil, the large number of unchurched
Evangelicals is not due to nominalism (people on their way out),
but rather to people who may be on their way in. Meanwhile, they
attend the more spectacular evangelical stadium events or special
meetings, as uncommitted church "tramps" or "seekers." In such
places, a large harvest has been reaped of people tenuously related
to GR churches, but not yet brought into the fold (Deiros 1994).

THREE

How Grass-Roots Churches
Get Started

The hot, narrow road heading east from Managua, Nicaragua, to the Atlantic leads to Rama, where travelers board a riverboat to the Atlantic coast. Along one lonely stretch Lancocho Lazo was among the homesteaders who had begun a new life on Nicaragua's "frontier" by carving out his farm in the virgin forest near the town of El Coral. He came across missionary radio station HCJB on his battery-operated radio one night and during the third broadcast of an evangelistic campaign from Quito, Ecuador, he and his wife accepted Christ.

Radio as the Leading Edge

Later he discovered a Nicaraguan station, YNOL, with the same message, and learned to pray and sing the hymns. He would go into El Coral and hold meetings in homes. A year later CAM International missionaries came across the group which already had grown to 200. At the first baptismal service, 34 made public their faith in Christ.

Because of their age and health, Lancocho and his wife, Gilberta, left their farm to operate a general store and eating place by the highway. Though they had no children of their own, one boy whom they had raised became a pastor. Some of Lancocho's other spiritual children moved into yet other areas where new farms were continually opening up (Pretiz 1977).

Reports of churches started by listeners to Trans World Radio in Venezuela, or by HCJB listeners in Ecuador, are frequent. When these groups make contact with missionaries or pastors they may be very disposed to relate organizationally with an established denomination. Some denominations will permit the church to continue with its GR style; others will tend to impose their foreign patterns.

Sola Scriptura

Before the advent of missionary radio, earlier generations made their first contacts with the gospel through Bible salesmen-- "colporteurs." Methodist Bishop Federico Pagura tells of a GR church founded by his grandfather in Arroyo Seco in Argentina. In the 1890s Natalio Pagura, an Italian immigrant, having read a Bible bought from such a salesman, questioned the local priest about Biblical teachings that seemed to contradict the Church's dogmas. The priest asked for the book and burned it. After purchasing and studying a second Bible, Natalio left the church and started services in his home.

Not having any contact with Protestant tradition, he believed that he was the first in the world to initiate a truer form of worship. So, he built an altar in his home and decorated it with two candles and a picture of the Holy Family. Eventually this GR congregation became part of the Methodist Church.

Some GR congregations begin when a Latin American finds Christ through reading a Bible or a tract or hearing the gospel on a radio program, and starts a church in his *barrio*. This is how some GR congregations begin. At times there is minimal contact with other Christians. But in most cases the process is more complex.

Breaking with Rome

The 16th century Protestant Reformation set in motion a process which has encouraged ongoing defections en masse from Rome. Some Latin American groups remain very Catholic in their orientation, while others become Evangelical.

Barrett in 1982 listed ten current autonomous Catholic groups in Latin America that had broken with Rome--in Argentina, Brazil, Guatemala, Mexico, Puerto Rico and Venezuela. Totaling the estimates in each of the W.C.E.'s tables, we arrive at over two million adherents among the ten groups.

The largest by far is the Brazilian Apostolic Catholic Church (ICAB), with an estimated 200 churches and a million members (ibid., 191-193). During World War II, D. Carlos Duarte Costa, Bishop of Botucatu, initiated a nationalist religious movement, socialist in spirit and openly critical of the government and Roman Catholic links with the Axis. In 1945, he was excommunicated and founded a church that countenanced divorce, abolished celibacy and confession, permitted its priests to have other jobs and celebrated its services in the language of the people. Hardly evangelical in its soft stance towards spiritism, this GR church spun off some short-lived sister churches in Venezuela, Panama and Guatemala (Hortal 1990).

This movement has subdivided and one of its branches is the National Network of Catholic Missions which has gained visibility through its two TV programs (Assman 1988, 86).

Another, the Orthodox Catholic Apostolic Mexican Church, was founded in 1926 at the height of President Plutarco Calles' virulent anti-Roman Catholic campaign when two defecting priests founded a church that enjoyed government favor (Acevedo 1984, 329). This so-called "national church," although it boasts some

750 congregations, 40,000 members and 60,000 adherents, has been in decline (Barrett 1982, 490-491).

A New Wave of Defections

Across the years individuals have also been renouncing Roman Catholicism, but it probably was not until the 1970s and 1980s that a new wave of Roman Catholics in Latin America left Rome collectively. In most cases these were entire communities of Catholic charismatics who had tasted of a personal experience with Christ and found their understanding of the Scriptures and their personal encounter with the Holy Spirit to be in conflict with the teachings of Rome.

Alexis Alvarado, a handsome Costa Rican dentist with a trim red beard, tells how during the 1970s he and other teenagers were drawn to Saturday Roman Catholic charismatic meetings because of the singing and the Scripture readings. Part of the group visited Evangelical churches secretly until their priest told them "not to read the Bible so much." At the negative reaction to this warning, the priest expelled them.

A Methodist missionary invited the 40 young people to hold meetings twice weekly in a nearby church without interfering or forcing them to become Methodists. For five years they met, many of them university students now, inviting Evangelical pastors to teach them. In 1981, they bought property and built the Shalom Missionary Church, now a thriving charismatic congregation of about 1,000 members in Hatillo, a poor area of the capital city, San José.

Alvarado, now pastor of the church, an avid self-taught Bible student, only recently began theological studies at a Nazarene seminary. No isolated sectarian, Alvarado has been member of the executive committee of the country's Evangelical Alliance and president of Costa Rica's pastors' fraternity.

Alvaro Muñoz, an Assemblies of God pastor in the same country, has had a ministry that consists of giving counsel to similar groups defecting from Rome. He laments the empire-building attempts of various denominational groups that have tried to capture these movements for their own cause. But many resisted these takeovers and for a while identified themselves as neither Catholic nor Protestant until they defined their position as independent Evangelical GR churches.

Noting that Catholics now conduct a large weekly televised charismatic mass (*La Hora Santa*) in his town of Alajuela, Muñoz believes that if such meetings had been held several years ago, Rome would not have lost so many followers.

Family Secrets: the Rebellious Children

But Roman Catholics are not the only ones to suffer loss from break-offs. A list of Protestant denominations in many Latin American countries will include denomination "X," related to a U.S. mission or church. But there are also churches of the *national* X denomination, churches that have broken from the U.S.-related group. Like parents of rebellious teenagers, missionaries and their organizations are often embarrassed to acknowledge many churches they founded have "flown the nest," never to return.

Are these GR churches? In many cases they are not. They may continue with the theological orientation, worship style, and organizational patterns of their foreign parents, even though estranged from them. However, in other cases they adopt leadership and worship style patterns that are highly contextual, thus becoming dynamic examples of GR movements.   As mentioned earlier, the Chilean Methodist Pentecostals, though Methodist in origin, broke from their parent denomination in 1909, and have had many years to develop into a clearly GR movement.

Schisms and break-offs are not new, but in the 1960s and 1970s several forces accelerated the disengagement of many mission-founded churches from their organizational parents.

1. "We Want More Life!"

With modern communications, the news of charismatic renewal in Roman Catholic and Protestant churches elsewhere quickly spread through Latin America. A major renewal movement in Argentina became the flame that spread to numerous countries. Many mission organizations with non-charismatic constituencies and rigid theological mind-sets regarding the Holy Spirit proved to be wineskins unable to contain the spiritual experience of their Latin American daughter churches.

In Brazil, for example, renewed Methodists separated to form the Wesleyan Methodists (Pentecostal) in 1967. Baptists of charismatic persuasion formed the Restoration Churches in 1961, the National Baptist Convention in 1965, and the Signs and Wonders movement in 1970, among others. And within the Presbyterians there developed the Maranatha Christian Church in 1970, the Renewed Presbyterians in 1975, and other groups (Fernandes 1993, 18-20).

2. "You're Too Modernistic"

Latin American daughter churches, sometimes suddenly aware of the fact that their parent organizations were affected by liberal theologies, and fearing that future missionaries would be theologically liberal, cut nearly all ties with their parent groups.

Such was the case of the major Presbyterian groups in Mexico and Brazil.

3. "You Don't Let Us Grow Up"

A few Latins, attracted to Liberation Theologies with a vision of social and political change, rejected their conservative parents to form more radical movements. However, more common was the tension between conservative mission boards and evangelical daughter churches who looked over the fences to discover a wider world of relationships. They discovered ecumenical and Roman Catholic Christians, people of other views on eschatology, Christian responsibility in issues of society and justice and other areas considered off limits to the narrower vision of some missionaries.

Washington Padilla, an Ecuadorian, in his history of Protestantism in his native country (1989, 407), described a national's view during a mission-church crisis in his republic in 1965: "There were foreign missions which considered themselves owners of the church and infallible standards of orthodoxy. No one could dissent, neither in practice nor in doctrine."

Then a club of evangelical young people exploded a "bomb" on Easter Sunday, by publishing a bulletin called *Despertar* (Awakening), with hard-hitting attacks on missionary paternalism. Those who distributed copies were labeled "subversives" by the missionary community. The shock waves tore into the country's Evangelical confederation and eventually closed down the Inter-Mission Fellowship (W. Padilla 1989, 407-413).

With the long-time emphasis on the need to establish "indigenous" churches, it is remarkable that mission-church tensions still exist. Many break-off GR groups are the result of

serious misunderstandings between missionaries and the churches
to which they had given birth.

In the early 1970s the word *moratorium* exploded upon the
world missionary scene when John Gatu, an African Presbyterian,
proposed that there be a halt to sending and receiving missionary
money and personnel for five years ". . . for each side to rethink
and reformulate . . . their future relationship," and to allow Third
World churches "to find their own identity." Other leaders picked
up the strain, especially in conciliar circles (Anderson 1974, 133-
141).

In Latin American Evangelical circles no one was ready to go
that far, but this concept added fuel to other contemporary fires--
Castro's Cuba and the Latin guerrilla movements, the
decolonization of Africa and the expulsion of missionaries, the
uncertainties about the implications of Vatican Council II, and the
charismatic movement. These all converged to create an
atmosphere of uncertainty throughout mission circles, while
nationals began to question the whole mission-national church
arrangement.

Robert ("Al") Hatch of Mission to the World (Presbyterian
Church in America) in Ecuador was concerned about rising
church-mission tensions. He edited a bulletin, *El Puente* (The
Bridge), to bring issues to the surface for frank and prayerful
discussion. He also brought together church leaders and mission
executives for face-to-face encounters.

One such gathering of Evangelical missionary leaders and
national church representatives from the Andean countries was
held in a Catholic retreat center near Santafé de Bogotá,
Colombia. Out of the gathering came the "Bogotá Declaration"
of November 1980, much of which is still valuable reading.

- The introduction recognizes the value of missionary efforts,
    despite the mistakes made. The ultimate goal ". . .must be

the total integration of foreign missionaries and national leaders, of Church and mission agencies, in one organism. . ."

- The analogy of mission-church relations in the father-son image is a limited one. The Third World Church may have very mature Christians. We are all in the process of spiritual maturity ". . .and there is no guarantee that the missionary is further ahead."

- "A missionary structure separated from the Church can only be justified as a temporary condition. . ." New ministries should be joint efforts between the Church and the mission agency.

- "Theological and general Christian education belong to the Church. . . educational methodology must equip the students in the use of appropriate tools . . . rather than indoctrinate them in a perpetuation of foreign theological dependence" (*Puente* 1980).

Tensions, ugly splits and violent break-offs could be avoided by these postures. Heavy-handed paternalistic relationships were condemned. National churches were to take front stage and mission structures recede into the background.

There is little in literature to prepare new missionaries for the reality of these tensions. W. Harold Fuller's *Mission-Church Dynamics* (1980) is one of the few books that deals frankly with this issue.

Grass-Roots Missionary Efforts

But not all GR movements are born in conflict. GR churches are expansionist. It is only to be expected that new preaching points and new local churches are continually being planted by the major GR movements. However, these missionary efforts are seldom the kind of institutionalized programs characteristic of missions from North America.

A Guatemalan evangelist, Gumercindo Melgar, had a successful evangelistic campaign in Costa Rica and turned over the results to José Luis Madrigal, a local believer with virtually no theological training. But a movement was launched, the Rose of Sharon Christian Mission, which met on the second floor of a business building in 1976. It has by now become a congregation of some 1,200, meeting in the unfinished basement of what is projected to be a sanctuary for 6,000 people (Bieske ca. 1985, 78-85).

How a single event such as an evangelistic campaign, a local leader with no formal background and only a tenuous relationship with the spiritual founder in Guatemala could have resulted in one of the largest congregations in the country is something missions should study with profit. We will consider the various forms of GR missionary expansion in chapter 14.

Elbowroom and Vision

Most GR movements originate, not as a result of any formal missionary strategy, nor entirely in reaction to a parent church's paternalism or theology, but in the heart of a Latin American who finds his own church or mission structure too confining for his vision.

The lack of elbowroom is not limited to missionary-dominated churches. GR churches themselves may be very confining. The usual highly authoritarian pastor may allow promising young men in his congregation to enter into theological education. But since there is no room at the top for a second gifted leader, the young man's only recourse in this kind of structure is to break away and start a new group.

Often the new leader may have a larger vision than that of the church structure he leaves. One Ecuadorian leader who "thinks big" speaks with disdain about churches of only 100 to 400 members after years of ministry.

In tiny Tres Ríos, Costa Rica, the founder of the Pentecost Missionary Center, Pastor Róger Castillo, had a vision of founding a center from which the gospel would spread throughout the entire world. Since the founding of this ministry in 1978 the congregation has grown to over 500 (*ibid.*, 88-93). What world impact will come out of Tres Ríos remains to be seen. But this kind of thinking "big" is what created a congregation of 500 in what was a small, conservative Catholic town, traditionally resistant to the gospel. Although no missionaries have yet been sent out, the church is promoting missions through FEDEMEC, a Costa Rican mission society.

In addition, the founder of a new movement often has a "vision" in the most literal sense--most often the result of a personal crisis and its resolution through prayer, fasting and what he affirms is a divine revelation. Latin Americans often follow spiritual leaders, not necessarily those with academic credentials nor with years of experience. Rather, they respond to those who have what is often termed the "unction" of the Holy Spirit, or some other deep religious experience.

Who Said We Can't?

An important reason for the growth of the GR movements is not so much the presence of some contributing factor as the absence of barriers. The prevailing Catholic tradition is fraught with obstacles, especially for laymen taking initiative to perform priestly functions. By way of contrast, a prevailing Latin American business climate is one in which the unofficial entrepreneur sets up his tortilla stand without asking anyone's permission.

The absence of the centralized control found in the Roman Catholic Church releases Christians to preach the Word and plant churches as they are led to do so, without the church traditions that would limit the adaptation of church patterns to local culture. No centralized control is the genius of Protestantism in contrast with Catholicism.

And so, common people, moving into a new urban housing development, or homesteading in a farming community, with an intense desire to spread their new-found faith, feel no reason to check with authorities, or seek credentials and training to start a GR Christian community.

One rather traditional Mexican church of our acquaintance did little to encourage lay participation. Some of the people were too bored to remain as passive members. Others had conflicts with the pastor. They lived in unchurched *barrios* and initiated home study groups on their own. Eventually the church claimed the groups as potential daughter congregations, as if it were their idea in the first place.

When spiritual experience is real and intense, the apostolic burden is shared: "We cannot help speaking about what we have seen and heard" (Acts 4:20).

Given the existence of many *evangélicos* unidentified yet with a church, the growth of nominalism, the rapid changes in the Protestant scene, and the general difficulty of gathering statistics, taking an inventory of the GR churches and their members will never be easy. But in many places, the numbers are large and growing.

FOUR

Early Grass-Roots Movements

Because so many GR churches are of recent origin, we listed this phenomenon in a previous work as the fifth and most recent wave of Evangelical advance in Latin America (Berg and Pretiz 1992). The first GR movement to our knowledge arose in the 19th century. Several major movements whose origins are related to the rise of Pentecostalism in the U.S., Puerto Rico, Brazil, Mexico and Chile began to appear early in the 20th century.

First GR Stirrings in Brazil and Mexico

In 1863, an educated Brazilian Roman Catholic priest, José Manuel da Conceição, became an Evangelical and began evangelizing, visiting village after village on foot (Hollenweger 1972, 94). Presbyterian missionaries already at work in Brazil tried to accommodate this itinerant evangelist into their Presbyterian framework of ministry without success because of his vision of itinerant evangelization (Pierson 1994).

In 1879, the Brazilian Evangelical Church was founded by Miguel Vieira Ferreira, a politician who was converted in the Presbyterian Church. Historian Hans Jurgen Prien (1985, 821) says he was relieved of his duties as presbyter when he could no longer maintain his mystical experiences in silence. No link has ever been proven to exist between him and any Pentecostals. He directed his congregation in Guanabara and the movement extended to other states until his death in 1895.

However, the first GR movements in Mexico had more permanent results. The magnificent *Paseo de la Reforma*

(Reformation Boulevard) in Mexico City honors the transformation of Mexico into a modern state by President Benito Juárez. But the fallout of his social and political revolution also included the seeds of a religious reformation.

The resistance of Mexico's Roman Catholic hierarchy to liberal reform led to serious state-church confrontations. Relations with the Vatican were severed and religious liberty was proclaimed in 1860. Soon after Juárez' triumphal entry into the capital in 1861, he ordered the organization of an "independent reformed Catholic church" under Mexican control.

Jean-Pierre Bastian's *Los disidentes*--The Dissidents--(1989, chapters 1 and 2) documents the government's confiscation of several Catholic churches in order to turn them over to this new group. The Iglesia Mexicana de Jesús Church, which included the participation of several ex-priests, was born. While part of the movement continued Catholic worship and practice, a parallel lay movement emerged composed largely of government workers, Freemasons, veterans of the war against pro-Catholic forces, artesans and, in some places, Indians. Congregations sprang up in Zacatecas, Monterrey, Veracruz, Puebla and elsewhere. Bastian estimates that in 1872 there were fifty such "societies" with memberships ranging from ten to 300 (*ibid.*, 48).

Government encouragement of the movement suggests an original top-down initiative, which eventually evolved into a lay movement. Some adherents no doubt were simply affirming their anti-Catholic protest. "Only men attended, and they were anti-Catholic masonic forums at which speeches were read, no hymns were sung nor offerings taken" (*ibid.*, 40), describes a typical meeting.

However, contacts with an Anglican missionary, Henry Riley, some Protestant foreigners and the Bible Society resulted in a solid representation of spiritual life in these societies. It was upon the foundations these groups had laid that the first Evangelical missionaries who entered Mexico built their denominations.

Congregationalists attached themselves to the societies in Guadalajara and Monterrey, Methodists to several units present in Mexico City, and Presbyterians to groups in Zacatecas. Although their original inspiration may have been largely political, the work of the major historic denominations in Mexico is founded on this GR movement.

To Central America via Canada:
The "Apostles and Prophets" Churches

The very first pentecostal foreign missionary to Central America may well have been "Federico" Mebius, a Canadian influenced by the Topeka, Kansas, pentecostal revival. Well before Pentecostals had defined their practices or established their denominations, he went to El Salvador in 1904, and founded a number of churches of the "Apostles and Prophets" stream. An example of a missionary who "went native," he married a Salvadorean, earned his keep as a cobbler, and to our knowledge, never returned to his homeland. The movement is marked by prominence given in each congregation to the offices of apostle and prophet. No structures link the churches, either within a country or internationally. Nicaragua has among its denominations five groups descending from this movement. This is not the result of any divisions, but is due to the high degree of autonomy of each church as they were never linked even from the beginning.

The movement still exists in four Central American countries. In El Salvador there are 224 churches of this group (a DAWN survey, *Despertar '93,* 1993, 30). Though started by a missionary, given his immersion into the life and culture of the people, the time elapsed since his direct influence, the absence of international links and a doctrine that gives unique authority to lay people, the churches today are unquestionably correctly identified as GR movements.

From Azusa Street to the World

The Azusa Street revival of 1906 in Los Angeles, usually considered the birth of the Pentecostal movement in the U.S., produced spiritual results far beyond the nation's borders. Due to industrialization and urbanization, the early twentieth century seemed to be marked by corruption, crime, and working-class alienation from the churches (Villafañe 1992, 87).

With this situation came a heightened sense of expectancy regarding Christ's soon return, and of a special outpouring of the Holy Spirit resulting in global revival. Hispanics present at the Azusa Street meetings carried the flame to their communities. Eventually, the missionary spirit generated at Azusa Street took the gospel to other Latin Americans, sometimes along very circuitous paths. It is to this same phenomena, seven or eight decades later, that scholars attribute openness to the pentecostal message in Latin America.

To the Caribbean via Hawaii: The Pentecostal Church of God and Other Puerto Rican Groups

Pentecostal missionaries on their way to the Orient in 1912 stopped off in Hawaii, and evangelized some Puerto Ricans working at a government experimental station. One of their group, Francisco Ortiz, became their pastor. Another member, Juan Lugo, who had joined the group in 1913, returned to the mainland. While in San Francisco he had a vision of himself on a hill overlooking the city of Ponce in Puerto Rico (González 1969, 110). On his way back to the island he met with Assembly of God officials in St. Louis.

Lugo's first efforts to minister in San Juan were unsuccessful. He began praying for a co-worker. Meanwhile, another Puerto Rican who had been in Hawaii, Salomón Feliciano, felt a burden to go to the Dominican Republic. In New York, however, a Christian brother told him that first he was to minister in his own land. Lugo made his way to Ponce, and found that Feliciano arrived the very same day, answering his prayer. That evening in 1916, they began with a street meeting. Ortiz arrived from Hawaii in 1917 and a "council of churches" (the term in Puerto Rico for a denominational organization) was formed.

To Adopt a Grass-Roots Movement or Not?

One of the most interesting examples of a U.S. denomination's trying to relate properly with a GR movement took place at this time. Although the unique relationship of Puerto Rico to the U.S. complicates the situation, this segment of history offers insights into the kind of problems that can develop.

At first the movement begun by Ortiz, Lugo and Feliciano, the Pentecostal Church of God, received assistance from the U.S. Assemblies of God. The denomination helped this GR movement organize, and sent a few missionaries to assist in the work. Nevertheless, no organic tie was formed between the U.S. denomination and the GR group.

At this stage in history the Puerto Ricans wanted stronger ties with the mainland denomination. This may be typical of a historical period previous to the rise of nationalism, or simply the innocent desire of any new group for more spiritual and organizational direction.

However, in reply to their request, a letter from the Assemblies of God to the Puerto Ricans said, "Your organization is national, sovereign, and your tie with us is spiritual, voluntary and very appreciated" (Moore 1969, chapters 5, 16). Such a loose arrangement did not satisfy the islanders and in 1947, they begged for "organic status." If they had been considered a "district" of the denomination, like the various districts of the Assemblies of God on the U.S. mainland (and not being related loosely and perhaps colonially with the Home Mission Department), history might have been different (Wilson 1994).

In 1955--about four decades later--the Assemblies of God sent a delegation to Puerto Rico to communicate the denomination's change of position. It now wanted a readjustment towards more union--what the islanders had requested earlier. But meanwhile the Puerto Ricans' position had also reversed. The post-war era was marked by an independence movement with regard to the island's political status. The Church had already begun to think sovereignly and the "desire for union had waned." Thus, in 1956 the Puerto Rican Church declared its sovereignty (Moore, *op. cit.*).

The whole process may have been providential. The original loose arrangement with the U.S. denomination may have been sufficient to give the Puerto Ricans needed help in the early stages of their growth. One missionary couple sent to the island was the respected Frank and Aura Finkenbinder family, whose son, Paul, became the well-known evangelist, "Hermano Pablo."

At the same time, the national group possessed enough freedom and authority to develop its own leadership and style. The 1956 "declaration of independence" seems to have released energy for the Pentecostal Church of God's missionary expansion into Central and South America, the U.S. and Spain. With over 66,000 members in 480 churches (Johnstone 1993, 459), this GR group is the largest Evangelical community in Puerto Rico. A spin-off from this group is the Pentecostal Church of Jesus Christ in Puerto Rico.

An Aztec in Puerto Rico

Another pioneer in Puerto Rico who also faced the problem of relating to a U.S. mission society, was the "Great Aztec," Francisco Olazábal. His ministry with hispanics began under the Assemblies of God in the U.S. Southwest. During 1923, in what was perceived as a question of whether an anglo or a hispanic should become superintendent of a district, Olazábal with many others left the denomination (Villafañe 1992, 90-91). He founded the Latin American Council of Christian Churches and engaged in a vigorous preaching ministry.

In 1934, his healing and evangelistic campaigns in Puerto Rico led to the formation of the Missionary Church of Christ and the Church of Christ of the Antilles (Piepkorn 1979, 141). Other groups that trace their roots to Olazábal include the Assembly of Christian Churches and the Universal Church of God (Burgess and McGee 1990, 395-396).

Following these early pioneers, dozens of other GR movements have arisen in Puerto Rico.

Across the Border to Mexico: The Apostolic (ACFCJ) and the Light of the World Churches

The Topeka and Azusa Street revivals, much like Pentecost, seem to have attracted people from various origins. Instead of Parthians and Medes, there were blacks and hispanics as well as anglos. And these, too, took the flame back to their homes. "No one was surprised to see Mexicans around the Azusa St. meeting

. . . here were some who had recently arrived from Mexico, and by the turn of the century they found themselves displaced in an environment controlled by the Gringo culture and language" (De León 1981, 89). The Spanish-language services in California that followed were home meetings (Manuel Gaxiola 1970, 157).

The first Mexican preacher out of Azusa Street was Juan Navarro. He baptized Francisco Llorente, who became the first "Pastor General" (presiding bishop) of the Apostolic Church of Faith in Christ Jesus (ACFCJ). It was one of the early GR denominations in Mexico.

The story of this movement began with Romana de Valenzuela, who received Christ in one of the California home meetings in 1912. She carried the message back to her home in Villa Aldama, near Chihuahua, Mexico, where twelve of her family responded. Anxious to find a pastor to minister to them when she left to return to the U.S., she looked up a Methodist minister in Chihuahua who became convinced of the pentecostal message and led the group for two years. Miguel García, a barber, then took over the congregation, called at that time "The Spiritual Evangelical Church." He preached enthusiastically, often until midnight, baptizing people on the spot.

At the time García left for the U.S., a period of fanaticism prevailed in the various churches of the movement. A Pedro Durán claimed he was the Messiah. Two prophets, "Saúl" and "Silas," appeared, bearded, uncombed, in long robes and sandals, insisting that all who entered the services remove their shoes. During this period some taught that Christians should just listen to the Holy Spirit and really did not need the Bible. Manuel Gaxiola's book *La serpiente y la paloma* (1970; also in English, *The Serpent and the Dove*), documents the history of the denomination and suggests that such periods of fanaticism may be common at the beginning of autochthonous pentecostal movements. Says Gaxiola, "If such extremes persist, the movements become separatist and do not grow" (*ibid.*, 15).

"We Weren't Invited to Nicea"

The ACFCJ denomination formalized its organization, practices and beliefs and now boasts 1,520 churches and 76,000 adherents (Johnstone, 1993, p. 379). Although some U.S. hispanics came to help in the early 1920s, and there is record of the involvement of one Irish missionary, Jos Stewart (Maclovio Gaxiola 1964, 29-30), the Apostolic Church is unquestionably a GR group, started by common people in the deserts of northwest Mexico. Ties with the U.S. Apostolic Church (which did not organize until 1930) were always fraternal. Neither church dominated the other.

Churches of the group look and act like most pentecostal congregations except for a thorny item which has kept other groups aloof from them. Like the United Pentecostal Church (the "Jesus Only" people), they are part of the "One-ness" stream of Pentecostals which baptizes only in the name of Jesus. Thus, their views regarding the Trinity have been unorthodox. However, being a group that had almost no connection with traditional Christianity in its formative years, it could well be said, "We weren't invited to Nicea, so why should we be bound to the creed?" This seems to explain their position.

For many years the movement was characterized by small, rural churches in northern Mexico, shepherded by untrained lay pastors. A 1969 study revealed that 99% had no studies beyond high school. Many believed that no book except the Bible should be read. Eventually the nature of its ministry began to change. A Bible school was established, and some leaders even left to study abroad (Manuel Gaxiola 1970, 92). The movement has spread down the Central American isthmus. In some countries the church mixes well with other evangelical bodies. In Mexico, however, Evangelicals do not include it as part of their fold.

Incidentally, in the U.S., according to researcher Clifton Holland, the sister Apostolic Church is no small group among the hispanics. After the Assemblies of God and the various Baptist groups, it is the third largest hispanic non-Roman Catholic bloc. In southern California it has 108 churches with over 11,000 members, the second largest single denomination among hispanics there (conversation with Holland, 1994).

A visit to a Central American Apostolic church reveals a best-for-the-Lord ethos in its furnishings. While there is an attempt to adhere to an "early Church" style in some respects (lace head coverings for the women, no women with slacks, makeup or jewelry), there is no hesitancy to use modern technology. The sound system is so powerful that the vibrations are felt in the pews. An outdoor baptistry tank in the church's front yard is graced with the words of Mark 16:16 painted on it: "Whoever believes and is baptized will be saved." Unquestionably, entrance into the church's fellowship is no private ritual. The neighborhood is witness to everyone's decision.

A New Rome for Mexico

During the Apostolic Church's more fanatical period, a soldier, Eusebio Joaquín, was evangelized in his barracks in Torreón by an "Apostolic" fruit vendor. "Saul" and "Silas" baptized him and encouraged him to preach. He deserted the army, moved to Tampico and then in 1926 made a long trek on foot to Guadalajara. Adopting a new name, Aarón, he founded the Light of the World movement.

In 1936, Aarón bought 10 hectares (about 25 acres) on the edge of Guadalajara and established the *Hermosa Provincia* (Beautiful Province). He encouraged literacy and helped his people raise their living standard. Many had very mobile occupations, such as traveling salesmen who could roam the area, or as artisans or housemaids who could easily change jobs. These became missionaries of the *Aaronista* movement as it is popularly called.

The *Hermosa Provincia* was laid out with its elegant, marble-floored temple as the hub of a wheel, with streets like spokes leading away from it where members built their homes. Seating some 3,000 people, it was for many years the largest non-Roman Catholic church in the country.

At least one observer has been impressed by the group's focus on the Bible.

"It is the only book ordinary members are permitted to use besides the hymnal. The memorization of Bible texts is the hallmark of every part of their religious activity and from the smallest child to the oldest grandparent, everyone seems intent upon memorizing and reciting the Bible . . . special arrangements between the church and local government officials allow the children to be released from government school for an hour each day to attend Bible classes in the church.

". . . So schooled are these people in the Scriptures that as soon as a speaker on the platform begins to quote a Bible verse, the whole audience breaks out in unison and helps him finish it. Preaching takes on an antiphonal quality . . . the overall effect is awesome" (Greenway 1978, 51-52).

Roger Greenway also notes the high moral standards of the group. The Hermosa Provincia is safe and clean, and the people are noted for their industriousness and honesty.

A visitor to a Light of the World church in Costa Rica is likely to be impressed by the contrast between its extravagant modernistic architecture and its humble members. An aisle separates the sexes, worship style is simple, people kneel to pray, women wear head coverings, no instruments are used, the little choir sings a capella in four parts. Some of the hymns are well-known turn-of-the-century gospel songs. But standing beside a worshiper and joining him in a lesser-known song praising the "Anointed One," the "Sent One" or "The Prince," one suddenly realizes that this is no song to worship Christ, but rather to honor the church's leader in Mexico.

And it is at this point that the movement most clearly departs from orthodox doctrine. Aarón, whose body "sleeps" in the Guadalajara church's garden, is idolized. His word is accepted as the fountain of truth. When visiting a branch church during his lifetime, he was met at the door by "virgins" dressed in white, and flower petals paved the aisle where he walked. His birthday in August is the date for the annual celebration of the Lord's Supper, held only in Guadalajara. It is an occasion for the faithful to make pilgrimages from Mexico and other countries to bring him gifts. Guadalajara has become a new Rome for this movement which has spread, followers say, to all of Latin America as well as to Italy and France.

Such a highly centralized and personalized organization naturally leads to an authoritarianism and legalism that excommunicates those who fail to submit. One evangelical missionary in Mexico found many people *"contristados"* (broken in spirit). Ex-members of the movement, having been taught that excommunication meant they were irrevocably lost, were hard to reach for the gospel.

A Mexican Church Instead of a Roman Church?

To help develop a national identity in Mexico, Mexican President Plutarco Elías Calles (1924-1928), a strong nationalist, is said to have dreamed of establishing a truly Mexican Church. His persecution of Roman Catholics was based on the conviction that their Church showed little allegiance to Mexico (De la Torre and Fortuny 1991, 34). Of all the church groups, the Light of the World movement is certainly one of the most Mexican. But its lack of contact with other Christian churches has undoubtedly contributed to its doctrinal aberrations.

To Brazil via South Bend:
The Brazilian Assemblies of God

Less directly related to Azusa Street, but clearly in the wake of the revival of the first decade of the 20th century, is the story of the beginnings of the largest denomination in Brazil, the Assemblies of God.

Two Swedish immigrants to the U.S., Daniel Berg and Gunnar Vingren, had met in pentecostal revival meetings in Chicago. Later Berg went to visit Vingren in South Bend, Indiana, where the latter was a Baptist pastor. In their common experience of praying in tongues, both found themselves enunciating "Pará" and sensed that God would lead them there, wherever that was. As they looked up the word in the atlas of the town library, it became obvious to them that they should go to the state of Pará, by the mouth of the Amazon River in Brazil.

A collection taken at church supplied enough money for them to get to New York. According to the *História das Assembleias de Deus no Brazil* (no author identified, 1960, 13-16), there they were providentially provided with the exact amount, ninety dollars, for passage to Brazil.

Vingren and Berg attached themselves to the Baptist church in Belem. Their teaching on the Holy Spirit led to their expulsion and the founding of the first Assemblies of God church in June 1911. Since then, this denomination has grown to become the largest Evangelical body in the country, with 85,000 churches, 6 million members and 14 million in its Evangelical community (Johnstone 1993, 128).

Is it a "GR" church? Assemblies' missionaries assure us that it is. One Pentecostal scholar and Assemblies of God leader, Everett Wilson, said it was "absurd" not to place it in this category. Control of the denomination is entirely in the hands of Brazilians. Its organization into "ministries" with a highly authoritarian *"Pastor Presidente"* (President Pastor) over each group of churches (and only a tenuous connection between these ministries) is unlike the organization in other countries where missionary influence is strong.

There are only seven U.S. missionary couples serving in the denomination in this vast country. They are engaged exclusively in programs of theological education by extension while exercising little influence in the church's government. Although it began with foreign personnel, time has erased the original influence of Berg and Vingren, hardly professional missionaries in the usual sense anyway. If we were to add this group of six million adherents to the "GR" category, it would double the number of such churches in the country.

Besides describing the early beginnings of another non-historic Latin American church, we included the Assemblies of God of

Brazil to show how the matter of definition of one major group can change the picture. But following Barrett's lead, we do not include this large group in our list of GR movements.

To Chile via India and Norway:
The Methodist Pentecostal Church
and Other Chilean Groups

Publications and correspondence following Azusa Street carried news of Pentecostal revivals around the world. In 1907 a pamphlet, "The Baptism of the Holy Ghost and Fire," was sent by a Minnie Abrams in India to a former Bible school classmate, Mrs. Willis Hoover, of Valparaíso, Chile. Miss Abrams had shared reports about the Welsh revival with Indian girls in her charge, and she wrote about the pentecostal phenomena observed among them. The Hoovers, Methodist missionaries, began correspondence with early Pentecostal leaders, including one from Norway (Kessler 1967, 111-112).

The 1906 earthquake had destroyed the church of which Willis Hoover was pastor, and a new building seating 1,000 people had been dedicated early in 1909. Hoover was already convinced of the teaching of a baptism of the Holy Spirit, accompanied by visible signs. He expected that with the new building God would pour out a special blessing. Saturday night vigils finally led to experiences of tongues during Holy Week.

This was followed by public confession, payment of debts and reconciliations. But later meetings were also accompanied by excesses which led to divisions, sensationalist newspaper accounts and resentment against other missionaries for opposing the new teachings. The manifestations moderated, but the die was cast and opposition by the denomination led to Hoover's resignation in

1911, and the subsequent withdrawal from the Methodist conference of several churches in Valparaíso and Santiago.

Hoover continued his involvement with the new Methodist Pentecostal Church until his death in 1931. Interesting vestiges of the original Methodist practice still exist--the Episcopal structure, infant baptism, even the nomenclature of the branch churches as "classes," as Wesley had called such groups in his day. But the contextualized style, the leadership, the strong identification with Chile's poor masses by the Methodist Pentecostal Church and its spin-offs combine to convince all observers that these are genuine GR movements.

John Kessler has produced a genealogical tree which sorts out the numerous divisions (and divisions of divisions) and new groups--no less than 34 at the time of his study--which have been derived from the original Methodist Pentecostal group (Kessler 1967, 316).

In 1962, Ignacio Vergara, a Roman Catholic priest who studied Protestants in Chile, counted 2,760 *"iglesias populares"* (people's churches, 2,317 of which were Pentecostal) in Chile with a total of nearly half a million adherents. This contrasted with 885 traditional Protestant churches with 66,716 adherents (Vergara 1962, 247- 248). Twenty years later the *World Christian Encyclopedia* identified 1,181,900 members of Chilean GR churches contrasting with 168,500 members belonging to traditional groups (Barrett 1982, 191).

Many students of these Chilean GR movements have admired the zeal of its members in street-corner preaching and the energy of the bicycle teams that pedal out to evangelize country villages. The rungs of the ladder by which men can rise to become pastors are based on experience and effective ministry rather than academic studies, thus creating a clergy that is close to the people. Not only the loyalty of the members to their bishops, but also the recognition conferred by the Chilean government upon these movements by celebrating the annual Te Deum thanksgiving service in the pentecostal Jotabeche Cathedral (as well as in the Roman Catholic cathedral), demonstrate how much these churches have become part of the country's life and culture.

"On Strike," Pro-Pinochet or Independent?

The political influence of these enormous movements has been a subject of continuous discussion. Christian Lalive, in his classic sociological study, *The Haven of the Masses* (1968), discovered that at the time of his study 85% of Chilean Pentecostals felt that a Christian should not be involved politically or be a member of a political party. He makes a case that these largely GR movements are on "social strike." Yet the fact that these movements are almost entirely composed of the working class population makes it hard to believe that many did not vote for marxist President Salvador Allende. Indeed, we heard of a Pentecostal lay pastor who, as a union organizer, taught factory workers how to make Molotov cocktails to repel the inevitable right-wing reaction to the Allende regime.

However, most of the world's attention focused upon the massed prayer meetings that preceded the fall of Allende in 1973, the Pentecostals' support of Pinochet, and the dictator's cutting the ribbon at the inauguration of the Jotabeche Cathedral. Roman Catholic criticism of Pinochet's disdain for human rights seemed to ally the government with the Pentecostals, who not only raised no voice against him, but gave him some aura of respectability when he made such appearances. Paul Hoff (1993, 25) hints darkly that Chile's left-wing political leaders have not forgotten the Pentecostal support of Pinochet.

However, this more recent survey (Fontaine-Beyer 1991) indicated that 53.6% of practicing Chilean Protestants (of which nearly 90% are GR Pentecostal) have a negative opinion of Pinochet. The same study shows an equal number (about 15%) on each political extreme--right or left--24% in the center, and 46% independent. Perhaps Chilean Pentecostals are not so much on "social strike" now as they are independent or centrist, neither so marxist nor so radically to the right as some leaders would have us believe.

Methodist Pentecostals Today

The mother church of the 400,000 Methodist Pentecostals is the "Jotabeche Cathedral" (named for the street it is on), a few blocks from Santiago's busy Central Railroad Station. It is a large, simple building. Two small towers and some tinted panes in the windows are the only concessions to our concepts of a cathedral-like building.

Ample areas are reserved for the choir and the orchestra. One large painting portrays Christ the Shepherd and another depicts an open Bible on a rock resisting waves of opposition.

Most men attend in coats and ties. Only a few women wear jewelry. But there are few young people or children, even for Sunday School. Familiar hymns are sung, but often there is a surprising twist to their rhythm. None of the choruses popular among Evangelicals are sung. An occasion for praise brings the congregation to its feet in the ritual of three exclamations of *"Gloria a Dios!"* (Glory to God).

Bishop Javier Vásquez' message is simple and evangelistic. Sunday School and morning worship are unmarked by pentecostal manifestations.

No Lack of Critics

But outsiders, even Pentecostals, often question the "Jotabeche myth" created by the church's admirers. Its many pastors are forbidden to study any literature beyond that of the Bible. Street meetings, its major evangelistic activity, now attract few listeners. Some criticize the fact that the church's 44 satellite congregations ("classes") are not given their autonomy. They are supposedly kept dependent so that their contributions can flow into the coffers of the cathedral, giving it vast financial power and depriving the daughter congregations of the chance to grow. Also, the denomination remains isolated from the rest of the Evangelical community.

Despite the critics, others believe that this and similar Chilean movements are still growing because of the momentum generated by their sheer size.

To Brazil via Chicago:
The Christian Congregation of Brazil

In addition to the Swedish immigrants to the U.S. who went to Brazil to found the Assemblies of God movement, another immigrant to the U.S. midwest was Louis Francescon. An Italian, he came to know Christ in Chicago at about the same time as Vingren and Berg. Like them, he, too, was called to share his faith in South America.

He first went to Argentina, and then to the state of Paraná in Brazil before reaching São Paulo where he attached himself to a Presbyterian church. His views on the Holy Spirit caused a division, and in 1910, the *Congregacão Cristã* (Christian Congregation) was born. Francescon was a layman who made frequent trips to Brazil witnessing to the Italian immigrant community there, but he did not make the country his home. The congregation kept meeting and grew to become one of the largest early GR movements in South America. About 1935, it switched from Italian to Portuguese and is no longer a church confined exclusively to an ethnic subculture.

Throughout São Paulo, Brazil, little standardized blue and white Christian Congregation churches with their narrow gothic windows reflect the style of the great mother church located in the old Italian section of the city. The principal building, with a capacity of about 4,000, is a handsome mix of gothic windows with Italian opera-house-style balconies. Eight tall columns rise from behind the large baptistry pool on the platform. The church's organizational simplicity merely requires that a person have accepted Christ, be 12 years or older, and be single or legally married, in order to be eligible for baptism.

Women with head coverings are seated to the left, men to the right. The racially-mixed congregation is well-dressed. An all-male orchestra, dominated by brasses, seated in the center of the congregation, lends a solemn air to the slowly-sung gospel hymns. Testimonies, spoken from the front, are given seriously and the congregation punctuates the close of each one with an "Amen," spoken in unison.

At the appropriate moment for the sermon, the leader routinely asks whether anyone has a message. No one responded at the service we attended, and so the leader proceeded with a simple exposition of a Bible chapter. Prayer is said kneeling and the service ends with the holy kiss (Rom. 16:16), men kissing each other lightly. The women also, in their separate sections, follow this custom.

The grandiose building and the formality of the service contrast with the simple quality of the church's organization. There is no clergy as such. No offerings are taken. There is no published literature, no training institution and no formal evangelistic effort. People are won as members feel led to speak to others about their faith. Tongues may be experienced by those being baptized, but there are few other manifestations in the general services.

Barrett (1982) lists one million members of the group, but no records are kept, except a head count at the annual communion service. So anybody's estimate is just that. Thousands gather for an annual Easter assembly and two large buildings (one still under construction) behind the church are built to house the delegates-- the elders and "cooperators"-- from the many related congregations.

While the Brazilian Evangelical community accepts other Brazilian G.R. movements, many of them quite "disorderly" and with questionable practices, the Christian Congregation, despite its formality and seriousness, is the one most commonly referred to as a "sect." Its refusal to recognize or relate to any other group translates into "you can only be saved in our church," and this is perceived by many as salvation through membership in the group or baptism into it, rather than by grace. Their members (the *"glorias,"* as they are popularly known) solemnly refer to their church as *"la obra de Deus"* (the work of God) in a manner that seems to exclude everyone else.

Other critics see traces of Brazilian *illuminism* in their approach to the Bible. The Scriptures are their only text, to be interpreted by a kind of personal inspiration. Without any correctives that could come from the insights of others, the lay preachers may "use some odd formulations about baptism, spiritual gifts, and other cardinal doctrines" (Read 1965, 40).

And here, too, as in the case of the Chilean Methodist Pentecostals and some other early GR churches, what began as a movement marked by spontaneity and freedom in the Spirit has become an inflexible structure. Attending a service in churches in movements of this kind is to step into a scenario created forty or more years ago, given the formality of the congregation's dress, the worship style and the general mindset of the church toward the world. It continues to exist and to grow by the sheer momentum of its size--but is increasingly out of touch with the age in which it lives.

FIVE

In Spanish Latin America: Cattlemen and Urbanites

Much recent attention has been rightfully drawn to Latin America's world-class cities and their need, almost to the neglect of attention upon the rural areas. In God's providence, GR movements have arisen in both contexts of Spanish-speaking Latin America.

Cattle Ranchers in Venezuela: the Apure Movement

The "Native Church" movement in Venezuela began with the baptism in 1927 of Arístides Díaz, a cattle dealer, his wife and seven others. That same day they founded a church in the state of Apure in southern Venezuela. Díaz had bought a Bible from a colporteur, experienced a radical conversion and legalized his marriage a short time before. A business partner, General José Domínguez, had him imprisoned for eight days to dissuade him from his decision to leave the business and dedicate himself to preaching (Ayerra 1980, 110-115).

Without any support from a missionary organization, this layman, by the time of his death in 1969, forty-five years later, had founded over 200 churches with over 7,000 baptized members (Ríos 1976, 153-154). By 1982 the *World Christian Encyclopedia* estimates there were 150 churches of this group with 15,000 members and twice as many adherents (Barrett 1982, 740-741). Membership numbers will be hard to come by, because

according to P. J. Ayerra, a Catholic priest who has studied
Venezuelan Protestantism, this information is not readily shared.
Say their leaders, "In the book of Acts the names of the churches
Paul founded were listed, but never the number of their members"
(Ayerra 1980, 111).

Venezuelans observe that Apure is the most evangelized state
of the country--90% may be Evangelicals or have close contact
with the gospel. Their numbers include some of the richest cattle
owners and community leaders.

Pastoral training consists of sending a candidate to a new field
to start a church. As people are converted, they eventually name
him their pastor, a position he holds for life. Pastors are laymen
and no offerings are taken for their salaries.

The headquarters of this often-called "Native Church"
(officially the "Evangelical Missionary Apostolic Christian
Church") is the "Bethel" farm in San Fernando. This is not an
Indian group, but rather a people's movement of *mestizo* (mixed
Spanish and Indian descent) cattle raisers, living on isolated farms,
and for whom regular festivals of believers are important. Five
thousand may meet for New Year's Day or Holy Week at Bethel.
This occasion is not just for spiritual refreshment, but also for
conducting a market for the sale of clothes and food. Three or
four cattle are slaughtered each day to feed the assembly.

Allergic to Pentecostals

The Apure Church is determinedly independent, not permitting
other groups to penetrate it. One missionary who tried to attach
himself to the group and exercise some control was isolated.
Asked regarding their relation with Pentecostals, they indicated
that the baptism of the Holy Spirit was demonstrated in a changed
life, not in pentecostal manifestations, pointing out that at

Pentecost it was Peter's preaching that convinced the multitude. There is prayer for the sick, but preaching the Word is foremost (*ibid.*, 114-115). It may be, says a friend of the movement, that they are particularly "allergic" to Pentecostals because such outsiders have robbed them of many of their churches. They are not members of the country's Evangelical council, nor do they cooperate in united evangelistic efforts (Nieves, 1992).

Services may begin with a time of praise, men on one side of the chapel, women on the other, all expressing their praise to God in a big murmur. The movement developed its own hymnal. Many pastors cannot read, so someone reads a Bible passage and the pastor preaches from that text. In their simplicity they have no Sunday schools nor women's or youth societies.

On occasions, they rent buses and a group of five or six churches goes to a place to hold a week's evangelistic campaign. Says Gilberto Nieves (*ibid.*), a pastor who has gained their confidence, ". . . there is a law that force draws force. If there are people, more people will be drawn. So when 200 to 500 people go to a place and have a campaign, many [outsiders] are saved."

No New Blood

But all is not well in the Apure Church's simplicity and isolation. In a church composed of many members well over 60 years of age and where only elders are trusted, the youth feel that they "are not people," and go elsewhere. Some who have left the church have become capable professionals. Nieves has related to the group for 18 years. "I love them. I help them. I took one of their leaders on a tour to Israel and the U.S. He became president of the area cattlemen's association" (*ibid.*).

But, he says, "Without leaders this church will disappear." Their General Pastor (much like a bishop) is also appointed for

life. "His son," says Nieves, "will continue" [in the leadership].
It is this ingrownness that Nieves also regrets. Self-government
or autonomy, especially if a church closes itself off to new blood,
cannot be its one and only goal (*ibid.*).

Nieves himself is a leader of a GR movement, the Emanuel
Church, which in five years has grown to 40 churches and 100
congregations in eight Venezuelan states. Seventy percent of this
group's income goes to missions. They support 17 missionaries
working among tribal groups (Landrey 1994).

Apathy and Stirrings in the Southern Cone

Buenos Aires is the most urbane of Latin cities. The least
Indian, the most European and cosmopolitan of the continent's
large cities, the birthplace of the famed tango, and home of many
intellectuals, it hardly seems a likely locale for pentecostal GR
movements to flourish.

The Tommy Hicks healing campaign (1952) during the Perón
administration made an impact. The renewal movement in many
established churches in the 1960s, led by Juan Carlos Ortiz,
introduced charismatic manifestations and questioned old
organizational structures of the Church, but did not make much
impact on society.

The proportion of Evangelical Christians in "BA" was always
low. But God began stirring Argentine society through evangelist
Omar Cabrera.

To Reach the 87%: The Vision of the Future Church

The pastor of the Vision of the Future Church appears on the
platform with well-groomed gray hair, a clerical collar, a purple
shirt (a bishop's colors), and a gray business suit. Unlike many

Pentecostal pastors, Omar Cabrera preaches in a conversational tone to the thousands gathered in the former Cuyo Cinema in downtown Buenos Aires.

The message is on "binding and loosing." While a typical pentecostal message might only emphasize the binding of demonic powers and a person's deliverance from them, Cabrera also speaks of unleashing God's blessings. He testifies about going to a city and praying that the spirits that control the city be bound. But he also prays for the release of God's blessings, prosperity, health and power on the place. This positive message is reinforced by the neon sign in the cinema's lobby: "The peace of God surrounds me now."

Another surprise is his irenic attitude towards Roman Catholicism. "God calls a man and gives him a message. My message is love, especially for the lost sheep of the Roman Catholic Church." His target is the 87% of Catholics in Argentina who do not attend church. After attending his services he notes that some Catholics become more faithful in attending mass. "I put them up against the wall . . ." he says, challenging them to be committed to Christ in one church or another. "I don't believe a person has to be an Evangelical." Until other Evangelicals understood his ministry, Cabrera says that neither the Evangelicals nor the Roman Catholics would accept him. Now he has friends among the bishops, and his movement is part of ACIERA, the Association of Argentine Evangelicals (Cabrera 1994).

Multitudes of People and the Presence of Angels

Cabrera's original interest was in architecture, and through a miracle of healing he was converted. His training was in Pentecostal Holiness schools. But it was at a World Vision-sponsored pastors' retreat that he was challenged by Bob Pierce's description of phenomenal Presbyterian church growth in Korea. "Why doesn't this happen in my ministry?" he asked himself. For nine months he then studied the book of Mark, underlining the many passages referring to the *multitudes* affected by Christ's ministry, becoming convinced that he should expect multitudes to respond.

A campaign in the city of Concordia was the first opportunity to see God work in answer to his faith. He rented an Anglican chapel to begin his campaign which soon exploded into a revival resulting in thousands of conversions. But 540 consecutive nights of preaching and praying for the sick left him in a state of collapse. "I didn't know about intercessors," he says.

Further study in Acts awakened him to the frequent mention of angels in the ministry of Christ and the apostles. While many Pentecostals are conscious of the demonic, his ministry began to take into account the counterpart kingdom, the angelic. According to Cabrera, people reported sensing angelic presence in some of his meetings. "Omar's new doctrine" was criticized until Billy Graham's book on angels appeared.

His healing ministry brought accusations of hypnotism, illegal practice of medicine and abuse of people's credulity. But he was cleared of all charges. Another kind of threat came from urban guerrillas during periods of political crisis.

Vision of the Future Churches

Eventually his ministry consolidated into a network of churches in 160 cities and towns with a total attendance of over 85,000. "I don't accept members or preachers from other churches," Cabrera (*ibid.*) says, supporting his claim that he reaches the 87% who are really unchurched. New believers are shepherded through three stages of Christian orientation. His associate pastors are well cared for with a house, car and health insurance. Part of the ministry's income is from book and cassette sales. A radio ministry reaches out from 60 stations. A published daily devotional guide is attractive.

Cabrera, like many GR leaders, does not mention social action unless someone brings up the subject, but is actively engaged in social service on an ongoing basis. Vision of the Future conducts courses on AIDs, provides meals for needy children, attends to abused women and gives assistance to orphanages of other churches.

There is something low-key about the Vision of the Future ministry. Cabrera never gives a formal evangelistic invitation, but people keep responding and testify of the miracles God is performing in their lives.

The Door Opens after the "Dirty War"

The Argentine military regime during the years 1976 to 1983 was one of the most repressive in contemporary Latin America. Thousands of people disappeared in the torture chambers during their subversion. Evangelicals' access to the media or liberty for large public gatherings was severely limited. Then the country's defeat in the Faulklands War and the mishandling of the economy left discredited both the military and the Roman Catholic Church, whose chaplains generally had stood with the military in its atrocities.

When the return of democracy in 1983 gave Evangelicals greater freedom for large meetings and for broadcasting the gospel, God raised up an unlikely evangelist. His name is Carlos Annacondia, a manufacturer of nuts and bolts from La Plata. A Baptist pastor (Prokopchuk 1994) shared his impressions when he first attended one of Annacondia's tent campaigns. "It was raining, but the tent was full. The short message--only 15 minutes--was Christ-centered, followed by prayer to rebuke the demons. People *ran* forward at the invitation." He went on to describe healings, even in the case of skeptical journalists who came to report on the campaign, and the positive reports by the press of the thousands who responded.

Actually in this evangelist's meetings there are often three invitations: (1) A call to conversion, (2) a call for the sick to come forward (in the case of those unable to attend, friends or relatives bring some item of clothing from the sick person to be blessed), and (3) a call for those who are in need of exorcism. These are taken to the "spiritual intensive care unit" tent where there is special prayer for them.

The number of signed professions of faith in one city, Córdoba, was 65,000 (Bush 1989, 20) and in other cities tens of thousands have accepted Christ.

While Annacondia never founded a church, others copied his methods and capitalized on the new openness to the gospel by founding new GR movements.

Feeling Pain for Buenos Aires: The Waves of Love and Peace Movement

Swarthy young Héctor Giménez (1994), involved in drugs since age 13, was shot on his way to a robbery. At a home where he received medical attention, a Christian friend led him to Christ. He began taking addicts, prostitutes and others into his home. In 1986, he woke up crying when he felt God had made him feel pain for Buenos Aires.

Through unusual circumstances he was given time on a Buenos Aires radio station and the use of a theater. Reports on

TV of healings swelled the crowds and three months later, his followers numbered 5,000.

He continued with daily services, and meetings all day on Sundays which drew standing-room-only crowds at the 1,800-capacity theater. Giménez claimed (1994) that the 120,000 members of the movement were mostly new people, because visitors from traditional churches, missing the formality of their liturgies, tended to return to their own churches.

Giménez told us that the Waves of Love and Peace church "adheres to old doctrines but employs new methods," explaining, for example, how he keeps track of the members by having them punch time cards in order to record their attendance. Five thousand trained workers, he said, handle visitation and carry out other duties. As of the time this was written, there were serious misconduct charges against the leadership and the future of this movement was uncertain.

Trying Not to be a "Church": The Calacoaya Cultural Center

We visited the Calacoaya Cultural Center in Mexico City before the current revision of Mexico's legislation which has given churches more legal rights. It was one of the many Christian groups that found it advantageous then not to be a "church," but rather to register as a non-profit cultural organization.

In its appearance, the Calacoaya Center, located in Mexico City's northwest suburbs, is likewise hardly the typical church. Like a number of large GR congregations in Latin America, it meets in a tent. This one seats 3,000. No dirt-under-foot circus tent atmosphere here; the center has a paved floor and permanent installations. Young women with tambourines lead the singing, accompanied by an electronic instrumental group.

How it Began

Founder of the center, former publicity agent Gonzalo Vega,
and his wife were part of the Roman Catholic charismatic
movement. As they read the Scriptures they experienced the new
birth. With six others they began Bible studies in their home in
1976. When the group grew to seventy, they began renting
locations, and when attendance was 120, the group broke from
Catholicism. The first tent with a capacity for 1,500 was already
too small when it was put to use (Flores 1989, 21-22).

Vega traveled to various countries to study churches,
including David Cho's church in Korea, generally considered to be
the world's largest Protestant congregation. While gleaning ideas
from other church models, Calacoaya seems intent on becoming
part of a current opposed to the style of traditional Evangelical
churches (*ibid.*, 26).

Vega is not called "pastor" or "minister." There is a reaction
against all *"templismo"* (church-building-centeredness) and all
ceremony. There is no Sunday school, no printed teaching
materials. A few attend midweek services, but the emphasis is on
the single service on Sunday morning (*ibid.*). Long commuting
times in one of the world's largest cities and little time available for
people during the week make the usual midweek activities difficult
to attend.

Low-Key but Effective

Commitment to the church, according to Héctor Flores (*ibid.*),
is "somewhat ambiguous," unlike the pressure of many churches
for high involvement. In fact, he says Sunday morning service is
reminiscent of the single weekly mass that Catholics are used to
attending. Despite the low-key atmosphere, Vega has found 400

people to help him in the center's sixty ministries (*ibid.*, 27). Special conferences and the circulation of audio and video cassettes available for members to borrow provide the group's Christian education ministry.

The only regularly printed material is the monthly bulletin which is a mix of inspiration, listings of ministries such as counseling and evangelistic breakfasts, courses in such subjects as English and computer science, and a "bulletin board" which includes recommended medical services and reliable mechanics. While the focus of the church is upon reaching middle-class suburbanites, programs such as literacy classes represent the center's outreach to the rural peoples still in the area--people engulfed by Mexico City's urban sprawl.

The Little Churches, Too

Having looked at some of Spanish America's large churches-- with Brazil's even larger movements yet to be described--we could easily overlook the fact that most GR activity in Latin America takes place not in the large movie theater or the tent, but rather in a small storefront, a refurbished restaurant or a remodeled home. A church "within walking distance" is important for the majority of Latin American Christians. The sense of community or family that the small church provides is still one major attraction for lonely people in an unfriendly city.

SIX

In Brazil:
Megachurches in a Megacountry

The largest country in Latin America, land of the largest Roman Catholic population in the world, Brazil is also home of some of the world's largest evangelical churches and largest GR movements. The Brazilian Assemblies of God (though not considered a GR movement in our study) and the Christian Congregation churches have already been described. We now turn to some of the newer movements.

Immensity with a Heart: The Brazil for Christ Church

Never say:
I can't
I'm afraid
I don't have faith
I am weak
I am defeated.
Come and feel the Holy Spirit
A relaxed atmosphere
Come and make friends

This is the welcome sign in front of what some believe is the largest church building in the hemisphere. The Brazil for Christ (*O Brasil para Cristo*) congregation meets in a hangar-like building in São Paulo where four 727s could fit. John Vaughn

(1984, 253) says the building was designed to seat 15,000, but as many as 30,000 have crowded into it.

The adjoining patio and buildings that house offices and a small restaurant are attractive. But despite attempts at decorating the cavernous echo-filled auditorium with fountains and other ornamentation, there is nothing to make the hangar hospitable until the warmth of the service and the thousands of voices join in praise offering the atmosphere promised on the billboard outside. For some who might be uneasy about entering, certain services are video-projected on a huge screen outside the church.

Today a song celebrating the Lord's resurrection is sung by the assembled people with motions like a children's action chorus. The congregation then raises its hands agreeing to ask God's blessing for a pregnant woman. The service today features the reaffirmation of the wedding vows of 35 couples who had been married before coming to know Christ. The pastor's wife gives each "bride" a rose. Announcements herald a coming evangelistic campaign, but also a collection of warm clothing for the needy.

In his office Pastor Paul Lutero de Mello fed a video cassette into a player and showed us images of tons of food, separated into family-sized packages (including a Bible), being distributed to 3,000 needy families.

Manoel de Mello, Paul's father and founder of the movement, was no stereotyped pentecostal preacher. He began as a tent-meeting evangelist with a strong healing ministry, and became widely known because of a daily live radio program in the 1950s. In addition to his preaching, he exposed corrupt politicians and denounced other public abuses (Read 1965, 150-151).

His movement was organized in 1955. Politicians saw the potential of de Mello's large following and one obtained land for his projected church in exchange for support for his presidential candidacy. After the church was built, the Roman Catholic hierarchy pressured the donor to withdraw his gift, threatening him with political ruin. The candidate did an about-face and without warning, bulldozers attacked the church building and destroyed it in a few hours (*ibid.*, 151) forcing de Mello to start over again--but this time with plans for an even larger sanctuary. His mission was accomplished with the construction of the present building.

However, this grievous experience did not inhibit him from political activity. He promoted the campaigns of Evangelical candidates. At the same time, his political views were undergirded by a sensitive conscience about society. In an interview with Roberto Barbosa (1975, 145-154) he criticized both communism and capitalism. Churches that offered the gospel without bread were "false" just as were those offering bread without the gospel.

He advocated turning empty church buildings into schools on weekdays. In an interview with Walter Hollenweger (1972, 101), de Mello stated that Rome brought idolatry to the world, Russia the terrors of communism, and the U.S. the demon of capitalism. Brazil, however, nation of the poor, will bring the gospel to the world.

The hierarchy-inspired destruction of his church building likewise did not inhibit him from joining with Catholic clergy to denounce injustice, from rejoicing in Catholic Biblical renewal, nor from meeting regularly with Catholic pentecostals (*ibid.*, 150-154). All of this cost him severe criticism by other Evangelical churches.

To cause even more consternation among fellow Evangelicals, he plunged into the milieu of the World Council of Churches--to learn about social action and to try to teach ecumenicists something about evangelism.

The founder died in 1970 and his son, Paulo Lutero de Mello, continued to lead the church out of the typical pentecostal mold.

"Anyone who asks for the Holy Spirit will receive Him," he says (1994), "and tongues are not necessarily a sign." The typically strict pentecostal dress codes are relaxed--at least in the movement's urban churches.

Back to One's Roots

Soon, Pastor de Mello confessed, something of the fire began to die out. In February 1994, he devoted two weeks to services of prayer and deliverance. Monday night healing services were restored, and consequently, the church experienced renewed growth, applying a "marriage" of pentecostal emphases and social concern. His father's relationship with the World Council was a source of division among the movement's rural pastors, so de Mello withdrew, calling his present relationship with the ecumenical movement simply "fraternal" (*ibid.*).

As for relating with Evangelicals, the Brazilian Association of Evangelicals (AEVB) states that although Brazil for Christ is not a member, there is a "dynamic relationship" with the movement.

The headquarters church houses a Bible school and de Mello feels other Pentecostal churches will follow, maturing and requiring theological preparation for their pastors. De Mello's own background is in business administration, and his theological preparation is the sum of many short programs and seminars.

Although he does spread the word among his churches that one of their members is running for a seat in the state senate, he says there is "much less" now of the kind of political activity that characterized his father's ministry.

But in this maturing process, he does not want to see Pentecostal groups become traditional churches, declaring that "the world needs both kinds." At the same time, he will not be critical of the *Igreja Universal del Reino de Deus* (Universal

Church of the Kingdom of God), a more controversial GR movement, feeling that if this group can bring people to Christ by employing sacred objects (blessed oil, etc.), that is fine. But he predicts that in time, that church will have to suspend this kind of activity (*ibid.*).

Brazil for Christ, founded in 1955, is already one of the older GR Brazilian churches. Johnstone (1993, 128) estimates that it boasts a million members and another million related non-members. But it has not become inflexible, legalistic or sectarian. De Mello's vision is not just for the 650 churches in the movement, but for the whole Body of Christ in Brazil. Identifying with the other churches, both traditional and pentecostal, he affirms that Brazil will eventually become "the biggest Evangelical country in the world" (de Mello, *op. cit.*).

Primitive Needs and Raw Emotions: The God is Love Church

Looking at the crowd at the God is Love (*Deus é Amor*) Church in the heart of São Paulo, one has to ask, "What must it be like to be jobless and hungry? How helpless do you feel when your son is on drugs and your life is ruined by drink? How desperate would you be if you were tormented by a demonic presence, a spell real or imagined, cast upon you by a personal enemy?"

Only by trying to imagine these agonies can one explain the mass of crying, shouting, trembling, desperate people. The leader instructs each afflicted person to place one hand on his own head. The other hand is raised skyward. *"Saíd, demonios!"* ("Out, demons") and hands draw away suddenly from countless heads as if waving off the demons in a rite of self-exorcism. These are identified as demons of swearing, of sickness, of transvestism, of nudity, and of homosexuality, among other ills and vices.

Gone is any attempt at refinement or decor. The locale is a former factory close to the heart of the city. Eighty small arched doors allow passers-by to look through a forest of steel columns to the platform where the leader, in coat and tie, microphone in hand, is behind a glass booth, shouting "Alleluia" repeatedly for perhaps 15 minutes. Women are on one side, men on the other in this vast area. Official posted signs warn that the 27,000-square-meter building's capacity is 10,000 people, obviously because the limit tends to be exceeded.

There is little sense of community. As in a Roman Catholic cathedral, each person is wrapped up in his own personal worship or spiritual struggle. Some go forward for prayer towards the low platform in front.

Six "bookstores" are spaced throughout the church, but LP records and cassettes are for sale rather than books. This is a stratum of society where communication is still primarily oral. Radio is a preferred medium. Yellow plastic signs arranged horizontally over the platform represent the 140 stations on which God is Love programs are aired.

Fighting Enemy Number One

If the traditional Biblical enemies are the world, the flesh and the devil, it is more simple in the God is Love movement and in similar groups to identify the devil (and his hierarchy) as the Christian's Enemy Number One and to deal with him.

To comprehend the plight of the desperately poor, we must add an understanding of Brazil's preoccupation with the spirit world. Several writers contrast the development of Christianity in Brazil with that in hispanic Latin America (e.g. Itioka 1988). In colonial Spanish Latin America the town was the center. There the resident priest had control of religious belief and practice.

But in Brazil, widely separated estates had their own chapels, too remote for priests to visit frequently. African slaves on the estates tended to influence the religion of the colonists (Parke Renshaw's article, "A New Religion for Brazilians" in *Practical Anthropology*, July-August 1966, 126) to such a degree that even today spiritism is more pervasive than Catholicism. A more refined European spiritism was later added to the mix. Today's converts to the gospel in Brazil still refer to their deliverance from bondage to the spirits more often than to deliverance from ties with Catholicism.

Unlike other parts of Latin America where spiritism is practiced clandestinely, in Brazil it is institutionalized. Its temples and charitable institutions (including a center to receive street children) compete with Christian churches and institutions for public favor. Its leaders are organized, at least to counterattack the Evangelical churches that specialize in preaching against spiritism.

The president of the Brazilian Umbanda Federation, Manoel Alves de Souza, complains about Evangelical churches being planted near spiritist places of worship. Another spiritist leader, Nélson de Omulu, issued a formal challenge to debate with Christian pastors who purportedly encouraged "invasions" of spiritist worship centers, breaking images and disturbing their celebrations (Bottam's article *"Evangélicos umbandistas em 'guerra santa'"* in *"O Globo"* October 23, 1988, 24).

However crude the manifestations in the God is Love Church, perhaps only a person who has struggled against the oppression of spiritual darkness can understand how desperate is the struggle against darkness and sympathize with the spiritual warfare that takes place in these services.

No Soccer, No Visits after 10:00 P.M.

In addition to the simplicity of defining the Christian's enemy, this movement also simplifies the ethical choices that a follower must make. Every detail is defined in the God is Love Church's *Internal Regulations*. For women wearing shorts or bermudas, the first offense is punishable by 30 days excommunion, 90 days probation the second time, a year the third time, and exclusion from the church on the fourth occasion.

Young men may visit their girlfriends at their homes up to 10 p.m. No TV is allowed in the homes of the churches' workers, women can ride bicycles, horseback or motorcycles only in dire necessity and may not shave their legs. On and on the list goes regarding prohibition of marriage with someone outside the group, the height of women's shoe heels, use of tobacco, men's long hair, jewelry, soccer, circuses, participation in politics and other matters.

Every branch church must display the name of the movement's founder, "Missionary" David Miranda--incidentally, brother-in-law of Manoel de Mello--and the street address of the headquarters' congregation. Even a branch mission in Central America must announce that Brazilian street address on its outside sign.

We watched dozens of chartered buses one Sunday morning taking the faithful to a lake to the south of São Paulo for a mass baptism--sometimes as many as 2,700 in one day--where they will join the other 1.6 million members (Johnstone 1993, 128) of this movement.

Are there really that many people in these movements? Larry Kraft, an Overseas Crusades researcher in Brazil questioned the numbers that churches report in surveys. Exaggeration, church "tramps" who are registered on the rolls of various churches, and churches (like the Christian Congregation) that refuse to keep records, all make data gathering an imprecise task.

Just a Financial Empire? The Universal Church of the Kingdom of God (IURD)

The favorite Evangelical whipping boy of the Brazilian press is the Igreja Universal del Reino de Deus (Universal Church of the Kingdom of God). The alleged financial empire of this group and its Holy War against spiritism make it a continual source for news stories.

The run-down former movie theater in a shabby part of São Paulo hardly suggests a rich headquarters church drowning in millions.   The area formerly occupied by the movie screen proclaims that Jesus Christ is Lord. The music is quiet, played on a piano and a synthesizer. The congregational songs are simple, the leader reminding everyone of the upcoming line between musical phrases. A soloist sings *"A Bridge Over Troubled Waters"* with Christian lyrics. People drift in until it's "standing room only."

No screaming here: the preacher's style is conversational; he raises his voice only at significant points as he paces the stage, microphone in hand. The message is from 2 Corinthians 9:16 ("As ye sow, so also shall ye reap"), leading to an appeal for people to sow sacrificially if they wish to reap God's blessings. This is not "U.S. Prosperity Teaching" promising wealth in exchange for faith. It is the promise of God's blessing in exchange for cash brought down right now to the table in the front of the auditorium.

In Santiago, Chile, at another IURD church (branches are being established internationally), Monday nights are reserved for prosperity teaching. Here, too, an old cinema only two blocks from the Presidential Palace is the meeting place of discouraged people seeking some kind of prosperity. A leader dressed in a pullover sweater, speaking with a heavy Portuguese accent, leads in a few songs and launches into the message, touching briefly on the need to accept Christ. Then, since the gold and silver belong to Him, we are entitled to an abundant life. Self-exorcism, similar to that in the God is Love Church, is practiced as people repeat the words of a prayer, one hand on head, the other expelling the demons of discouragement, unemployment and poverty.

Latin American theologian, C. René Padilla, calls prosperity teaching "popular religion" (1993, 21), a term describing the primitive religion of a people. If popular religion is based, as many say, in making deals with God, trading some personal sacrifice for some favor from God, then the teaching of the IURD is indeed popular religion. Money offered to the church is traded for God's blessing.

The abundant coffers of the church make it possible to buy into the mass media for its evangelistic and missionary activities. In addition to 14 radio stations, the IURD bought São Paulo's TV Channel 7 (cost: $45 million). Its Copacabana radio station in Rio has climbed to fourth place in AM ratings (Bottam 1988, 24).

The IURD newspaper, *Folha Universal* (June 5, 1994), lists the churches founded through the IURD's missionary efforts--32 in Portugal, others in South Africa, France, other Latin American nations, and five in the U.S., including one on Second Avenue in lower Manhattan. But critics question why money is invested in some alleged non-church businesses.

The mass media and the church's message have won thousands of followers. Johnstone (1993, 128) estimates 2 million. In what is certainly an exaggeration, IURD leaders claim 12 million in Brazil and 20 million elsewhere (Claudio Ribeiro in magazine *Signos de Vida*, 1992, 10-14).

Bishop Edir Macedo, the IURD's founder, lives in New York City and goes to Brazil for major events, like the rally in the Macarena Stadium, when some 130,000 attended. "Throw your eyeglasses on the ground," he instructed the crowd, suggesting that such an act of faith would lead to restored eyesight.

A notice on the wall of the headquarters church quotes a passage in Isaiah where God tells the prophet to prepare a paste of figs to cure King Hezekiah's ailment. This verse leads to a notice about fig paste available at the church's entrance. Blessed oils, water from the Jordan and other sacred objects also characterize the Universal Church.

Many Evangelicals within and outside of Brazil call the IURD a sect, outside the stream of orthodoxy. But a surprising number, such as Paulo Lutero de Mello of Brazil for Christ, do not. A prominent Baptist pastor (anonymous source) confesses that the historic churches were not reaching the masses and that in "the providence of God" groups like the IURD have arisen. At the same time he is critical of the IURD's lack of teaching regarding sin, holiness and the cross.

Caio Fabio, President of the Brazilian Association of Evangelicals, is reported to have said (Kivitz 1994) that a person converted in the IURD stays only six months, unless be gets involved as a "worker." Some, seeking more spiritual depth, come into the historic churches, almost suggesting that much new growth in many Evangelical churches may come from people exposed first to the gospel in groups like the IURD.

Macedo has been jailed on occasion under various charges. Caio Fabio, as a Christian brother, has visited him in prison, trying to assure Macedo's rights, even though he and his church are not members of the AEVB (Brazilian Association of Evangelicals).

The legal charges, the sacralized objects, the Universal Church's purported riches and its "Holy War" against Brazil's spiritists are all fodder for the media. Is the Evangelicals' image damaged by all this? Some say it is. Others are convinced the public is aware of the differences among various Evangelical movements. Others say that the charges of corruption leveled against a number of Evangelical deputies in the national congress caused more harm.

Christian Rock and T-Shirts: The Renascer Church

Too new and too small a movement to appear yet in Johnstone's 1993 edition of *Operation World* is a younger generation Brazilian GR movement, the *Renascer em Cristo* (To be born again in Christ) based in São Paulo. This movement, under pastor Estevam Hernandes Filho, is making an impact on the young people who attend historic churches in coats and ties on Sundays and frequent Renascer Christian rock concerts in jeans on Monday nights. Middle-class yuppies who go to the beach on Sundays also find Monday nights convenient. But many of them end up joining the movement which after only eight years has gained an estimated 50,000 followers (80% of them under 27 years of age) who worship in 31 meeting places (article in *Veja*, São Paulo, June 8, 1994, 56-58).

Renascer, like many new movements, has taken advantage of vacant theaters that have become available for new churches. One cinema occupied by the Renascer Christians is on the street floor of the Copan building, an enormous S-shaped structure in downtown São Paulo which houses no less than 10,000 occupants.

The media (Dávila 1994 and Ruiz 1994) portray Renascer as a sophisticated commercial enterprise, headed by the pastor's flamboyant wife, Sonia Hernandes, who markets T-shirts proclaiming "If you feel tossed by the waves, let the Master be the keel for your surfboard."   "Gospel" (the word is in English, appealing to Brazilians fascinated by the U.S.) appears in the title of Renascer's various enterprises: Gospel Records, a Gospel communications network, Gospel clothing, a Gospel prep course for young people preparing for university exams, etc. In fact, the English word "Gospel" has been trademarked for exclusive use by these businesses.

Sonia closes every broadcast day on the Manchete TV Channel with her appearances, wearing heavily-jeweled designer clothes. The church has programs in 21 out of the 24 broadcast hours on an FM station, renaming it "Rádio Gospel" and raising its audience rating from 26th place to 14th. Not lost to the press is the fact that the late race driver, Ayrton Senna, often attended Renascer, and his sister, a psychologist, is an active participant.

However boisterous the Monday rock concerts, Renascer's moderately charismatic Sunday services are hardly an outrageous scene as depicted by the press. Choruses are sung to words projected on a screen, led by a young woman in jeans. A video projecting testimonies of people saved out of drugs and prostitution is convincing, as well as the video of the church's program feeding, bathing, and washing out the clothes of São Paulo's ubiquitous street children at the Copan building. The Sunday morning message is Biblical, the communion service is conducted seriously.

Two telephone hot lines connect 7,000 callers a month with Renascer. And in the Heliópolis *favela* (squatters' settlement) it conducts educational programs (ranging from literacy classes to computer skills), medical services, a sports program for children, food "baskets" for the needy, and, of course, gospel services. Renascer has started work, too, in Spain and France.

A New Generation of Churches for the New Generation

Renascer is not the only ministry that's breaking with tradition to reach Brazil's youth. Countless new ministries, some of them quite commercial, are capitalizing on young people's interest in the gospel. The Apocalypse video-games center in Rio de Janeiro offers players the thrill of killing Goliath. The *"Shopping Evangélico"* (mall) in Belo Horizonte offers a wide range of products. An Evangelical soccer team of Rio's Vida Nova Church plays in the city's second division, wearing uniforms emblazoned with Bible verses. There are numerous rock and funk music gospel bands (Dávila 1994 and Ruíz 1994).

In addition to Renascer, similar middle-class GR "Communities" are springing up. For several years Marco Antonio Rodrígues Peixoto, leader of one group, has run an evangelical *"bloco"* in Rio's annual Carnival parade. Most Evangelical churches schedule retreats to keep young people as far away from the Carnival as possible (article in magazine *Veja,* June 8, 1994, 57).

O.C. International (an interdenominational Evangelical mission) personnel find these autonomous communities hungry for fellowship and for training in church growth and missions. They are not sectarian, but rather look for fellowship in the AEVB.

The Charismatic Breakaway Denominations

Baptist pastor Ed René Kivitz of São Paulo offered us a convincing typology of Brazil's Evangelical churches:
1. The historic denominations
2. The charismatic breakaways from each of the major historic groups
3. The classic Pentecostals (e.g. Assemblies of God)

    4. The older GR groups (e.g. Christian Congregation)

    5. The newer GR groups (e.g. Renascer em Cristo)

What about the second type--the charismatic groups that broke from the historic denominations in the 1960s?   Barrett (1982, 191-193) considers them sufficiently different from their mother organizations to label them "indigenous." Luis Wesley, Executive Director of the AEVB, believes they are growing faster than their mother denominations. The Wesleyan Methodists, he says, are almost as many in number as the original Methodist Church in Brazil. "These groups are in tension," trying to agree as to which of the old forms and liturgies should be recovered and maintained along with the charismatic forms and practices they have discovered (Wesley, 1994).

José Bittencourt Filho, a Brazilian Presbyterian pastor and scholar, has developed an interpretation of the reason why these renewal movements developed in Brazil more than elsewhere (Bittencourt 1992, 49-51). In colonial Brazil "a vast syncretism" was born out of the mix of European Catholicism and African religion with its recognition of the spirit world. The Roman Catholic Church was able to live with this, but traditional Protestants, including classic Pentecostalism, negated this latent cultural "matrix." Grass-roots Pentecostals, however, recognized the underlying concern of Brazilians regarding this dimension.

According to Bittencourt, while they declare war on this religious matrix, at the same time they reinforce belief in the world of the spirits by affirming that they are "bearers of a superior spiritual power." But the historic denominations were not capable of dealing with this subconscious recognition of spiritual realities and therefore they were divided in the 1960s by the charismatic movements which did deal with these issues.

In addition to the cultural reality of this "matrix," there is a Biblical and theological reality in much of it. The spirit world must be recognized in order to minister fruitfully in Brazil. The GR movements, for all their apparent faults, failures and excesses, have discovered this.

SEVEN

Among Indians and Minorities

World War II suddenly brought some of the artefacts of Western civilization to the Melanesian peoples of the Pacific South Seas. A new religious form suddenly arose, mixing elements of Christianity with native beliefs, leading its followers to perform rituals on the beaches to hasten the arrival of ships that would bring them other Western manufactured goods for the taking (Turner 1981, 47). These *cargo cults* were more exotic examples of syncretism (mixing Christianity with non-Christian beliefs and practices).

It should not be surprising that in Latin America, too, native peoples have generated new religious movements, some of them Christian, others only faintly so, including a surprisingly similar cargo cult on the Panamanian isthmus.

Harold W. Turner (*ibid.*) indicates that since the first such movement recorded in Guatemala in 1530, perhaps one hundred new religious movements can be identified in Central and South America, ". . . up to the recent Mama Chi movement in Panama and the ongoing Hallelujah religion that began last century among the Akawaio Indians in the interior of Guyana."

A Cargo Cult in Panama

Turner describes a cargo cult in the mountains of Panama, up against the Costa Rican border, among the Western Guaymi Indians. In 1961, Delia Atencio had visions of the Virgin Mary and her "husband," Jesus, arising from the Fonseca River with a secret message for the Guaymi. They had five years to withdraw from Western contacts, reject polygamy, alcohol, their traditional festivals and fighting, and observe the Sabbath. Faithful adherence would bring them prosperity (*ibid.*).

Twenty-thousand Indians followed "Mama Chi" before her death in 1964. The movement has undergone adaptations since then, and rather than resisting Western ways, some institutions, such as formal schooling, have been adopted (*ibid.*, 46).

Two major Indian GR movements, definitely Christian in nature, deserve our attention.

"Reaching the Gentiles, Too": The Otomis of Mexico

On the high, arid plateau of central Mexico, just north of the capital, live 346,000 Otomi Indians in an area that spreads across five states (*Operación Samaria* 1993, 56-57). Venancio Hernández was the first of the tribe to hear the gospel while in the U.S. He returned to Mexico to be a foreman in charge of Indian farm laborers (McGavran 1963, 99).

Hernández lost his job for having led many of his workers to Christ and conducting Bible studies with them. Furthermore, under the threat of death, the *hacienda* owner, the local priest, and the unconverted Indians drove them off the farm. They discovered land in Ixmiquilpan between Mexico City and Guadalajara and first settled near an army observation post for protection. They acquired the land, paying for it by installments as a cooperative. Hernández taught masonry and eventually they left their cactus huts for more substantial stone homes. Organizing themselves in agricultural cooperatives and a textile factory cooperative, they quickly raised their standard of living (Hollenweger 1974, 44-45).

As the movement spread and a new church was built in another place, they would secure a government bulldozer and provide the labor to put a road into town, thus improving conditions for the whole community. "We are going to show you that we Christians are useful citizens." While on these road projects they composed songs in the "soft restrained style of the Otomi"--songs they continue to sing to remind them of their times of persecution (*ibid.*, 46).

The road projects followed a principle that evangelization of a new village starts with discovering the needs of a village, and then preaching the gospel, notes Donald McGavran (1963, 100).

In 1962, when the movement was twenty years old there were twenty-five churches in the Mesquital Valley and 25 others in the surrounding hills with an estimated 10,000 believers (*ibid.*). The churches tie in loosely with the Independent Evangelical Pentecostal movement which has its headquarters in Pachuca (Hollenweger 1974, 47). The Indians who were formerly day laborers on local farms now are farm owners, masons, owners of small businesses, truck drivers and mechanics (*ibid.*, 48).

The movement's pastors are untrained, mature men, and work as laymen, critical of Catholic priests who are not involved in "regular work" exposing themselves to criticism that they minister only for money. Regarding the possibility of being paid for their ministry, they reply, "What would our colleagues at work say? As a full-time ministry we would become estranged from them" (*ibid.*, 48-49).

Services are informal, lasting four or five hours. The movement is strong enough to be spreading "to the Gentiles" outside the tribe (McGavran, *op. cit.*, 98-101).

Converting the Missionaries:
The Tobas of Argentina

For over 300 years the Tobas of the Argentine Chaco region responded minimally to Christianity, whether to the missionary efforts of the Jesuits or to the Mennonites who later attempted to evangelize them (Turner 1981, 47). They had suffered the loss of their lands under various Argentine governments, were negative to approaches to them by the whites and lived in isolation (Bollatti 1994). Early in the 1940s they came in contact with Pentecostal churches in cities along the Paraná River and came back with the message to their own people. They organized their own GR movement, the United Evangelical Church completely under Toba leadership (Foerster, 3-4).

Anthropologist William Reyburn noted that the Toba church ". . . assumed a form . . . different from that of the mission group . . ." and it took no little work for the missionaries to ". . . harmonize their program with it" (Smalley 1979, 37).

The Toba movement was, however, the Indians' ". . . own church, with Indian pastors and leaders recognized by the other churches in the area" (Foerster, 4). The Tobas are taking the gospel to other Chaco peoples, the Matacos, the Pilagás and the Mocovi in Argentina and the Maká of Paraguay. Their churches have followed the Indian migration to the cities of Formosa, Resistencia, Santa Fe, Rosario and Buenos Aires (*ibid.*). Barrett lists 62 congregations with 4,000 baptized adults and a community of 15,000, comprising 80% of all Toba Indians (Barrett 1982, 149-150).

In 1981, the Church outlined its basic doctrines:
  1. The Bible is the Word of God.
  2. Jesus is Savior and Healer of all our illnesses.

3. Jesus removes evil from our heart and puts love in its place.
4. The believer does not waste his money.
5. The believer does not drink, because getting drunk is wasting money and destroys all human relationships.
6. Power comes from God through the Holy Spirit.
7. Prayer is the fundamental way to face every felt need.
8. A sincere believer attends church regularly, participates in the singing, the dance, prayer, and by giving his testimony.
9. The sincere believer reads the Bible, if he can read.
   (*ibid.*)

There is not much emphasis on the Lord's Supper, and baptism is related to healing (Turner 1981, 47). An examination of the creed and practices of the Toba reveals the extremely practical, down-to-earth nature of their faith. Rather than theological pronouncements reminiscent of Western creeds, their statement is life-related.

Hollenweger (1972, 458) observes that their contextualized Christianity enabled them ". . . to change from a nomadic life to that of cotton planters without having to give up the mystical and magical conceptions that were important to them." But country villages are being abandoned as the Toba move into town (Bollatti 1994). This unusually homogeneous tribal movement has recently been fractured with the entry of other Protestant and Roman Catholic groups (Rooy 1993).

Descendants of the Incas Unite

Participants in the 1992 Latin American Congress on Evangelization (CLADE III) in Quito, Ecuador, were blessed by the special music sung in Indian rhythms and tonalities of colorfully dressed indigenous peoples accompanied by their unique instruments. For a few days before the congress, they had celebrated their own congress of Evangelical Indian groups, an expression of a new phenomenon: para-church GR Indian movements, which do not fit our scheme of GR churches.

For years denominations and faith missions have been evangelizing within their own mission-defined territories of the Quechuas, descendants of the great Inca empire. Lately, however, Indian Christians have been looking over these arbitrary fences to discover their cultural ties with other Quechuas of other denominational stripes. Music festivals to share Christian Quechua music were often the first events to bring these peoples together, often through the coordinating efforts of Rubén ("Tito") Paredes, a Peruvian Christian anthropologist/missiologist of Quechua descent.

These groupings of Christian Indians in Ecuador and Peru are authentic GR associations which have gained the allegiance of their peoples. This is despite the fact that ecclesiastically their churches are still related to the missions and denominations that brought them the gospel.

In Ecuador, the group is FEINE (*Fraternidad Ecuatoriana Indígena Evangélica*--Ecuadorian Evangelical Indian Fraternity), which has often adopted a political orientation, backing a political party it believed compatible with Indian interests.

In Peru, the corresponding group is Tawa Tintsuyu (Empire of the Four Corners of the Earth, a term evoking the ancient Indian empire), and their principal emphasis has been that of recovering their cultural roots and ties.

In Guatemala, such interdenominational GR Indian Christian groupings seem to be more local, rather than national in character. They see the advantage of retaining the institutional links with the denominations. But on the local level there is much relating across denominational lines. Some of it is to rediscover, as Christians, their cultural roots and how much of the ancient Mayan culture, for example, can still be retained and even integrated into their Christian faith, without going off the edge into syncretistic patterns.

The 500th anniversary of the conquest of the New World and the attention focused on the Indians of the Americas has given them a heightened sense of identity in many places. This even entails in some circles a legitimization of their ancient beliefs. Greater communication between the groups exists and there is bound to be increasing Indian grass-roots activity of one type or another.

GR Movements among Ethnic Minorities

"You won't find any grass-roots movements among the immigrant peoples," we were told in South America. Many immigrants find it comforting to maintain close ties with their homeland churches. Their churches are faithful transplants from the home country. These minorities are often Protestant groups that relate to corresponding Protestant churches abroad.

But when immigrant people find Christ and have no connection with a homeland Evangelical community, these are fertile ground for GR movements within their ethnic enclaves. Here we cannot speak of "grass-roots" in terms of contextualization within the general Latin American culture, but certainly contextualization within a subculture.

The Christian Congregation of Brazil, already described, began as an Italian people's movement. Barrett (*op. cit.*, 149-150) also lists the Christian Assemblies, an Argentine Italian group. A reading of the Buenos Aires evangelical directory (Saracco 1992) reveals Korean, Japanese and other churches seemingly unrelated to churches in their homeland.

The West Indian English-speaking black populations in Panama and the Caribbean coasts of other Central American countries is another example. The dominant Spanish-speaking Roman Catholic *mestizo* population has traditionally kept these peoples in a second-class status. Many with roots in the Caribbean islands have brought their denominations with them to Central America--Anglican, Baptist and Methodist. But GR movements, such as the Christian Mission of Panama, have also arisen.

However, like many ethnic churches in the U.S. that did not shift gears into the dominant language, these will tend to disappear after a few generations unless they make the change. The Christian Congregation of Brazil switched from Italian to Portuguese and became a major GR movement.

GR Movements among Students

The perennial problem of what to do with the results of a witness to university students is present in Latin America. New Christians at this social and intellectual level may not find a church that meets their needs, and opt to start their own movement.

A Colombian movement, the Cruzada Estudiantil y Profesional para Cristo (Student and Professional Crusade for Christ), headed by Ecuadorian Néstor Chamorro, broke from its Campus Crusade origins and became a unique GR denomination. In attempting to reach upper social classes and not offend Catholics, it has been repudiated by Evangelicals who also react against a liberal lifestyle (regarding social drinking, dancing, etc.) which this group countenances. The Roman Catholic hierarchy likewise does not recognize it.

In Costa Rica, an Evangelical witness to students turned into an ecumenical movement, *Arbol de la Vida* (Tree of Life), now directed by Roman Catholic lay people. Although not officially a church, this GR movement is perhaps "church" to many of its middle- and upper-class followers. It represents a kind of supplementary para-church community providing serious Bible study and an evangelical style of fellowship to others who continue attending mass. *Evangélicos* are also involved.

The Navigator movement in Latin America has also developed fellowships of people with a style that seeks to appeal to the "secularized person." These home Bible study circles (*turmas* in Brazil) are still mentored by Navigator missionaries. So, although they are not a GR movement, they and the other university movements represent a possible new level of GR activity that will grow in Latin America.

While GR movements by definition seem to suggest movements of the masses, in this chapter needed recognition has been given to the churches and movements that arise from Latin America's subcultures.

EIGHT

Things Can Go Wrong

"The fear haunts us that if we allowed our converts, though they might be illiterate men, to teach freely what they had learned, the doctrine might spread like wildfire, and the country might be covered with multitudes of groups of men calling themselves Christians, but really ignorant of the first principles of Christ, and that thus the Church and her doctrine might be swamped, as it were, with a flood of ignorance" (Allen 1963, 52).

Roland Allen, in his classic appeal for an indigenized Church, verbalized the missionary's fear of an uncontrolled and doctrinally suspect wildfire spread of inadequate or impure teaching. Then he went on to press for more freedom, indicating that a genuine experience with Christ was less prone to heresy than the teaching of dead doctrine.

He comes close to saying that once a church is unleashed from foreign control, nothing can go wrong. There is a quality of pristine faith in a believer's first love that should be emulated. With this is the need to be more sensitive to the Holy Spirit's illumination of the simple believer. We can be grateful for new-found perspectives by believers in the GR church.

But they are subject, as are all of us, to the deception of the enemy and the temptations of the flesh. There are many other examples of movements that have lost their moorings, in addition to those already described. Church history since New Testament

127

times indicates things can go wrong as long as a church is composed of human beings, regenerate though they may be.

Davidic Dances and New Jerusalems

Characteristic of many movements worldwide is a believer's break with the prevailing culture, a loss of identity, and an unconscious attempt to relate to another stream of history and tradition. Many Latin Americans who have discarded Roman Catholic traditions and history reach back and practice Old Testament forms. This apparently gives them a sense of being part of an even older tradition.

In Costa Rica, TV audiences are exposed to Evangelical music festivals in which Psalms are sung to purported "Davidic dances," with the waving of palms and Old Testament costumes. One 1991 event was held in the National Gymnasium, coordinated by the San José Christian Center, at which an "ark of David" was demonstrated. The concert was followed by preaching and a healing service (*Maranatha* #114 in 1991, 17).

Singing Psalms has a strong precedent, and Davidic dances are harmless. A non-Latin might wish that such attempts to relate to history would not overlook identification with the history and cultural treasures of the Protestant tradition since the Reformation. But then again, performances of Lutheran chorales and Handel's "The Messiah" do not match the colors and rhythms of the so-called Davidic dances!

There is a serious tendency to adopt Old Testament-like legalisms with respect to behavior, and preaching styles that echo the authoritarian pronouncements of judgment by Old Testament prophets. But yet more critical is a regression by some to Old Testament forms and a yearning for an earthly Jerusalem. Much has been said about the greater identification of African Christians

with the nomadic, animal-herding tribal culture of the early Old
Testament than with the Greek and Roman urban atmosphere of
the New Testament. This may be invoked by Africans to justify
polygamy, animal sacrifices, a priesthood, and a Jerusalem-like
center of worship.

Howard W. Turner (1981, 48), who studies "New Religious
Movements" worldwide, classifies these movements as *Hebraist,*
some of which reject the New Testament entirely, believing
themselves descendants of the ten lost tribes. Such, says Turner,
are the main Maori movements in New Zealand (*ibid.*). Hebraist
expressions are also found in Latin America.

A New Israel in Peru

Ezequiel Ataucusi is the founder of the first religion to emerge
in modern Peru. He was born in 1918 in the Arequipa area, one
of fourteen children. He completed grade four in school, and
worked as a miner, cobbler and carpenter. His early skepticism of
Roman Catholic practice led him to skip confession when in
school and in military service. From age 12, he reported having
visions and at age 30, he acquired a Bible. For a year he related
to the Seventh Day Adventists, but when he shared his visions he
was expelled.

Manuel Marzal, a Peruvian priest-anthropologist who has
studied Ataucusi's movement and interviewed the founder, reports
(1988, 342-373) on Ataucusi's alleged elevation to the third
heaven, his vision of the Trinity, and divine instructions as to the
sect he was to establish and its name: the Israelites of the New
Universal Covenant. Other visions permitted him to see Ellen
White (Adventist founder) and Joseph Smith (founder of the
Mormons).

Kenneth David Scott, a Scottish missionary, one of the few Evangelicals who has studied the movement carefully, has written two books about it (1990a, 1990b).

In 1959, according to Scott, Ataucusi met Alfredo Loje, who had had contact with the Chilean *Cabañista* (Tabernacler) movements (*ibid.* a., 25). They attract curiosity because of their yearly celebration of the Jewish Feast of the Tabernacles in which a month is spent in shelters away from their homes. Loje, also expelled from the Seventh Day Adventists, founded a movement that did not gain as much fame as Ataucusi's. Loje did not believe followers should have to wear long tunics, nor offer Old Testament sacrifices--although the Old Testament feasts were still to be celebrated (*ibid.* b., 30).

While the *Israelites* of Ataucusi's movement baptize in the name of the Trinity (*ibid.* b., 84), other rituals and celebrations all come out of the Old Testament: the Sabbath, New Moon festivals and the major feasts of the Passover, Pentecost, and in October, the Atonement ceremonies and the Feast of the Tabernacles. Their major center in Cieneguilla, 22 kilometers outside of Lima in a desert, is the site for Old Testament animal sacrifices (*ibid.* b., 55-75). Their diet, too, is based on Jewish law, and they abstain from liquor and tobacco (*ibid.* a., 23).

Long hair, blue pants and a white shirt or robe identify well the participating men (Marzal 1988, 353). Since Peruvian Indians are anatomically incapable of raising a full Abrahamic beard, the thin growth on male followers of the Israelites of the New Universal Covenant sect makes them look somewhat oriental.

They sometimes drop into Evangelical churches and will join in singing the choruses if they are based on the Psalms. In order to be able to take time off for their many services and feasts, most *Israelites* are self-employed (*ibid.* a., 64).

Many of the *Israelites* have sold out and moved to one of the colonies in Peru's eastern jungle that have a semi-communal structure. The families work half a day on their own parcels of land for their family crops, and half a day, following the Andean Indian custom, on communal projects (*ibid.* a., 35-44).

Discipline and a work ethic characterize the colonies. As the movement developed they organized cooperatives, established a bus and truck transport company, and a school system, hoping some day even to launch their own university. This is despite an original anti-educational posture origin (*ibid.* b., 54-55). In a concession to modernity, the *Israelites* also opened medical clinics, offering "chemical," "natural" or "spiritual" healing (*ibid.* b., 57).

Hardly a movement with its head in the sand politically, it launched its own party (the *Frente Independiente Agrícola*). Its platform presented the enforcement of Saturday as a non-working day in addition to its moralistic aims (anti-drugs, anti-alcohol, and anti-terrorism) and its anti-imperialist stance--to ignore Peru's foreign debt and the demands of the International Monetary Fund (*ibid.* a., 61).

Scott traces many of the movement's theological roots to pre-Christian sources. The *Israelites* often refer to the moral law that the legendary prophet Manco Cápac taught the Incas before the conquest (*ibid.* b., 42). Pentecostal-like tongues and prophecies may be evidence of God's favor on *Israelites* who faithfully keep His law. Buddha, the prophet, and the signs of the Zodiac are part of the mix (*ibid.* b., 113). Bizarre numerologies and Old Testament interpretations lead to eschatalogical date-setting (*ibid.* b., 100-102).

The Trinity is invoked at baptisms, and the historicity of Christ's life, death and resurrection is affirmed (*ibid.*, 113-114). Christ is the Way, but the way by which *Israelites* can fulfill the

Old Testament law. There is an absence of serious interpretation regarding the meaning of His death. Ataucusi is a precursor of the Christ who will return--to Peru--and will experience death and resurrection. And so, he is given high reverence (*ibid.* b., 117).

Isaiah 19:18's reference to the "City of Sun" (according to the older versions) is interpreted as referring to Cuzco, a sacred city known also as the "Navel of the Universe." This and other arguments magnify the country, referred to as "Privileged Peru." It is a strong motive for followers to look forward to the Inca Empire's recovery of its ancient leadership and splendor (*ibid.* b., 43-49).

During a period of social and political reform in the late 1960s, the Israelites began to grow rapidly. The movement now has extended into Bolivia. In 1992, Catholic authorities considered them the third largest non-Catholic group (after Evangelicals and Seventh Day Adventists) and the fastest growing, having gained 100,000 followers since its founding only 24 years earlier (Pérez 1992, 54).

Chilean Zionists

A group in Chile by almost the same name (Evangelical Church of the Israelites of the New Covenant) is one of two movements there that trace their beginnings to Juan Chavarría. His background was Methodist and Seventh Day Adventist. These groups observe the Old Testament Feast of the Tabernacles and spend seven days each September living in tents. Known popularly as *cabañistas* (*cabaña* was the word in some older translations for such tents or tabernacles in Leviticus 23), they keep the Jewish calendar and claim to give a new covenant perspective to all the feasts.

The other *Cabañistas* are the "Zionist Church" from which the above group broke. The Zionists separated from the Seventh Day Adventists. They identify with the Jews in Chile, aspiring to emigrate to Israel, some of them already having gone there (Vergara 1962, 150).

Soldiers in White

In a crowded downtown plaza in a Central American capital a tourist may find him or herself politely accosted by men or women in white uniforms soliciting contributions. Intent on their fund raising, they may not have literature to explain who they are nor spend time explaining their identity. These are members of the *Bando Evangélico de Gedeón* (Gideon Evangelical Band), or the *Gedeonistas* (Gideonites), originating in pre-revolutionary Cuba.

Founded in the early 1930s by Ernest William Sellers ("Daddy John"), a former Bible-distributing member of the Gideon organization, this movement was most successful reaching Jamaicans and other West Indians on the island as well as the poorest of the Cubans. It is a mix of adventism, sabbatism (strict sabbath observance), pentecostalism and a lifestyle that prohibits all forms of entertainment.

Missionaries of the movement, all Cubans at first, were expected to turn over all properties to the organization and live from a common fund. The first *bati-blanco* (white-robed) missionaries were sent in 1950 to Panama and Mexico. On the eve of the 1959 Cuban revolution, they claimed 20,000 followers, 600 full-time workers and meetings in 325 churches or missions in Cuba. In some rural areas they were the most prominent religious group, even exceeding the strength of the Roman Catholic Church (Ramos 1986, 455-456).

Obviously the Gideonites clashed with the revolutionaries, beginning in 1960. Their common-fund Christian communism was not compatible with state communism, nor was their refusal to bear arms nor their Sabbath observance. The movement's workers would not give up their uniforms or their vocation. Many were fined or imprisoned, most of their missions were closed, and many fled the island. We have no estimate as to their present numbers or strength.

Eventually, compromises were made by both sides. To continue their overseas missions, the headquarters was moved to Miami--where they are in great prominence working the corridors of Miami International Airport. To minimize confusion with the better known Bible-distributing Gideons, in the 20 countries of Latin America, Spain and Germany where they have spread, they are known as the Soldiers of the Cross (*ibid.*, 556-557).

The Miami headquarters of this group makes it no less a Latin American GR movement, having been founded in Latin America and led by Latins. Of course, there are those who, in any case, will claim that Miami, too, "is Latin America."

The "Incarnation of the Holy Spirit"

The Father did not have to be incarnate. The Son had already become incarnate. According to followers of the Mita movement, it remained for the Holy Spirit to be incarnated in a Puerto Rican woman, Juana García, the "Mita," founder of a movement that began in 1942. "Mita" was the new name she was given in accordance with Revelation 2:17. She believed she would not die, but her tomb, where she was buried in 1970 just outside the headquarters church in Hato Rey, reminds us that she was indeed mortal. At her death the movement suffered a division. The present leader, Teófilo Vargas Sein, whose adopted name is "Aarón," claims to succeed her as the Holy Spirit in person.

"Aarón" has taken the Mita message to seven states in the U.S. Other branches now exist in the Dominican Republic, Colombia, Mexico, Venezuela, Costa Rica and Panama.

Worshipers dressed in white fill the large six-million-dollar headquarters temple where a brass band creates an atmosphere of power and militancy.

> "They are legalists with regard to dress and hair-style; they dress in white to go to church as a symbol of purity. In every meeting prophecies abound; they are very united, show affection to everyone, and morally are very strict. They believe in spiritual gifts, and respect the laws of the country. They do not tithe, but give offerings at receptacles at the entry of the church. The money goes mainly for the poor. The mother church is supported by various businesses that belong to the group" (*Maranatha* #116 of 1991, 2).

Instead of a Sunday school, the Mitas have a Saturday program for children. But there is no Bible school or seminary because ". . . if God has called someone, God will instruct him" (*ibid.*).

The movement's wealth is no doubt a target for anyone with designs for a takeover --hence, Aarón's bodyguards. At his age (70 in 1992), another power struggle upon his death is not unlikely.

The *World Christian Encyclopedia* (1982, 581) estimates there are 5,000 followers. A knowledgeable Puerto Rican church historian and leader, Carmelo Alvarez (1992), estimates there are 80,000.

"Vivazos" and Visionaries

"Nowadays any *vivazo* ("sharpie") can gather a dozen families around him, convince them to tithe, and make an easy living as their pastor." So stated a leader (an anonymous source) in a country where people are open to religious change. Without the need for academic credentials or denominational oversight, such *vivazos* can easily introduce aberrations of the kind we have described.

Others, like Jim Jones of the Guyana massacre fame, begin in established movements and then lead themselves and their followers astray.

Zacarías Pérez, a thin, rough-hewn Costa Rican with a drooping mustache, formerly a pastor with a recognized denomination, started his own ministry in the town of Barranca as the Roca del Pedernal church. Soon it became a GR movement of 30 congregations.

Reports began to filter back to the Costa Rican Evangelical Alliance that at services of the sect, lights were dimmed and physical contact between the sexes was encouraged as part of the group's "spiritual union." Visits by Alliance officials confirmed the stories. Unfortunately the media also discovered the *Zacarianos* and a TV channel produced a documentary exposing the group (Moya 1992, 6A-7A).

Local unbelievers, as a result of seeing the exposé, formed a mob that pillaged the Barranca church (article by Moya and Rodríguez in *La Nación* July 18, 1991, 10a). Pérez was charged with immoral acts, and the Alliance had to publish newspaper articles disassociating itself from the group (*La Nación* July 25, 1991, 27a). Such events do not necessarily discredit the group in the eyes of its followers. We are told that the *Zacarianos* have not only held their own, but have grown since the discreditation of their leader (Kessler July 1994, a conversation). This phenomenon occurs under certain circumstances, which has been observed and reported by sociologists (Festinger, et al. 1956, 4).

The uphill struggle by Protestants in Latin America to establish credibility is beset continually by wide media coverage of such events. But exposure or knowledge that is limited to this kind of GR movement has blinded many to the existence and the contribution of many movements that are Biblically sound. We only have to be reminded that while the Mormons and Jehovah's Witnesses, also aberrations of the truth, are GR movements, many other made-in-the-U.S. denominations remain true to the gospel.

PART II
RISKING SOME GENERALITIES

Prologue: Older and Newer Generations

When we became acquainted with a South American reporter of a very prestigious newspaper, he was attending a respectable middle-class Presbyterian church. He had grown up in a poor neighborhood and had been converted in a simple Pentecostal GR church. Though now living in an elite suburb, he confessed that when he or a family member became sick, he would cross the tracks and resort to the prayers of the pastor and the people in the little church in the *barrio*--where faith was simple and praying for the sick was not hedged with too many qualifications.

New Christians often move upward socially as they give up wasteful habits, to invest in education and acquire discipline and purpose in life. Some, like the journalist, will look for churches that respond to their middle-class concerns, in neighborhoods where their cars will not be vandalized while they are worshiping. While enjoying the program of a more "respectable" church, however, they may look back wistfully to the down-to-earth application of a simpler faith of their early Christian experience, and bring elements of that experience with them.

The descriptions of the two Santafé de Bogotá churches in the first chapter illustrate the social extremes that characterize Latin American GR churches.

A Constantly Changing Picture

Not only do people advance upward socially, but churches do so as well. Sociology of religion takes note of the gradual transformation of spontaneous, sectarian storefront groups into respected institutionalized churches and denominations. GR churches often begin climbing socially, too, and so, like the proverbial river, they are never exactly the same each time one takes a look at them.

If the church does not move upward fast enough for some of its members, they, like the journalist, will leave. There are GR pastors who make no attempt to grow intellectually and spiritually. Their churches often remain stagnant, and younger and more educated members leave to find spiritual food elsewhere.

If these churches do rise socially, moreover, they may lose members at the bottom of the scale. But new storefront congregations will spring up to take their place and meet the needs of the poorest. Given the masses of Latin American poor, there will always be people hungry for the simplest message, couched in terms that they will understand and embrace.

"Generations" and Social Class

It is interesting to note that some of the "old generation" GR churches move upward socially. The Brazilian Christian Congregation movement looks as if it has ascended socially. Its people appear well dressed and come to church in their own cars. This is despite the fact that the church has remained sectarian in its isolation from the rest of the community and has maintained its original forms of worship. Most other "old generation" churches continue to minister to the poor.

The GR churches of the "newer generation" may also be classified by these two social classes.

But the fact that GR churches are found at various points of social institutionalization should not lead one to think that middle-class GR churches are very similar to middle-class congregations of traditional Protestants in North America or Europe. Most of these churches are charismatic/pentecostal. Also, given that Latins are more transparent with their emotions, these GR churches reflect a warm, spontaneous and expressive spirit in their life and worship.

GR churches not only vary as to their social level but also in their style. Some early movements have become rigid, legalistic and isolated from the Evangelical community--separating the sexes in worship and sacralizing their hymnals, thus prohibiting modern musical expressions. Even in their antiquated ways, they may erect magnificent buildings. Frequently their congregations are composed primarily of older people, as young people seek fresh, contemporary forms of life and worship. What had been spontaneous manifestations of pentecostal gifts are so controlled that they almost disappear.

Newer movements are creative, employing mass media and modern musical instruments, frequently adopting current theological innovations such as prosperity teaching, and effectively appealing to youth and middle-class people.

A Two-Variable Classification

With these two general groupings and added three-level descriptions, we attempt to classify some of the churches already mentioned:

	"Older Generation"	"Newer Generation"
Lower social class	Methodist Pentecostal Apostolic Church Light of the World	Waves of Love and Peace Universal Church of the Kingdom of God Bethesda Missionary Center
Lower middle class	Apure movement	Brazil for Christ
Middle class	Christian Congregation	Vision of the Future Renascer Church on the Rock

With this background, we introduce the following chapters. The first three offer perspectives from social scientists, from Roman Catholics, and from Protestants. This is followed by generalizations about theological issues, their churches, and their outreach.

NINE

Issues that Intrigue Social Scientists

While the Latin American Protestant movement was small, meeting in churches that looked like outposts of North American or European denominations, they attracted little attention from the sociologists or anthropologists. Perhaps they were written off as foreign enclaves, not worth studying.

As the Latin American Evangelical movement gained momentum, it was often identified as anti-cultural, an exotic implant. Sociologists discussed whether it really contributed to the region's modernization. Then, with the explosion of the GR movements, especially the large Pentecostal churches, social scientists began to make an about-face regarding their previous indifference.

Protestants are no Longer "Anti-Cultural"

Bastian (1992, 335-336) quotes Alberto Rembao, a Mexican of an earlier generation, who described Protestantism in 1949 as ". . . transforming a deep, corporative and vertical society and democratizing it by creating a new type of man and woman, morally regenerate as well as active and disciplined economic agents, creators of socially redistributed wealth, and political subjects of a sovereignty yet to come."

In other words, Protestants in their social relations, instead of authoritarian, aimed to be democratic. Family and community loyalty is overshadowed by individuals seeking personal progress. Ethics is seen as a part of religion. Discipline replaces dissolution.

143

Charity supplants selfishness. Allegiance is shifted to Christ's coming kingdom. All of this cuts radically across the grain of Latin American culture.

Rembao for some reason did not get around to many other facets of Protestantism that seemed anti-cultural--the solemn worship style of the traditional Protestant churches, the appeal to reason and study, and the very foreignness of the *gringo* missionaries who brought Protestantism south of the border.

"It was for this reason that Protestantism, in the 1920s and the 1930s, did not progress numerically, even though its minorities had been very active politically, educationally and socially," concludes Bastian (*ibid.*, 336).

The charge that imported Protestantism was anti-cultural needs no rebuttal. But then Pentecostals took center stage, especially the GR movements. Many elements of their churches were congruent with Latin American culture. For example, the authoritarianism of the GR pastor is comfortable for people accustomed to their country's power-wielding President, or even perhaps to dictatorships.

The greater family spirit of the Pentecostal Church reflects Latin Americans' sense of community.

--   Ethics and moral discipline do get imposed, but outbursts of passion in a service parallel the frenetic dance and excitement of the fiesta of the local culture.

--   All-night prayer meetings evoke the personal sacrifice formerly invested in arduous trips to distant shrines.

--   The wonder of tongues-speaking and pentecostal ecstacy (rather than a cerebral approach to religion) reflects the many mysteries to which people have been exposed all their lives in the Roman Catholic Church.

Now that the Protestant movement is large in many cities, the great evangelistic campaigns, in addition to winning new people, provide the crowd excitement of Latin Americans watching soccer games or bullfights. Evangelical parades and massive street meetings are ways to *tomar la calle* (take over the street) as a show of force that reflects Latin American political rallies or Roman Catholic processions.

Some wings of the Roman Catholic Church have promoted the transformation of social and political structures. However, while purportedly speaking in behalf of the masses, they often talk "over the heads" of the people. So it can be said in many places that GR Protestantism is not only attuned to the culture, but may be even more a part of it than Catholicism, which has always maintained that it was an essential element in Latin American culture.

Karl-Wilhelm Westmeier (1993, 76) quotes two Latin Americans, Samuel Palma and Hugo Villela, who affirm that ". . . official Roman Catholicism actually runs counter to the religious feeling of the Latin American masses."

All the time-worn arguments that Protestantism is to be resisted because it is destroying Latin American culture are empty at this point in history. Pablo Deiros (1994) believes that in fact Protestantism is already shaping Argentine culture. Statements of non-believers and public officials, like that of the President, now include evangelical expressions such as "May the Lord bless you." Of course, Evangelicals have not yet made significant contributions, Deiros says, in the arts, in literature or secular music. "But pentecostalism is the great expression of post-modern culture" (*ibid.*).

While we have emphasized the fact that Protestantism in its GR manifestations has touched the deepest veins of the Latin American psyche and culture, the other side of the coin is obviously the change that Protestantism has undergone. Paraphrasing the title of David Stoll's book, *Is Latin America Turning Protestant?* Quentin Schultze in his chapter on "Orality and Power in Latin American Pentecostalism" (in Miller, ed., *Coming of Age, Protestantism in Contemporary Latin America*, 1994, 66) raises the inverted question: "Is Latin American Protestantism turning Pentecostal?"

But What is Latin American Culture?

The fact that the tiny Central American countries across the years have failed to unite to form a logical political unit is, among other things, a recognition that there are cultural differences, for example, between Guatemalans and Costa Ricans. Throughout the continent the *mestizo* is dominant. In some countries the faces, the clothing, the accent are Indian. In others, European or African cultures show through. In every country, despite the tradition of anti-Americanism, there is a social sector that identifies with everything made-in-USA.

Immigrant groups, social classes and the generation gap add to the pluralism of Latin American cultures.

Who can say, then, that Brazil's *Renascer em Cristo* GR movement, appealing to rock music fans, is not superbly attuned to this international youth subculture? Or that forms which other "newer generation" GR movements take are not meshing with today's urban society? With the exception of some of the more rigid "older generation" movements, the ability of the GR movements to adapt to their environment is remarkable.

GR Movements are Expressions of Popular Religiosity

With a rise of studies of Roman Catholic popular religiosity several years ago, another fact dawned on many observers. GR Protestantism is also a form of popular religiosity. The concept of popular religiosity is important in any study of GR movements.

Roman Catholicism, especially in Latin America, consists of more than official pronouncements of the Church, its theological confessions or its organizational structures. Practices originating with the common people as they respond to their immediate needs begin to form around religion.   These practices--popular religiosity--are the darker and, at the same time, the most visible side of Latin American Roman Catholicism. Examples include pilgrimages to shrines, taking home holy water from a particular spring, wearing miraculous medals, participating in processions and in the town's patron saint's fiestas, and sometimes even witnessing a crude reenactment of the crucifixion during Holy Week.

One other specific example is the *Basílica de los Angeles* in Cartago, Costa Rica. This church is "home" to the country's patron saint, a stone image of the virgin purportedly found in 1635 by an Indian girl by a spring. The shrine attracts people from the whole country to pray for physical healing, victory in a soccer match or safety at sea. A roomful of cases displaying little silver replicas of organs and limbs that have been healed (livers, hearts, arms, legs), soccer trophies and fishing boat models are part of the sanctuary.

Attempts to define popular religiosity abound and the various definitions reveal attitudes towards the phenomenon. Pope Paul VI was quite positive about it, calling it ". . . the particular expression of a people's search for God and their faith" (Deiros 1992, 118). Catholic historian Enrique Dussell (1981, 71) is more critical, calling folk catholicism ". . . a manifestation of an aware-ness of conscience not yet entirely Christian."

A Route to Real Faith?

With this new attention upon Catholic popular religiosity and the various new visions which have arisen as to what the Church should really be, the contrasts between the ideal and the actual church have been accentuated. Behind this study of Catholic popular religiosity (the real religion of Latin America's masses) is a question debated in Roman Catholic circles. Is this folk religion to be deplored and discarded? Or with proper guidance can it be tolerated and through it can people be guided towards a purer and more orthodox faith?

The Roman Catholic hierarchy, often expressing itself as temporarily tolerating the newest and perhaps crudest expressions of popular religiosity, sometimes fails to see that instead of the disappearance of these temporary concessions to uneducated people with time and maturity, many of these expressions become official and permanent.

High Religion and Low Religion

Roman Catholicism is not the only religious system in which there is a popular religiosity that is in contrast to the more official theologies and philosophies of its hierarchies. Missions anthropologist Paul Hiebert in *Toward the 21st Century in Christian Mission* (eds. Phillips and Coote, 1993, 253-257) points out that many religious systems such as Islam and Buddhism have their "high religion" and their "low religion." The former is the realm of the theologians and high priests who deal with ultimate realities. The latter is the version of the same religion that the common people practice, in their attempt to resolve their immediate problems.

Now that Latin American Pentecostals, mostly in the GR movements, have become numerous, it has dawned on many that just as Catholicism has its high and low forms of religion, so, Latin American Protestants have corresponding forms of their faith: (1) the traditional churches, formal and institutional, and (2) the GR churches, where the masses are looking for God's miraculous interventions.

Anthropologists and sociologists see little difference between Roman Catholic and Protestant popular religiosity. To them, both, in their unsophisticated soliciting of God's intervention in the resolution of immediate problems, are appealing to magic. Emilio Willems states: "Certain aspects of Pentecostalism in Chile . . . show continuity with the people's Catholicism, although no member of the sect would ever admit this" (1969, 202).

Pablo Deiros, an Argentine Baptist scholar, is one of the few Evangelicals who see a parallel between Catholic and Protestant popular religiosity. He devotes three chapters of his *Historia del cristianismo latinoamericano* to popular religiosity: one to the topic in general, one to Catholic popular religiosity, and one to Protestant popular religiosity (*ibid.*, 117-120).

Why are considerations of popular religiosity important to those interested in Evangelical GR movements? It may seem "unfair" to Evangelicals that the social scientists compare Catholicism's "low religion" with Protestant "low religion."

Abelino Martínez and Luis Samandú (1990, 43) state that ". . . pentecostalism suffers the same fate as the so-called Catholic 'popular religiosity,' which is looked upon with misgiving and suspicion by representatives of the 'official religion.' So there is a 'popular protestantism,' too, a deviation, and an 'official protestantism' which has a monopoly on legitimacy."

As we compare the phenomenon of popular religiosity in both camps, we see that many characteristics are shared.   Such comparisons can help us better understand the problems faced by Latin American GR movements.

It is no less important for Evangelicals, observing popular religion on the Protestant side of the fence, also to debate whether some of the GR movements with crude and more syncretistic forms should be rejected outright. Or should we wait for such movements to mature? And should we also rejoice at the large crowds being attracted, while winking at the apparently shallow Biblical perception and practice?

The Many Faces of Popular Religiosity

Since both critics and defenders of popular religiosity often touch different parts of the proverbial elephant, the various faces of the phenomenon must be examined.

1. Popular Religiosity: Owned by the Masses

The term *popular religiosity* carries the Spanish sense of the word *popular*. In Spanish something *popular* is not necessarily highly attractive (as a "popular rock star") or faddish (as in "pop culture"). The increasing appeal of GR Pentecostal churches to the masses who are less privileged economically or educationally makes them, too, a parallel expression of popular religiosity. Protestant popular religiosity is, in its way, similar to Catholic popular religiosity. But the Protestant version is also "popular" in another sense--the strong emphasis on the participation of its followers, instead of domination by the clergy. It is something the masses can appropriate as their own. In a definition of popular religiosity, Manuel Marzal, a Peruvian priest (Paredes 1989, 42), says that it is ". . . how the people or the great majorities of a country express themselves."

To the elite, popular religiosity is discredited simply because it is just that--the religion of the poor and the uneducated. As Martínez and Samandú said, Catholic theologians may look upon Catholic popular religion "with suspicion," while the Protestant establishment feels it has a "monopoly on legitimacy" (1990, 43).

To others, the fact that it originates with and appeals to the masses is the glory of it all. Harvey Cox (1973, chapter 6) traces his own personal pilgrimage, despairing of the modern world's growing secularism, and then uncritically celebrates the rise of all kinds of "people's religions" everywhere.

The great crowds participating in Roman Catholic processions affirm that they are indeed *popular*--activities of the masses. But in another sense and to a greater degree, Protestant GR popular religiosity also belongs to the people. Unlike Roman Catholicism, where only priests have authority, all believers in Protestant GR movements have access to God's power and spiritual gifts. The priesthood of every believer makes the faith, its blessings and responsibilities, the property of the masses.

2. Popular Religiosity: "Unofficial" until it becomes "Official"

Popular religiosity is often identified with the unofficial and the non-traditional. This, too, is a bane to some and a glory to others. Some marxists deplore popular religiosity as the most blatant form of religious opiate. Others applaud it because it is a people's religion, rather than that of the oppressive Catholic hierarchy (McIntosh 1986, 68).

Peruvian anthropologist Tito Paredes (1992, 205) makes the point that there is much unofficial activity in Latin American society. The informal business sector--sidewalk merchants, backroom manufacturing--represents 60% of his country's work force. To establish an official, properly registered business is to many entrepreneurs almost impossible, in view of government bureaucracy. Likewise other unofficial legal, political and even religious activities have to find their space when official options are closed or too rigid. In religion, popular religiosity fills a vacuum where official religion makes no provision.

Whereas official Catholicism offers no solution to the señorita looking for a husband, popular religion offers the intercession of prayers to San Antonio. Where traditional Latin American Protestantism seldom offers prayers for the sick, except in pastoral prayers in the church services, GR movements do.

But the boundary between that which is official and that which is folk religion is not all that well defined. Some practices of folk religion get officialized, some do not.

In Costa Rica a young boy in rural Sarapiquí regularly hears messages from the Virgin Mary accompanied by phenomena such as a so-called "Dance of the Sun," when an apparition of the Virgin in the sky is perceived by the faithful. Thousands of pilgrims trudge over muddy roads to the sacred grove. Mary's words, as transmitted through the boy, are transcribed and published in the newspapers.

The country's Catholic archbishop denounced these unofficial apparitions. Interestingly, this denouncement took place at the annual August 2 pilgrimage that thousands make to the aforementioned Cartago basilica, where a cult was established after an Indian girl also witnessed an apparition of the Virgin. Cartago is official, but Sarapiquí is not.

Just as Cartago's apparition has been officialized, other elements of Catholic popular religiosity have invaded Catholicism's official practices and beliefs across the centuries. Dussel (1981, 84-85) recognizes that popular religiosity has been seeping into official Catholicism since church and culture became intertwined under Constantine. Later, elements of European folk culture were added before Catholicism came to the Americas.

Paul Hiebert (1993, 259) observes that in addition to doctrinal issues, it can be said that it is precisely this accretion of popular religiosity--the sale of amulets and merits--that sparked the Reformation. Then, coming to America, Catholicism acquired elements of African and Indian cultures.

3. Popular Religiosity Seeps Upward

Just as elements of unofficial Catholic popular religiosity often become official, so facets of unofficial Protestant popular religiosity also invade traditional Protestant churches. In the U.S., negro spirituals are part of the musical repertoire in many traditional churches. The phenomenon is even more evident in Latin America. Congregations in many traditional denominations are singing choruses originating among the charismatics, although their doctrine remains unchanged. Others may clap as they sing, making it hard for a passer-by to determine what kind of church it is. And some traditional churches, like the downtown Presbyterian church of Caracas, Venezuela, have become charis-matic.

While many Catholics look upon the Protestant GR churches as unofficial "sects," Protestant popular religiosity also seeps into the Catholic Church. Many portions of *La Hora Santa*, a weekly telecast of a Roman Catholic mass on a Costa Rican channel, can hardly be distinguished from a Pentecostal service, with its borrowing of Evangelical choruses and other elements. In fact, says David Martin (1990, 176), Pentecostals accused Roman Catholics of attending their services "to steal their musical clothes."

Sociology of religion describes how new religious groups ascend socially and become as institutionalized as the older denominations. But official churches also reach down and adopt elements of popular religion, when perhaps they unconsciously sense that they have removed themselves too far from the masses.

4. Popular Religiosity: Contextual or Syncretistic?

The Puebla (Mexico) bishops conference (CELAM III, 1979) defined popular religiosity, in part, as: ". . . the form or cultural existence that religion adopts in a particular people" (Deiros 1992, 119). Here the emphasis is on the interface between religion and a particular people's culture.

Popular religiosity, as a people's religion, is by definition highly *contextual*, i.e. expressed in the culture of the people. But when a culture is so fused with a non-Christian religion, the missionary or Christian leader has to subject every point of contact with culture to question. When we identify the Christian faith as containing some cultural element with strong non-Christian connotations, we run the risk of identifying the gospel with some element of a pagan belief--which is syncretism.

How to sort out that which is acceptable in a Christian's worship and lifestyle and that which bears evidence of a former belief, is an age-old missiological problem. Volumes have been written on the subject. The chapter on critical contextualization (171-192) in Hiebert's *Anthropological Insights for Missionaries* (1985) and the section on accommodation (169-179) in Bavinck's *An Introduction to the Science of Missions* (1960) are some of the best.

Building a Christian church on the site of a pagan shrine did not, as early Catholic missionaries to Mexico and Peru expected, demonstrate the superiority of Christianity over the earlier faith, but rather confirmed the former faith. Do Indians today, centuries later, pray to Christian saints in that church or are they in some clandestine or unconscious manner paying homage to some other god?

Catholic popular religiosity is accused more often than the official church of such mixing of Christian and pagan elements. The annual Day of the Dead in Mexico, with its macabre sugar-candy skulls and "bread of the dead," and its underlying connotations (death as the final conqueror) and the tribute paid to the spirits of one's dead forebears, is not only anti-Christian but reflects some half-forgotten pagan system. Mexico's federal government, officially non-religious, nevertheless requires its schools to celebrate the Day of the Dead. Children are taught to bring food offerings to altars, where the spirits are said to come and smell the food.

Whatever system that may have been, and whether or not every Mexican *campesino* is consciously praying to the dead, the mixture of pagan fatalism with a Christian holiday (All Saints' Day) is syncretism.

Critics of some of the GR movements also see traces of syncretism in Protestant popular religiosity. The sacralization of specially blessed or anointed objects, for example, to bring healing or good fortune in some GR movements is perceived by many as a syncretistic form--a mixture of Christianity with a Catholic, if not pagan, fetishism.

Serving Two Masters

Not enough attention has been given to the human capacity to be committed to two or more separate religious systems at the same time. The Western mind finds it hard to comprehend an oriental's commitment to two distinct religions at once. But such a juxtaposition theory expounded by Enrique Dussell (1981, 67) may well explain the Andean Indian's acceptance of Catholicism while still practicing his ancient rites, or the Brazilian Catholic who still attends spiritist gatherings of African origin.

Traditional Churches More Syncretistic?

While GR churches are often accused of syncretism, some of their leaders claim that traditional Protestants are more guilty of syncretistic practices, commonly associated with popular religiosity, than the GR churches. Such leaders point to the ritual, the robes and the formality of some historic Protestant churches as evidence. GR churches are supposedly freer of these vestiges of Rome. Some GR churches do not celebrate Christmas, feeling this holiday is also a vestige of a pagan holiday.

More serious, however, was the charge of a Peruvian GR church leader (Nieva, 1993) who pointed out that pastors of historic churches in their congregations often have more problems with their members continuing to visit the local *curandero* (witch doctor) or engaging in pagan and superstitious practices, because their churches did not take seriously the issues of the demonic and the spirit world. His GR church addresses these issues and exacts a commitment from the believers to renounce all such practices.

In another Andean country, according to a well-informed anonymous source, officials elected to their posts in a historic denomination were reported to have waited until they could consult with the *curanderos* before confirming their acceptance of their election.

Brazilian Neuza Itioka (1987, 73-75) also notes the difference between traditional Protestants and Pentecostals regarding Brazilian spiritism. Traditionalists are unprepared to face the issue.   Pentecostals address the issue, but without an adequate theological orientation to undergird their practices.

How Much is Satanic?

The most serious charge against popular religiosity comes from those who see Satan's hand behind every manifestation. The following statement concerning popular religiosity, coming out of an evangelism congress in 1980, is an example:

> "The strategy of the diabolical spiritual powers is to follow remarkable techniques of contextualization. If we accept that the first 'pseudo-theologian' was the serpent in the garden, who first called for reflection on the Word of God, we will discover from then on the infinite variety of methods and expressions of satanism across the ages. From prehistoric primitive forms up to the recent worship of extra-terrestrials, including such popular manifestations as the *Difunta Correa* of Argentina and *La Aparecida* in Brazil, one sees that the spiritual powers have multiple forms of expression in all social levels and in all circumstances" (CLADE II, 1980, 351).

Obviously the framers of this statement were looking at the crudest forms of the phenomenon. Some forms of popular religiosity, such as the Brazilian Umbanda spiritist movement, have so much non-Christian content that they are satanic movements--an example neither of Catholic nor of Protestant popular religiosity. But they employ enough Christian symbols that untaught Catholics often see no contradiction in participating in their practices while at the same time believing themselves to be faithful Catholics.

We agree with the statement that any alliance between a form of Christianity and spiritist and pagan beliefs, must be recognized as satanic and be condemned. If any miracles in the various manifestations of popular religiosity are not of God, we must be suspicious and on guard.

But our use of the term popular religiosity is evidently wider than what is condemned in this CLADE II statement. The term is usually applied to a wide band of Roman Catholic and Protestant religious contextual practices that can be found even in evangelical movements. But since the "father of lies" is behind every distortion of the gospel, we must recognize that his influence, even though less direct and less obvious, can indeed make itself felt in every movement led by imperfect saints, even the most orthodox.

5. Popular Religiosity: Integrating All of Life

Paredes (*El evangelio en platos de barro* (The Gospel in Pots of Clay) undated, 51) points out that popular religiosity makes ". . . the presence of the religious experience as a way of life . . ." integrating the sacred and the secular, as well as personal and community life. Life in a traditional Latin American town is much more integrated than the compartmentalized life of a person in a more advanced society.

It is precisely this "wholeness" that characterizes almost all of the GR churches that are intimately connected with the poor-- meeting needs with a message of hope (Shaull, unpublished, undated lecture presented in Nicaragua). They carry out significant social programs always hand in hand with evangelization--literacy, community libraries, day nurseries, funds for expectant mothers, care of the sick and orphans. Hollenweger (1972, 79-80) goes on to describe the activities of a GR church in the São Paulo situation--a tile factory to provide employment, a community center with medical and dental clinics, instruction in typing and music, a hospital, a home for the aged, a secondary school and a Bible school.

The farmer sees that the prosperity of his crops, the soil and the weather are in God's domain. Or looking at it another way, the natural includes the supernatural and vice versa. The sacred is not separated from the secular.

On the other hand, however, missiologist Paul Bergsma sees in *Protestant* popular religiosity a "dualist mentality," where the sacred and the secular are indeed separate (*Religiosidad Popular*, unpublished undated paper). Christians in GR movements are often not permitted to engage in worldly affairs (e.g. in politics or sports). As a minority with a perspective different from that of the surrounding community, they create boundaries around particular areas of life, and life loses a certain amount of integration, especially in relationship to society. To belong to a minority, with a distinct world view and behavior, will always be disintegrative socially.

But many Evangelical GR movements are beginning to open up, recognizing that politics, the arts, science and other activities are parts of God's domain and can be legitimate areas of participation.

Individualistic or Part of a Community?

Paredes (1989, 51-53) perceives Indian popular religiosity to be particularly integrative of personal and community life. Much as early North American settlers made each farmer's barn-raising a community event, so is the Andean Indian's *minga*, an activity which draws the whole Indian community to repair a road or build a bridge. Andean Indian culture developed a popular religiosity that created a community awareness so that all personal decision making took into account a serious responsibility not only to one's extended family, but also to one's community. Here, too, the view is more Biblical, in that a high value is placed on love for one's neighbor.

Here, too, Bergsma (*ibid.*) and Deiros (*op. cit.*, 168) accuse *Protestant* popular religiosity of being characterized by individualism. In many GR churches even prayer time in a worship service is an occasion for each individual to pray aloud, presenting his own petitions to God, rather than a time of collective praise, confession and petition. Evangelical emphasis on a personal decision for Christ, personal devotions and a lack of a well-developed ecclesiology can make for weak commitment to the church and the Christian community, not to speak of little commitment to the broader community in which one lives.

Fortunately, a strong sense of family still exists in many Evangelical churches. This is a major attraction to outsiders. Uprooted rural peoples, finding themselves in a large city and missing the sense of community in their village, discover a new family of caring and concerned people in many an Evangelical church.

6. Popular Religiosity: A Tool for the Manipulator

Simple people, swayed by emotions and awed by what is perceived as miraculous, are easy prey to strong leaders with their own agendas. The Latin American Catholic Church, beset by its own divisions and losses to Protestants, seems at times to be appealing to a common denominator to keep it together--popular religiosity. An appeal for people to renew their participation in processions, *romerías* (pilgrimages to the shrines), and other practices of popular religiosity, seem to be part of a strategy to regain its spiritual and political hegemony. Said Dayton Roberts of the Latin America Mission: "One way the Pope tried to restore centralized authority . . . was by encouraging traditional Catholic piety, such as the cults of the Virgin Mary and the saints" (quoted in Stoll 1990, 40).

David Stoll (*ibid.*, 99-100) documents those who see manipulation of Latin American Protestantism by the C.I.A. and U.S. imperialism. This fails to recognize that the vast majority of churches, especially the GR movements, have their own spiritual agenda. But the temptation is always there for the U.S. political right and for people with other political agendas to capture these GR movements to propagate their own ideologies.

More present is the temptation for a leader with a charismatic personality to manipulate people at the level of popular religiosity for his or her own ends. In so doing, the person creates his or her own kingdom of followers and institutions without any serious spiritual or financial accountability.

"Protestantism no Longer the People's Opiate," say Some

Nineteenth century Latin American liberals welcomed Protestants because their work ethic and their schools could help the region's modernization. Protestant immigration would turn Latin America around, they thought, anticipating principles later expounded in Weber's *The Protestant Ethic and the Spirit of Capitalism* (1930 publication in English; original in German in 1904).

Protestants were associated with progress in Latin America until marxists began condemning all religion as the people's opiate. The GR movements displayed a religious form that seemed to isolate their followers from society--e.g. involvement in labor unions and political parties--and some of them still do. Hence, this could be construed to be anti-progress.

Christian Lalive d'Epinay's *Haven of the Masses* (1968) was a landmark study of Chilean Pentecostals that introduced "social strike" into sociologists' vocabulary, suggesting (*ibid.*, 146) that their faith isolated the believers from social involvement and progress. Eighty-five percent of the Pentecostal pastors studied felt that a Christian should not be a member of a political party (vs. 19% of other Protestants); thirty percent that he should not even join a neighborhood improvement committee (vs. 4% of the others).

Emilio Willem's *Followers of a New Faith* (1967) studied Pentecostals in Chile and Brazil and found that their faith helped them overcome anomie (a sense of loss and disorientation) when immigrating to growing industrial and urban centers, and cope with life there. The church became their new family.

One suspects that there is more than one vision as to what it means to contribute to the progress of a people. Is it to become an efficient worker within the system or to work towards change, including revolution?

David Martin (1990, 224) also admits that the studies regarding the contribution of Evangelicals to social progress are ". . . contrasting, some proving that the gospel restores social harmony, others that it is maladaptive, undermining group identity, promoting social division or acting as agents of U.S. culture."

Jaime Valverde (1990) studies Costa Rican Pentecostal churches and criticizes them for not encouraging their members to participate in banana company strikes or in protests against electricity rate hikes. "The determinism and eschatalogical pessimism in these churches is evident. In more general terms, the established social order is legitimatized" (*ibid.*, 66).

Taking a New Look

While Martin (*ibid.*, 205-231) reviews many studies that demonstrate that Protestant churches promote progress, historian Carmelo Alvarez (1992) states that social scientists are taking specific note of the positive social values of pentecostal GR movements. One is a book with a provocative title: *Algo más que opio* (Something More Than Opium) by a trio of Dutch anthropologists, Barbara Boudewijnse, André Droogers, and Frans Kamsteeg (1991).

To start with, at the level of the individual and his or her family, the social condition of the Christian often rises. Daniel Wattenburg (1990, 15-16) describes a down-and-out butcher who wandered into a church in Chile. The first move on the part of the believers was to cast out the "spirit of drunkenness" from him. The second was a word of prophecy that God would provide him his own butcher shop. When the shop materialized, the pastor loaned him money for equipment and eventually the man acquired a second shop. Wattenburg summarizes:

> "The reasons for the apparent link between Pentecostalism and modest upward mobility are varied. They include withdrawal from the Roman Catholic fiesta system; rejection of the Latin male ideal of hard-drinking, promiscuous, violent machismo; the mutual material support available within the Pentecostal faith community (the churches provide a network that often functions as a job or housing referral agency); and the acquisition through lay participation in church activity of skills (speaking and organizing) and attitudes (self-confidence, initiative) that assist professional advancement outside the church."

His honesty often gives him preference in job hunting. Where
the church, however, makes too many demands, it may result in
job loss. The weekly all-night prayer vigil in one GR church
leaves people too exhausted to do a day's work the morning after.
Such demands by a church often attract people who are not in 8
to 5 jobs, or encourage others to leave. Studies (Martin 1990,
228) have shown that GR movements are composed of a greater
number of self-employed people.

Another more subtle contribution of Protestantism is the
attitude that change is possible. Fatalism--*que será, será* (what
will be, will be)--characteristic of traditional Latin culture, is
replaced by a sense that with hard work and God's help one can
hope for change. A person can make plans and change conditions,
if not in society, at least in his or her personal life. And more than
offering people escape from fatalism, the egalitarianism of GR
churches (despite top-down pastoral leadership) gives
disenfranchised people a sense of power. Every believer can seek
the gifts and manifestations of the Holy Spirit. A Pentecostal
church in one Central American city quotes in large letters printed
on its facade the phrase in Acts 1:8: "Ye shall receive POWER."
This sense of spiritual power often translates into an attitude of
confidence in facing problems.

Anthropologist Angela Hoekstra (Boudewijnse et al, *op. cit.*,
50) asks why Roman Catholic popular religion does not satisfy
migrants to the city. She suggests that Catholic popular religiosity
is too rural, attached to saints of given localities. These get left
behind when people move. Protestantism is more universal and
equips people to live in the modern mobile world.

While there has been a disdain for religion in the secularized
West, Walls and Shenk (1990, 196) say ". . . the new religious
movements have been cheerfully unaware of these strictures
against religion." Religion has values which are ". . . prerequisites

to progress . . . self-restraint and thrift . . . personal discipline and integrity to be industrious and set goals . . . a spirit of self-determination and self-responsibility" (*ibid.*).

David Martin (*op. cit.*, 287) argues that although Latin American Pentecostalism does not constitute a movement that can change society in some macro-fashion, it will eventually create change. It is a "cell in society," he says, and throughout history groups "test" their practices in these "enclosures." Later the wider society may then pick up their ideas. He cites the development of pacifism in closed Quaker and Mennonite societies. Eventually many in the wider world adopted pacifistic perspectives.

In chapter fourteen we take up some of the GR churches' increasing entry into ministries that attempt to heal some of society's ills, and their more recent attempts to make a contribution politically.

The Social Scientists' Agenda

There are long discussions about whether Latin American Pentecostalism is a subconscious "protest" against the establishment or an accommodation to it. It is a question of whether it clings to outmoded patterns of society or breaks with them. Some criticize GR movements because they make people comfortable in a society that needs revolutionaries.

For a long period Pentecostalism was cast as a paid agent of the U.S. right wing. Anthropologist David Stoll (*op. cit.*, 319-320) put that concept to rest saying: "Despite the flagrant romances between pentecostal patriarchs and right-wing regimes, congregations tend to retain considerable autonomy in their dealings with state and society. They conform to outer restraints yet maintain a degree of independence, in a paradoxical way that critics have not quite captured . . ."

The social scientists' interpretations, however insightful they may be, make a reader conscious of their particular priorities. The nature of the social scientists is to study the effects of a phenomenon like religion within society. Given the limits of their field, they cannot probe into the deeper motives and purposes of people who are seeking God. They may observe that GR movements may be a subconscious protest against a prevailing system, the Roman Catholic Church included, but people do not accept Christ in these churches to protest. They are convicted of their sin and their need as they respond to the Holy Spirit. Their preaching usually does not include social reform--with the exception of preaching about reform in the basic social unit, the family. What one observer says about GR movements in India applies to Latin America:

> "This contextualization of Christianity was completely unanticipated and frequently opposed by the older churches and ecumenical leaders. These groups show little direct interest in the social questions that have concerned the contextual theologians of the last generation. Nevertheless, these groups are having a major social and economic impact in several respects" (Stackhouse 1993, 58).

He goes on to mention (*ibid.*) the creation of community, networks for finding jobs, developing leadership skills and other social benefits. "Of course, these benefits are by-products, not the core purposes of these groups. Their chief focus is on helping people develop a personal and saving relationship to Jesus Christ. . ."

These statements sum up the issues arising as social scientists and others look at the GR movement through their lenses. They perceive that by the very nature of GR movements they are inserted into a people's culture. In many cases they may be the most Christian expression of popular religiosity. And they are being recognized as contributing, in some measure, to modernization. But as important as this may be, the Church measures itself by its own criteria--its faithfulness to Christ and the witness that emanates from that faithfulness.

TEN

Divergent Views by Roman Catholics

"When the pope thinks of Latin America in the evening, he cannot sleep that night," observed a cardinal about the growing strength of the *Evangélico* Church (Buhlman 1977, 154).

The Roman Catholic view of GR peoples and churches is often included as part of its view of the *evangélico* movement as a whole. No doubt the typical Roman Catholic attitude towards all Protestants is shaped in some measure by those that appear to threaten the Church the most--the expanding GR churches.

As we shall see later, in many countries Roman Catholics learned to distinguish between the historic churches and the others. While more comfortable with the less-threatening historic churches, their views of all the expanding non-historic groups were even more specifically shaped by their fears regarding GR movements without necessarily looking at this subgroup in particular.

Yet more discriminating Catholic observers are beginning to refer to the GR churches themselves, especially in Brazil. Because of the size and visibility of these groups they are called "neo-pentecostals" and "*pentecostais autónomos*," as well as "native churches" and "popular churches."

Atheists, Communist Dogs, Separated Brethren, Ravenous Wolves

Recent history reveals an intriguing development of Catholicism's attitude toward the *evangélico* in general.

1. Up to Vatican Council II (e.g. from the Colonial period to 1962)

Before the mid-19th century, a Protestant movement was inconceivable in most countries of Latin America. The Roman Catholic view in the subsequent century preceding Vatican Council II can be described as passing through three stages.

a. With the efforts of politically liberal elements to encourage the immigration of Protestants, it was at first argued that people accepting Protestantism were simply taking a first step toward losing all religion and becoming atheists.

b. Beginning in the latter part of the 19th century, the prevailing opinion was to limit Protestant worship to foreigners.

The Costa Rica-Panama border was straddled by vast United Fruit banana plantations connected by a single narrow gauge company railroad which, in the 1950s, before the Pan American Highway was completed, was the only land connection between the two countries. There we ran across two men in jump suits, bumping their motorcycles over the ties toward Panama. As they introduced themselves, we discovered that they were Chilean priests, returning to their country from the U.S. by land. Upon finding out that we were Protestant missionaries, they commented on the surprising number of Evangelical churches they found in their trek through Central America. "You are doing a great work," they said, "but don't bother the Roman Catholics. Stay with your own people."

This was the more typically 19th century attitude-- Protestants were welcome to minister to the British, the U.S. citizens, or Germans resident in Latin America. But native Latin Americans were off-limits. There was a degree of wishful thinking even then, in the 1950s, that Latins would never respond to the drastic step represented by "changing religions."

c. Still later, with the Roman Catholic Church firmly on the side of the establishment and the wealthy, Protestants were identified as communist dogs. We remember being at a Pan American Christian radio network conference in Cali, Colombia, in the 1950s. Somehow a newspaper had come up with our names, perhaps through immigration offices, and listed the lot of us as undesirable elements in Colombia, namely "communists."

From Wilton Nelson's *A History of Protestantism in Costa Rica* (1962, 245): "It was also claimed that Protestantism led to Communism, and that the 'Roman Catholic Faith is the only invincible bulwark against Communism.' When Archbishop Odio [of Costa Rica] made this accusation in his Lenten Pastoral of 1954, the Evangelical Alliance answered by pointing out that in Protestant countries there is little Communism while in Catholic countries it abounds."

2. In the 1960s and 1970s

Vatican II (1962-1965) wafted warm ecumenical winds and rather suddenly, the *evangélicos* were described as "separated brethren."

From being the pariah of Latin American society to being accepted in friendship by priests and nuns in the early 1960s was a confusing and heady experience for many of us. The recollection of one of the authors is that "Whereas previously I was shunned or stones were thrown at my automobile during special religious seasons of the year, now I was invited to share a coffee break in a restaurant with a priest and say grace over a meal in an air flight by a nun seated next to me. I began praying regularly with a priest--something utterly inconceivable a few years before."

Latin Catholicism often perceived the *evangélicos* as manifesting a ". . . biblically based and personally appropriated faith" (Martin 1990, 288). At the same time, change was the order of the day. Divergent Catholic movements arose, such as the militant and fortress-like Catholic Action and Opus Dei, the socially-oriented Liberation Theology, and the middle-class Catholic charismatic movement.

As to the effect of this attitude change toward the *evangélicos*, "Those which until now had been rather contemptuously termed 'sects' are being taken increasingly seriously, because their extraordinary success shows that they are responding to a real human need. . . . People who used to feel insignificant, bored and frustrated in the official churches now no longer feel harnessed to an over-intellectual theology or held in check by patriarchal structures. . ." (Buhlmann 1977, 302).

Furthermore, there was across-the-board fraternizing, especially between Catholic charismatics and Evangelicals in the early 1970s in many countries. However, it is well to remember that while priests and pastors, theologians and leaders, participated in these contacts, by and large the average Catholic and Protestant Latin American did not mix.

Meanwhile, in the more radical liberation wings of Latin American Catholicism with their prior option-for-the-poor stance, Protestants were considered as standing for the status quo and reactionary to social change. Whereas the "communist" Protestants were formerly to the left of the Catholics, now we were generally perceived to be on their far right. Even as late as 1989, a conference sponsored by the Catholic Institute of International Affairs in London considered a paper on "Oppressive Christianity in the Third World" which implied that Protestants were a Trojan horse for imperialism (Marcom 1990).

3. Enter John Paul II

In the wake of this conservative and reactionary Pope, not only is there increasing alarm at Evangelical growth, but the ecumenical doors are near to being closed. Now, instead of "separated brethren" the *evangélicos* are back to where they were before, called "sects" and worse. In 1992 in Santo Domingo, Pope John Paul II, in an expression bound to become classic, referred to Protestants as "ravenous wolves."

A Sliver of Light

And yet, there is still a crack in the door. For one thing, there is growing recognition that all Protestants are not the same. Many mainline denominations or historic churches in Latin America have identified with the social reforms advocated by the Catholics. They also have attempted more ecumenical contacts with the Roman Church. Furthermore, because they have been generally less aggressive in evangelism than other non-Catholics, they are perceived by the latter as less threatening by the Roman Catholics.

So, while in some countries like Mexico, all Protestants are identified as "sects," in most other countries a distinction is made between the established historic Protestant churches and those "sects"--a term now applied to all of the other groups including churches established by foreign independent, interdenominational, and younger denominational mission boards plus Pentecostals and the GR groups. Generally in this classification non-*evangélico* groups are also included, such as the Mormons and the Jehovah's Witnesses.

Denial, Menus, and Legends

Although the Roman Catholic Church continues, as it has in the past, to attempt to keep change under control (Hollenweger 1972, 106), it is interesting to detect mixed signals.

On one hand, there is failure to accept the reality of the growth of the *sectas* and the stubborn, negative, sometimes bitter reaction continues.

An article appeared in the November 3-10, 1992, edition of *Esta Semana* (a San José, Costa Rica, weekly newspaper) about Monseñor Arturo Rivera y Damas, archbishop of San Salvador, in which he declares that 90% of Salvadorans are Catholic. He emphasizes that the modest increase of *sectas* in the past 20 years has merely caused division in the Christian Church. He defines *sectas* as groups that simply grow by "dividing themselves" and have no central direction. What is even more of a denial on the archbishop's part is the fact that El Salvador is a country where there has been phenomenal Protestant growth.

Also typical is the defense of the Catholic Church given by Monseñor Román Arrieta, archbishop of Costa Rica, who has said repeatedly in effect that there is no need to leave the Catholic fold because the Mother Church has everything. If you want a more ascetic, saintly life, we have that. If you want Christian social and political involvement, we have that. If you want the charismatic, we can offer you that.

Here is a menu of options for a Christian lifestyle, none of which rings out genuinely. This is a typical dominant Catholic attempt to control change--to say nothing of its paternalistic and condescending mood.

In *Los evangélicos: ¿nueva leyenda negra en América Latina?* (The Evangelicals: New Black Legend in Latin America? 1991), Samuel Escobar addresses the bad press the Evangelical

Church is receiving from wide circles of the Roman Catholic press, both from sources on the right and on the left. This charge has been supported from social scientists as well as in ecumenical circles.

Escobar calls it the new *leyenda negra* (black legend), looking back to the ancient black legend which described in extremely negative terms the treatment of the indigenous peoples by the Spanish *conquistadores* (conquerors) and the Catholic hierarchy in the war of conquest, exploitation and domination of Latin America. Traditionally, Catholics have been trying to rebut this "black legend." "We weren't all that bad."

According to this alleged *new* black legend, the numerical growth of Protestantism, especially among the non-historic groups and Pentecostals, is a new conquest and attempt at domination of Latin America funded by vast sums of money provided by the C.I.A., planned by certain U.S. imperialistic and politically rightist groups. In this propaganda assault, the word *secta* is not defined, but shrouded in ambiguity as Jehovah's Witnesses, Mormons and other such groups are all lumped together with the *evangélicos*.

Escobar (1991, 3) laments that "By ignorance or bad faith, versions of the legend have been multiplied, falsifying incidents, propagating half truths, or providing interpretations that do not do justice to the facts."

Learning from the Grass Roots

In other Roman Catholic circles, however, the spirit toward the GR churches, while still showing marked concern, is more open. Mention has already been made of ecumenical tolerance toward mainline Protestant churches that share a great commitment to social justice.

GR movements are a major part of the "sects" grouping after the historic churches have been removed and placed in a more favorable category. Yet many of the changes in worship style and evangelization being adopted by the Roman Catholics have more typically Pentecostal and GR characteristics. Even though the Catholics in their perception of the non-historic churches do not distinguish between the GR churches and other Evangelical churches, it is the characteristics of the GR churches that are being copied.

An example of this is what José Comblin (1994, 217-220), a Belgian priest who has worked in Brazil for many years, says about "What We Can Learn from Pentecostals." In mentioning personal caring, fraternal community, personal worth, religious expression, missionary outreach, and pastoral leadership, he is describing characteristics of the GR churches as well.

Cecilia Mariz (1994, 75-81) does essentially the same thing as she makes "a comparison of Catholic BECs (Base Ecclesial Communities) and Pentecostal Communities." Many elements she finds in her analysis of Pentecostalism coincide with the nature of GR churches, in general.

Peruvian Catholic José Luis Pérez (1992) provides a study of Catholic desertion in Peru, which is surprisingly sympathetic to Evangelicals. He mentions the vigorous evangelistic methods of Protestants, and disenchantment with the Catholic Church. He adds an interesting note that the *evangélicos* are offering an "informal church" to the masses (*ibid.*, 81-82)--so much like the informal way in which manufacturing, selling, and business are done in Peru, as mentioned by Tito Paredes in chapter 9 of this book.

Other voices resound as well. A review by Jeffrey Gros, FSC (1993, 492) of the remarkable book, *El protestantismo fundamentalista: una experiencia ambigua para América Latina*

(The Fundamentalist Protestants: An Ambiguous Experience for Latin America), emphasizes the importance of Roman Catholic author Florencio Galindo's attempts to dispel the widespread mythology in the Catholic Church about the GR churches. This mythology is portrayed as reducing these churches to political motivation, pseudo-spiritual movements or mixing them up with semi-Christian and non-Christian proselytizing groups. Gros adds: "His conclusions are much more self-critical for the Catholic Community, and positively disposed toward the authentic Christian needs met by these Protestant groups, than is most of this defensive literature."

Like the social scientist, who formerly looked with disdain upon these groups and now is discovering values in them, the Roman Catholic hierarchy, while always sensing the threat, is beginning to look more carefully at them to discover what it can learn in order to hold on to the masses.

In the fascinating July 1992 number of *Maryknoll*, the issue bears the title, "Is Latin America Turning Protestant?" The major author is Catholic Thomas Bamat, a sociologist who has served in Ecuador. Right up front there is recognition of the force and impact of the *evangélicos*. He estimates 10% of Latin America's 415 million are Protestant. Although acknowledging that they are expanding everywhere, he singles out Central America, Chile, and Brazil as the areas with greatest growth (*ibid.*, 10).

He also notes that, given its development in the past two decades, 25 or 30% of the total Latin American population may consider itself Protestant in forty or fifty years. He recognizes that this is already true in Guatemala (*ibid.*, 12).

However, from his own studies Bamat concludes that there will not be a Protestant majority very soon. The major reason, as he sees it, is the revitalization process under way in the Catholic Church.

Considering the various and sometimes bizarre Catholic explanations of the growth of the *evangélicos*, he believes it is much more complex. Among the explanations, he cites the social conditions in which this growth is occurring. Crushing poverty, massive displacements of people from a traditional existence to the insecurity of new rural patterns or migrations to the jagged edges of modern cities are all factors with which to be reckoned. He recalls the familiar refrain heard throughout Latin America: "What we have doesn't go far enough" (*ibid.*, 12).

Over 40% of Latin Americans do not satisfy their basic needs for food, health and housing. By the year 2000, opines Bamat, this figure could be 55%. Hunger, unemployment, the widening gap between the rich and the poor will lead to social violence, repression, and outright warfare in some countries (*ibid.*, 12-13).

In the light of these social realities, no one can ignore the widespread economic, political, and cultural influence of the U.S. Some see this as highly destructive while others idealize "the American way of life." Bamat also adds: "The well-financed, well-organized missions programs of fundamentalist U.S. Protestants--including carefully prepared methods for gaining converts and aggressive use of television and radio--are key elements in winning converts, as is the missionary zeal of newly converted evangelicals" (*ibid.*, 14).

He goes on to describe the other side of the coin. He emphasizes an obvious parallel factor--the inability of the Roman Catholic Church to cope with the situation. He mentions the relatively few priests and the centralized, clergy-dominated structure of the Church. These factors work against responding to the religious needs of the people (*ibid.*).

What Bamat seems to fail to recognize is the great, ground-swell grass-roots movement stemming from the people themselves, without any kind of foreign assistance and support.

Franz Damen, Belgian Catholic missionary to Bolivia, has observed that ". . . the Protestant groups that grow faster are either indigenous to the continent, or, if they had an origin in North America, they have quickly become 'Latin-Americanized' in both leadership and financing" (Escobar 1992, 31).

Is the Roman Catholic Church Turning Protestant?

What is the Roman Catholic Church learning from the GR people? What changes in attitudes, methods, and organizational models are being made?

1. **First, there are the charismata and the concept of the gathered Church.**
       One Roman Catholic admits that Brazilian Pentecostals had adopted Catholic truths which had long been forgotten, such as speaking in tongues and the distinction between the "semi-believers" and the charismatically equipped born-again believers--a distinction which he claimed was seen in the writings of the early church fathers (Hollenweger 1972, 102). Not everyone in the geographically-defined boundaries of a parish were really a part of the church.
       The Roman Catholic charismatic movement in Latin America was stimulated in the early 1970s by the visits of Father Francis McNutt and others from the U.S. (Their ministries also markedly influenced Protestant missionaries.) No doubt much change has been the product of the Church's internal awareness of the necessity of making its language the language of the people, whether literally--the use of the vernacular since Vatican Council II--or figuratively--in worship styles and in the issues it addresses.

2. **The second lesson is the importance of teaching, the involvement of laity, and a festive atmosphere in the church.**
In a 1991 Vatican conference called to discuss the various non-Roman Catholic confessions in Catholic countries, Mexican Cardinal Ernesto Corripio Ahumada said that to stem the flow from Roman Catholic ranks the Church had to engage in a more intensive work of teaching its doctrine, involve the laity in the ministry, and make its masses more joyful (Sheridan 1991).

Father P. J. Ayerra, in his 1980 study of the Protestant movement in his country, *Los protestantes en Venezuela* (The Protestants in Venezuela), typifies an attitude increasingly sympathetic and open to learn. He affirms that not all Protestant movements are a conspiracy, but rather deserve respect. One can learn from them. Indeed, there is increasing recognition of the Protestant spiritual experience.

There is also increasing recognition that the *evangélicos'* ability to mobilize lay people for mission is why they are growing.

At the *IV Conferencia General del Episcopado* (Fourth General Conference of Latin American Bishops) in Santo Domingo, Dominican Republic, in 1992, a new evangelistic strategy was sought. It begins with a new concept of the parish. A passive pastoral posture will not be followed as before. There will be an emphasis on the dynamics of small groups.

Costa Rican Archbishop Román Arrieta returned from the conference proposing to make parishes become training centers for organizing small groups. "The parishes will be converted basically into centers of spiritual formation for laymen who will work in the creation of small Christian communities" (Guevara 1992).

The unmistakable *evangélico* mark is on these strategies, even though they would not have admitted this at that conference.

Evidences of a more festive style among Roman Catholics include large charismatic rallies, occasional healing campaigns, and Christian rock concerts in some countries. In this sense, then, the Church is "making its masses more joyful."

3. **There is the use of the mass media which the** *evangélicos* **have utilized to a large extent.**
The revitalization process occurring in the Catholic Church in Latin America appears to be, in large measure, a Catholic backlash seen locally in paid ads, street marches, sermons denouncing the *evangélicos,* and even some sporadic persecution in scattered areas. "The stress that Pope John Paul II laid on the Protestant challenge during his 1991 visit to Brazil and the intent to which the Vatican has retooled to combat it--including plans for its own electronic church, Lumens 2000--underscores the seriousness with which this Pentecostal expansion is regarded within the Catholic Church" (Winn, 1992). It is clear that even though the Catholic Church is reacting against the *evangélicos*, it has nevertheless learned from them the importance of the use of the mass media.

It is interesting to note that the Roman Catholics are installing a TV ministry (Channel 11) in Costa Rica, well after Evangelicals already have two channels. This is history repeating itself. Several years after the first Protestant radio station (TIFC) was established in 1948, the Catholics inaugurated their own Radio Fides, now heard on an adjacent frequency.

The influence of Latin American pentecostal worship styles has touched Catholic church worship as well as local weekly telecasts.

4. **A fourth lesson being learned is the compassionate care for the individual in the Evangelical movement.**

There has been considerable social ministry by Catholics in Latin America. What is different about the *evangélicos*? They are less institutional, more personal, more lay and less professional.

It is recognized by some Catholics that *evangélicos* are not winning entirely by default. Rather, they offer elements that appeal to the oppressed and believing people. These are seen to be:

a. Simple answers and consolations are supplied in face of suffering and uncertainties, based on irrefutable truths involving a literal understanding of the Bible.

b. They affirm the dignity and importance of ordinary people in their prayer meetings and in the expressions of their emotions. People become somebody through religious experience--they become human beings.

c. They offer means for improving poor people's social and economic well-being. Examples of this include: overcoming alcoholism and domestic violence and networking mutual support, including economic help to migrants (Bamat 1992, 15).

"The changes fundamentalists call for are largely matters of personal improvement, more readily within reach of ordinary people than commitment to struggles for widespread social or political change" (*ibid.*, 16). This is in sharp contrast to Catholic social teaching which stresses action for justice and participation in the transformation of the world as an integral element of the preaching of the gospel.

One priest in Brazil, Rubens Chassereaux, said that the Roman Catholic Church has considered herself the great *senhora*, "over everything and over all peoples, manipulating politics and morals," having never learned how to relate the spiritual and the political, its preaching and its pastoral activities (Dermi Azevedo 1991). Brazilian Bishop Helder Camara is even quoted as saying that the measures taken to contain the advance of the new groups "are too late" (*ibid.*).

In conclusion, what will be the effect of these changes in the Roman Catholic scene on GR churches? Our predictions are tentative.

1. *The Catholic Liberation Theology wing will probably not affect the GR movements directly.* For all practical purposes, it is in disarray. Cuba and Nicaragua, which were to be models of liberated peoples, have failed LT followers.

Several writers, in fact, document the move of people from the LT-dominated BECs (Base communities) to grass-roots and Pentecostal churches. Guillermo Cook refers to research done by an ecumenical agency (CEDI) in Brazil to support this (Cook 1994, x).

This is not to say that guerrilla warfare or political unrest in Latin America will cease. Quite to the contrary, the great social revolution of this century in Latin America, sometimes violent, at other times by peaceful changes through elections and legislation, marches relentlessly on.

2. *The Roman Catholic charismatic movement will not likely influence GR churches.* As in the case of the CEBs, the flow has been out of this movement to the Evangelical fold. It could be argued that most Catholic charismatics who have had enough courage have already left. The freedom in worship and the personal relationship to Christ which are generated in charismatic circles lead to more freedom--not less.

3. *The traditional Catholic parish or a similar center of life and ministry, if it is revitalized in large measure and becomes more Christ-centered, could become a force that would slow*

down the growth of the GR movements. Its projected mass media outreach, vital small groups, and a good number of regenerate clergy, could make a large impact.

If, in fact, Roman Catholics' conclusions about the reality and strength of the *evangélicos'* spiritual experience (e.g. Pérez 1992, 27-30) is taken seriously, revival in the Catholic Church could break out. Even now this Church is ". . . recapturing many people with its greater seriousness, teaching, and reconversion. Much depends on the [local] priest" (R. Padilla 1994).

John Kessler's studies in Costa Rica (Kessler 1990), which indicate a number of individuals who state they were "former Evangelicals" and some who have returned to the Roman Catholic fold, flash a danger signal. The Evangelical movement in Latin America has not kept watch on its back door.

How deep was the commitment of these "ex-Evangelicals" to the gospel? Did they consider they were Christian just because they raised their hands in an evangelistic crusade? Or had they been baptized members of a church? Whatever the situation, the threshold for entering into the Evangelical fold is now easier than ever before. The traditional persecution and social stigma are much less. But when it is too easy to enter through the front, it can become easy to leave through the back.

While this regression or return to the "mother church" is evident, it may be only one of the reasons for the phenomenon. From our Mexican studies presented in chapter 2, we see a certain nominalism in force. Some calling themselves *evangélicos* are wrestling with the costliness of following Christ. While in Argentina, as mentioned earlier, Deiros (1994) uncovers another reason. Some are simply not yet in the fold. They attend services, but often float from church to church. In both cases, they call themselves *evangélicos*.

Since the beginning, Latin American *evangélicos* have made the uncommitted or nominal Roman Catholic their principal target. Now it is possible that a revitalized Roman Catholic Church may not only try to "re-evangelize" its own people, but also make nominal *evangélicos* its target.

Latin America's Roman Catholics prefer to relate, if at all, with the historical churches rather than the GR movements. While the latter are their greatest threat, at the same time, they end up being the models that the Catholics find themselves imitating.

ELEVEN

Looking Askance: Protestant Views

"Look at the grass-roots churches," we said. "Somehow they have captured the enthusiasm of the people so that they really sacrifice for the Lord. Some of them have built enormous buildings, and they are filled with people."

"I really can't believe," replied the Central American pastor of a traditional Protestant group, "that the poor in these countries are raising the money to construct those churches. They *must* be getting money from abroad."

In Chile, a colleague who was an evangelist and whose background was that of a U.S.-related denomination, had heard quite enough about the authoritarianism, the nepotism, and the well-publicized rumors of sexual misconduct in the leadership of one Chilean GR church. In addition, he had observed a very legalistic understanding of the gospel on the part of the group's members. He blurted out: "I don't know if I want to call these groups 'Christian.' Well--maybe 'sub-Christian' would be a better word."

Misinformation, denial, prejudice, honest criticism and sometimes high regard are all part of the views and attitudes that Latin American *evangélicos* and Protestants elsewhere have of the GR churches.

A brief historical review of the development of missions may help establish the background against which we can understand the reaction to the rise of the GR churches. Let us make a thumbnail sketch of: (1) the search by missionaries for guiding principles in their ministry, (2) the emergence of the grass-roots churches, (3) the various points of view that Protestants have adopted regarding them, and (4) the issues of church growth and contextualization as they relate to the reaction to these autochthonous movements.

1. The Goal: Indigenous Churches

From the beginning of modern Protestant missions in the seventeenth century, missionaries have viewed their task as essentially one of preaching personal salvation. Historically, Protestant missions originated in the pietist movement. In reaction to formalism and intellectualism, pietism stressed Bible study and personal spiritual experience.

Pietism began in the 17th century in Germany when aftereffects of the Thirty Years' War and a hardening of orthodoxy robbed the Church of much of its spirituality. Principally through John Wesley, it had a powerful effect on the English-speaking world and later on Latin American Protestantism, primarily through missionaries from North America.

Peter Beyerhaus (1979, 15) analyzed this by noting the strengths and weaknesses of the missionaries of this type. "Their strength lay in their sincere and self-sacrificing zeal to win souls for the Lamb; their weakness was in their spiritual concept of the Church and the small importance they attached to its visible form and ministry."

Saving Souls

J. Verkuyl in his *Contemporary Missiology* (1978, 176-181) skillfully traces this single purpose of saving souls as it was reflected in the fathers of early pietism (Philip Jacob Spener, 1635-1705, and Herman Francke, 1663-1727) and later pietism (Nicolaus von Zinzendorf, 1700-1760), in the hundreds of missionaries, a result of this movement in many countries. It was also clearly manifested in the pioneer missionary work of Henry Martyn in the Muslim world (1781-1812) and William Carey in Asia (1761-1834), as well as the American Student Volunteer Movement which under leaders like John Mott, Robert Speer, and Herman Rutgers sent missionaries to the six continents. This basic motivation and singular goal for mission, the saving of souls, was the dominant emphasis at the beginning of the "great century of mission," the nineteenth.

But during that same century, there was a reaction to the emphasis on personal salvation to the exclusion of building up the church. As emphasis was placed on the church, paternalistic structures developed. Native Christians became both spiritually and materially dependent upon Western missionaries and their organizations to maintain their mission-founded churches. In essence, the expansion of these churches was limited whenever the sending bodies reached the limit of their personnel and financial resources.

Another Goal: Indigeneity

The corporate life of churches planted in distant lands had to be strengthened and developed along with the winning of individuals to Christ. But more than that, the churches had to be "indigenous," as defined in recent days by Alan Tippett (1979, 85): "When the indigenous people of a community think of the Lord as their own, not a foreign Christ; when they do things as unto the Lord, meeting the cultural needs around them, worshiping in patterns they understand; when their congregations function in participation in a body, which is structurally indigenous; then you have an indigenous Church."

This early awakening to the need for indigeneity began in the thought and work of two leaders of prominent mission organizations--Anglican Henry Venn (1796-1873) and American Congregationalist Rufus Anderson (1796-1880). They began about the same time to articulate a goal for mission that sought to build up the Church wherever it is found. What emerged is the so-called three-self (3-S) formula--self-governing, self-supporting, and self-propagating characteristics of a church. Congregationalist Anderson sought to apply these principles directly to the autonomous local church. Anglican Venn, however, had in mind not only local congregations but application of the 3-S principles to a whole diocese under its native bishop.

This was a clarion call for Western missions to make indigenous churches their goal. "Missions are instituted for the spread of a scriptural, self-propagating Christianity. This is their only aim. But it includes four elements: (1) converting of lost human beings (2) organizing them into churches (3) providing the churches with competent native ministers (4) conducting the churches to the stage of independence and (in most cases) of self-propagation" (Verkuyl 1978, 186).

Guidelines at Last

Pierce Beaver noted that for two hundred years prior to Anderson, North American missions had been operating without any principal guidelines. Anderson was the first to develop a theory and carry it out (Verkuyl 1978, 187).

The "3-S formula" received wide acclaim. It was embraced by virtually every mission agency throughout the world from the mid-nineteenth century to the mid-twentieth century. Until World War II practically all mission agencies and their missionaries paid lip service to it.

A Difference of Opinion

Before the end of the 19th century, however, German Gustav Warneck wrote several books on missiology which broadened the scope of mission outlook, instead of limiting it to a simple application of the 3-S formula. He called the Christian Church "the institute of healing for all humanity." His view had a place, not only for the church, but also for education and medicine (Verkuyl 1978, 27-28). In fact, Warneck noted that some churches developed by the 3-S formula were stagnant or had collapsed (Beyerhaus 1979, 17-18).

To counteract this weakness, Warneck developed a long and detailed process of missionary education. In effect, he adopted the 3-S formula. But it was an ideal to be reached *gradually* through education--rather than a goal to be met as soon as possible (Beyerhaus, *ibid.*).

The Three Selfs with a Vengeance

Anglican missionary to China, Roland Allen (1912), reacted strongly to Warneck's conservatism in missionary methods. Allen's pronouncements came on the heels of the 1910 Edinburgh Conference in which the native church received renewed attention. Allen made an even more radical claim for the validity of the 3-S concept than did its originators, Venn and Anderson. Warneck and others made allowances for the nature of some races and their alleged instability or lack of experience in directing organizations. Such factors may impede progress in the development of church autonomy, they believed.

These anthropological and sociological factors counted for little with Allen. He emphasized that the church is a body endued with the power of the Holy Spirit. "A church that has the Holy

Spirit, its own clergy, and the sacraments, will be a self-supporting, self-governing, and self-extending church according to Allen" (Kasdorf 1979, 82). These elements should more than compensate for any deficiencies.

Allen contended that "The danger to the church's autonomy lay not in the character of the Christians, nor in the risk of heresy, but rather in the cautious and paternalistic attitude of the missionaries" (Beyerhaus 1979, 18).

Years later, Melvin Hodges (1953, 102) makes the point that many missions actually stop short of taking the necessary steps towards "devolution," his term for the process of turning over the reins of government to the national believers.

As the 3-S formula received more and more attention, more questioning voices were raised as to whether it completely described the basic purpose of missions. Despite this appropriate question, all mission leaders were generally agreed that the planted churches "belonged" to the people in the area.

2. Exploding Indigeneity

While missionaries and mission boards were fumbling around to put in practice the 3-S concept--including how best to grant autonomy to churches already planted as well as how to initiate a work in such a way that the eventual elimination of the missionary's leadership and funding would go smoothly--two dynamic realities appeared that were not covered in standard operational procedures.

The first phenomenon was the revolt of many national leaders against missionary domination. In many places, this resulted in ugly breakaways from the mission organizations. (We look at the causes of these splits in chapter 3.)

Often nothing could be done with the group of believers who formed another church that broke from the mission station's moorings. Sometimes a second generation in the splinter group would overcome the pain and bitterness, re-establishing some contact. In most cases, however, it did not work out that way: no resolution to the problem was found, if sought. Some became type-B churches. (See chapter 3 in comparison with the Introduction.)

Indigenous? We Were Never Anything Else

At the same time, there was the second phenomenon for mission organizations to consider--the independent rampaging groups spreading like wildfire. Again, how missions should react and relate to these congregations was not found in their mission policies.

"Missions and mission churches . . . usually do not know quite what to think of them or do about them" (Smalley 1979, 48). Missiologists seemed to discover the emerging independent churches in Africa first. In that great continent, the "nativistic" movements are large, colorful and sometimes bizarre.

One of the earliest comprehensive missiological studies is David Barrett's *Schism and Renewal in Africa: An Analysis of 6000 Contemporary Religious Movements* (1968), a study of both breakaway and spontaneously generated churches.

On a broader scale, Harold W. Fuller did pioneer research in the field and created a center of study at Selley Oaks College in Birmingham, England. Files have been collected on "New Religious Movements," ranging from South Sea Island cargo cults to the peyote cults of the North American Indians.

In addition to Eugene Nida's aforementioned *The Indigenous Church in Latin America* (1960), there is *Historia del*

Cristianismo en América Latina (History of Christianity in Latin America) by Argentine Baptist Pablo Alberto Deiros (1992). A relatively small section (751-763) is devoted to *El Protestantismo Autóctono* (Autochthonous Protestantism). But its focus is essentially limited to the development of Pentecostalism, failing to consider the broader nuances of the grass-roots phenomena.

The GR churches are also presented as a definable and significant movement (the "fifth wave") in *The Gospel People of Latin America* by Berg and Pretiz (1992), as mentioned earlier.

Ready or not, traditional missionaries and missions were forced to open their eyes to the burgeoning movements springing up all around them.

3. What's the Verdict?

Unlike the courtroom, there isn't just one jury. The reaction to the GR movements in Latin America has been a mixed bag.

Maybe It'll Go Away

For some mission practitioners in Latin America, the first stirring of this GR phenomena produced denial. Then, with the reluctant recognition of its reality, some of us absurdly hoped it would soon pass off the scene. Just as Archbishop Arturo Rivera y Damas denied it, so did we. After all, it did not fit any of our patterns.

We shall never forget a conversation in Brazil some years ago with a missionary colleague who had served with a non-historic denominational board for almost two decades. On being asked about the strength of the GR churches in his area of that huge country, he responded in utter honesty: "What churches?" In his case, it was a question arising from a ghetto mentality. The same mentality about the significance of the movement prevails among a few at the present time.

It is interesting to note that in the major Protestant work, *Diccionario de la historia de la iglesia en la América Latina* (Dictionary of the History of the Church in Latin America) (Nelson, General Editor, 1989), there is no article about autochthonous (i.e. grass-roots) churches.   Articles about *Pentecostales,   Iglesias*   (Pentecostal   Churches)   and *Pentecostalismo en América Latina* (Pentecostalism in Latin America) do appear.   But no direct mention is made of the movement. The same lack is true of the aforementioned *Crisis in Latin America* (Núñez and Taylor 1989) as well as CEHILA (*Comisión de Estudios de Historia de América Latina*, a Catholic/ecumenical study group).

It is Still Here--and We aren't Crazy about it!

The sources of criticism of the GR movements are varied: some from conciliar and liberal circles, some from anti-Pentecostal fundamentalists.

A common concern from some Latin American Protestant leaders is that the GR movement is, by and large, an "Evangelical popular religiosity"--much like its Roman Catholic counterpart. Extreme practices such as exorcism and undue emphasis on the *culto* (church service) in itself are some of the charges.

Others underscore the pride and bitterness manifested in some GR leaders, to the point that one critic says: "When we evaluate the personality and the messages of these leaders we sense their personal ambition. The majority are sick people, pathological cases of personality disorder, fanatics, egotists. . ." (da Gama Leite F. 1990, 121). da Gama Leite Filho also condemns the coercive methods of these movements, their taking advantage of people's misery, weakness or ignorance, the bartering of temporal benefits for people's faith, their aggressive proselytism, the exaltation of their leader to a semi-god status, and the lack of academic and theological knowledge of the leaders.

Still others are critical because of lack of political and social concern and involvement by grass-roots churches, particularly on an institutional basis (i.e. change of societal structures). Jaime Valverde telegraphs his attitude with the title of his book: *Las sectas en Costa Rica, pentecostalismo y conflicto social* (The Sects in Costa Rica, Pentecostalism and Social Conflict) (1990), and addresses this theme.

A Growing Awareness and Openness

From the earliest appeals for recognition by Eugene Nida (1960) and Ralph Winter (1970, 21-35) to the more recent publication by Pablo Deiros (1992), there is generally growing openness among *evangélicos* to recognize GR movements. The Brazilian Evangelical Association as well as other national councils, federations or alliances of *evangélicos* have welcomed these movements unless they are too self-sufficient or proud to join or unless they are definitely outside the Evangelical stream.

Pastor Ed René Kivitz (1994) in Brazil feels that in "God's providence" these movements have arisen because they are reaching the masses.

Deiros (1994) says that in Argentina ". . . most new people were converted in a [GR] megachurch or a campaign, where perhaps they were healed. But they became aware of their need for the Word, more order, and better discipleship. . ." and so, for many people who eventually join traditional churches, these movements are a point of first contact with the gospel.

Relating to the Community of Faith

On the other hand, highly sectarian groups usually develop impermeable boundaries around their flock to isolate them from contaminating doctrines and influences. This is particularly true of the GR churches of the older generation. To keep its followers doctrinally pure, Brazil's Christian Congregation forbids them to watch or listen to TV or radio programs.

Brothers and sisters . . . sometimes. Others may attend a local conference with an outside speaker or participate in a united campaign if the visitor is a "star"--like David Cho of Korea, or Argentine evangelist Alberto Motessi. For the most isolationist groups the only contact with outside influence may be on a personal level. A Honduran pastor shared his concern with us regarding GR leaders. He described how he cultivated their personal friendship, loaning them books and tapes.

Part of the family. However, many have a healthy relationship with other Evangelicals, joining alliances or councils at a local or national level. This is particularly true of the middle-class churches of the newer generation.

In Chile, the president of the Evangelical Pastors Council is Bishop Francisco Anabalón of a GR church. The president of the Evangelical Confederation of Colombia is Héctor Pardo, pastor of Faith Tabernacle in Santafé de Bogotá. Internationally, the president of the Women's Commission of the World Evangelical Fellowship is Marfa de Cabrera, whose husband founded Vision of the Future in Argentina.

Both Cabrera and Giménez identify themselves with the larger Evangelical community by publishing articles in their magazines by internationally known leaders such as Luis Palau, or inviting them to their conferences. Darío Silva of Santafé de Bogotá's Church on the Rock values his contacts with Billy Graham.

While leaders of historic churches may engage in some communication with the Roman Catholic Church, GR groups are by and large completely closed to this. Manoel de Mello of Brazil for Christ maintained personal friendships with members of the Roman hierarchy and suggested cooperation with the official Church in issues of social justice. But he was an exception, just as the GR churches that have related to ecumenical networks are also not typical.

A Courtship in the Making?

The interest of the international Protestant community in GR movements is marked with apprehension--note title of Donald Dayton's (1988) article: "Yet Another Layer of the Onion, or Opening the Ecumenical Door to Let the Riffraff In." Dayton is a serious student of pentecostal movements. He suggests that ". . . in many parts of the Third World, where alienation from American Pentecostalism is sometimes strong, many Pentecostals are eager to demonstrate their independence by embracing the ecumenical movement." Here is a clear reference to the differing style and attitude of non-U.S.-related Pentecostals--i.e. grass-roots Pentecostals.

A major earthquake in Chile in 1960 resulted in massive relief from both ecumenical and evangelical world organizations. To many observers this was an effort by each group to win over the large Chilean GR churches, without much success on either part. According to Francisco Anabalón (1994) of the Pentecostal Apostolic Church, it only caused "distortion" in the life of the church and corruption since local leadership had no experience in relief distribution.

Evangelicals generally expect that the GR churches, most of them charismatic and pentecostal, would naturally join the more evangelical international movements. Ecumenists would probably agree with this premise, as evidenced by the surprise of one ecumenical leader, Franklin Clark Fry, who, according to Bishop Chávez of the Pentecostal Church of Chile, ". . . almost fell off his chair. . ." when Chávez announced that his church would join the World Council of Churches (Hollenweger 1972, 439).

As it turns out, Chávez had set about listing reasons for distrusting the ecumenical movement, feeling that it tended to move Protestants back to Rome which had persecuted them for so long (*ibid.*, 438). But after his study of the movement, he and his church voted in favor of joining.

Those not joining often give other reasons for not relating to the ecumenical movement: the alleged connotations of marxism and lack of the manifestation of faith.

These reasons notwithstanding, the following major Latin American GR churches joined the ecumenical movement through CLAI (the Latin American Council of Churches) and/or WCC (World Council of Churches): Brazil for Christ (which later reduced its relationship to a "fraternal" one); the Church of God in Argentina (not related to any of the Church of God denominations in the U.S.); the Pentecostal Church of Chile; the United Evangelical Church in Argentina (the Toba Indian Church).

Why do these Evangelical churches hook up with the ecumenical movement--in addition to Dayton's aforementioned reason? Is it that these groups believe that in the light of their movements' size and influence, they merit recognition in larger and broader spheres than what the World Evangelical Fellowship, for example, can offer? Do they perceive greater respect and freedom to express themselves than in the typical Evangelical gathering?

Dayton lists factors he believes makes the ecumenical movement attractive: ". . . the frustrations of many being heard only through the evangelical networks, anger at years of marginalization and manipulation" (1988, 8).

It is not that the GR churches in the WCC find the atmosphere all that inspiring. Manoel de Mello of the Brazil for Christ Church attended the WCC gathering in Uppsala, Sweden, and ". . . felt like Ezequiel in the valley of dry bones." Livening up the services would not be enough in his estimation. But he stated that the Brazilian Church needed the WCC to fulfill its function as a prophet and a reviver of social and political conscience. "Why not transform the hundreds of church buildings into schools on weekdays and even into trade unions and associations to train people?" His movement was the largest WCC-related member denomination in Latin America. De Mello expressed the hope that prejudice towards the WCC could be broken down by "ecumenical prayer meetings" (Hollenweger 1972, 102).

Other groups also had some messianic hope that they could change the WCC and give it life.

But other members of the Pentecostal movement worldwide were not pleased about this Brazilian church joining the ecumenical camp. Meanwhile, the ecumenical stream is sponsoring frequent consultations with Latin American Pentecostal groups, mostly of the GR stripe.

Across the tracks, many GR churches are members of national alliances, councils, or federations of Protestant denominations. These groupings are often members of CONELA, the Latin American Confederation of Evangelicals, which in turn relates to the World Evangelical Fellowship. But the links are sometimes missing. Brazil for Christ, for example, is not yet a full member of the Brazilian Association of Evangelicals. And the latter is not a member of CONELA at this writing, although it is a member of the World Evangelical Fellowship.

In some countries like Costa Rica there is an active Protestant alliance. GR churches (like the Shalom Church mentioned earlier) are participants. In Chile, where there is the greatest concentration of GR movements, there are a number of groupings that claim to speak for the Evangelical churches. But the GR movements there are large and self-sufficient, not really committed to any interdenominational relationship.

There are other networks--the occasional world congresses on evangelism or Latin America's own CLADE (Latin American Evangelism Congress) meetings. The 1988 Lausanne II Congress in Manila included among its participants Omar Cabrera (Vision of the Future Church, Argentina), Héctor Pardo (Faith Tabernacle, Colombia), and Manuel Gaxiola (Apostolic Church in Mexico) among others, but these constituted a small minority within the Latin American delegation. Whether it is the failure to take Latin American GR leaders into account in extending invitations to these events, or a lack of interest on the part of GR leaders in attending such meetings, is a matter for serious study.

Why do some of them join local groupings or participate in larger gatherings? They enter into this kind of fellowship mainly if they have a voice in the group and if there is a climate and history of cooperation. Or if the GR church is a small, denominationally unconnected church that recognizes its need for spiritual relationships. Or if the government imposes certain legal requirements upon smaller denominations or churches, in which case a national alliance can offer legal counsel or coverage. The Peruvian Evangelical Council has been providing this kind of service (Merino 1992).

Church history shows us clearly that older, traditional churches have almost always looked askance at upstart new movements in the Church--the Anglicans' less-than-positive attitude toward the Methodists in the early days of spin-off, the Lutherans' reaction to

the Anabaptist movements in Europe, the cold reception given by
historic denominations in the U.S. to the early Holiness churches,
the earlier Evangelical reaction to Pentecostal denominations. We
are slow indeed to perceive that God works in many different
ways and forms in His Church for the purpose of sharing the good
news of the kingdom.

4. Telling Us What Church Growth and Contextualization *are* All About

How Come So Big?

Missiologists focusing on church growth studies have begun
to examine these autochthonous groups for what they can teach
Christians elsewhere about the subject.

For example, Peter Wagner of Fuller Theological Seminary's
School of World Mission has made frequent reference to the
significance of this point in Latin America (1973, 1983, 1988,
1991). In speaking of the phenomena in general, he says: "By far
the most rapidly growing segment of Christianity on all six
continents is a kind of a church which does not fit traditional
categories or classifications. Missiologists have recognized its
presence for some time, but it is such a recent phenomenon that
they have not yet even agreed upon a name for it" (Wagner 1994,
1).

Wagner continues: "Whether large, small or in between, these
churches represent the cutting edge of the Kingdom of God today"
(*ibid.*, 2). He mentions Berg-Pretiz research on these Latin
American churches (1992) commenting on the classification:
"The first four waves would be the immigrant churches, the
mainline denominations, the faith missions and the new
denominations. . . 'Fifth wave' might fit Latin American churches,

but not so much their counterparts in China, the U.S.A. and elsewhere" (*ibid.*, 2). After reviewing several possible generic terms to identify these churches, he suggests the term "postdenominational" (*ibid.*).

John N. Vaughan, in his *The World's 20 Largest Churches* (1984), studies the patterns of Evangelical "super-churches" and looks closely at the Jotabeche Church in Chile, and the Christian Congregation, God is Love, and Brazil for Christ in São Paulo, in addition to churches elsewhere in the world. One reason for Brazil for Christ's growth, according to Vaughan, is one not often mentioned in mission texts: ". . . the controversy generated by the pastor [Manoel de Mello] as he attacks abuses of society and government policy" (259).

The Whole Picture

A crop of missiologists with an anthropological bent has also been applying its insights to mission theory. As Roland Allen appealed for an indigenous Church, this new generation of missiologists cries out with the same fervor for contextualization. Where earlier mission theorists promoted the 3-S definition for indigenization, these point out that churches can be self-supporting, self-governing, and self-propagating without essentially expressing the gospel in the culture of the people--and therefore are not fully indigenous. (See Kraft 1979 and Hesselgrave and Rommen 1989 for a general presentation of contextualization.)

Charles Kraft (1979, 277) quotes David Barrett as follows: "High on the list of reasons why 5000 or more African independent movements have broken away from missionary Christianity is the fact that the mission churches, preoccupied with the concerns of Western theologies, did not pay adequate attention to matters of health and illness--matters which are to the African highly theological."

Looking at Latin America's churches, we, too, have seen that health issues--praying for healing--are important in a continent of physically sick people. But it may take a long time for traditional churches to recognize this.

Dynamic Equivalents

One concept this new breed of missiologists espouses is described as "dynamic equivalence." In Bible translation a strict literal translation is not always effective in communicating the original idea. For a culture where "greet the brethren with a holy kiss" may be disturbing or at least confusing, Phillips' very British paraphrase, "a hearty handshake all around," may more effectively convey to certain cultural groups enthusiastic acceptance of a Christian sister or brother.

Likewise, in planting new churches, they say, we must not woodenly carry over church patterns or styles directly from the New Testament first century into the new churches. Rather, it is better to discover the dynamic equivalents in church organization, worship styles, and Christian marriage and family patterns.

Some church strategists, however, will balk at the idea that patterns of church government--such as the institution of elders and deacons--can find their equivalent in some entirely different way of organizing in another culture. For example, if the culture demands strong authority figures, which is generally true in Latin America, should a pastor be authoritarian and the roles of elders and deacons diminished? (Kraft 1973)

Falling into the Same Trap?

Such an anthropological missiologist might appear to be making an idol of contextualization just as Roland Allen did with indigenization. But the questions raised are very useful in our study of Latin GR churches. Tortillas and coffee for communion? A spiritual dance to praise God instead of or along with singing an anthem? How much application of dynamic equivalence can we accept without falling into the dark pit of syncretism?

Under the chapter title, "Doing Theology in Latin America: Contextualization," Emilio Núñez and William Taylor effectively discuss the issue of contextualization in their classic work, *Crisis in Latin America* (1989, 311-347). After addressing the meaning and challenge of contextualization, they focus specifically on Latin American evangelicalism and contextualization.

Núñez and Taylor (*ibid.*, 318) refer to Paul Hiebert's ". . . concerns about embracing 'an uncritical contextualization'" with his question: "If the gospel is contextualized, what are the checks against biblical and theological distortion? Where are the absolutes?" (Hiebert's article in *The International Bulletin of Missionary Research*, July 1987). Obviously ". . . it is necessary to make a distinction between noncritial contextualizers [i.e. contextualization] and critical contextualizers" (Núñez and Taylor, *op. cit.*, 319).

Naturally, just as the GR church is often a model to the church growth enthusiasts, so it also becomes a rich source of study for those focusing on the implications of contextualization.

What is the attitude of Latin America's Protestant Church toward the GR churches? Varied to say the least. Nevertheless, there is a growing awareness among most *evangélicos* to accept them as sisters and brothers in our common pilgrimage in the bonds of Christ.

TWELVE

Doctrinal Variety, But a Common World View

A friend, when asked about the theology of the GR churches, replied, "Can you name one that isn't Pentecostal?" Yes, the Venezuelan Apure movement and a few others. But it is not enough simply to label them all pentecostal. There are many doctrinal variations. However, all of them are supported by a basic world view that is more significant than the visible differences.

In order to grasp these various distinctions in doctrine and practice among the GR groups, we will examine briefly: the place and use of the Bible; the person of Christ and His work; and salvation by grace and legalistic patterns and practices. After some examples of the doctrinal and practical weaknesses that are a result of the GR lack of connection with the main stream of Christianity and its history, we conclude with the particular and common spiritual dimension of their world view.

The Authority of the Scriptures

GR churches of the older generation, sectarian, isolated from corrective interaction with other parts of the Body, and without profound knowledge of the Scriptures, may tend to place greater authority on the leader's word than on the Bible. In some heretical groups, this is doctrinally formalized. In others, untaught people simply accept their bishop's word, rather than search the

Scriptures for themselves. In churches of the older generation the literalistic acceptance of Biblical authority often leads to rigid and legalistic adoption of forms such as the *ósculo santo* (the sacred kiss, as in Romans 16:16) or women's head coverings and other types of dress codes.

René Padilla (1986) underscores the danger of this tendency: "I believe in this area lies the greatest danger for a 'church of the masses' with no theological orientation, such as the Church in Latin America at this moment in history--the danger of letting itself be carried away by whatever wind happens to blow, with no criteria to discern what the Gospel demands in this situation."

Paul Hoff (his article in the July, 1991, issue of *Evangelical Missions Quarterly*, 246), director of a Pentecostal Bible institute in Chile, puts it well:

> "Lay pastors without formal training are seldom able to provide biblical teaching. This problem is intensified because the pastors' knowledge of the Bible is limited to what they hear from the older men, who themselves have had no systematic teaching and know little about proper biblical interpretation. The slim knowledge of the original leaders has gradually deteriorated. Further, dreams, visions, and personal revelations often are placed on a par with the Bible. Many sermons are simple exhortations and the biblical text is just a kick-off; the preacher utters whatever comes to mind and he believes it is inspired by the Holy Spirit."

The Person of Christ and His Work

The old generation churches, sometimes consciously depriving themselves of all the resources of theological thinking across the centuries, often reformulate theological truths, making comparisons difficult. So it is with the "oneness" teaching of the Mexican Apostolic Church. Others will unconsciously adopt theological thinking from heretical sources such as the Jehovah's Witnesses.

Such is the opinion of Paul Hoff (1993, 24) who detected Arianism in the theological outlook of one of his students, formerly chairman of the board of a large GR denomination. The student was surprised to learn that in orthodox theologies Christ was pre-existent.

Scott Horrell, a missionary-theologian in Brazil (1994), notes that the secondary place given to Christ in Roman Catholic teaching may sometimes be carried over into untaught GR movements. While Mary receives the greater attention in Catholicism, in some Brazilian groups the Holy Spirit preempts the place of Christ in subtle and non-explicit ways. The focus of the songs, prayers and praise can be on the Holy Spirit instead of Christ.

Salvation by Grace and Legalistic Practices

Even though a church subscribes to salvation by grace, the lack of careful teaching often leads its followers to adopt a salvation-by-works perspective, especially if the emphasis is on insisting on strict behavioral patterns. We have described the Israelites of the New Covenant in Peru who minimize the work of Christ by practicing Old Testament patterns.

Israel García (1991) notes another strict application of Old Testament law in the practice of some Puerto Rican churches of forbidding women who are menstruating from participation in the Lord's Supper.

Piepkorn (1979, 151) cites the statement of the Congregational Evangelical Church, Inc. based in Humacao, Puerto Rico:

> ". . .men may not wear their shirts loose, nor may wear neck-chains or shirts with short sleeves or with exaggerated collars. Women must wear moderate hairdos and may not cut their hair. Their dresses may not have short sleeves or expose too much of their shoulders and necks . . . they must wear stockings in public and at church services must avoid rings, necklaces, bracelets, wristwatches, expensive pins, all kinds of adornment, hoop skirts (ropa de kankan) and excessively expensive fabrics. Neither sex may wear the clothing of the other. A female member who submits to sterilization to avoid having children is to be expelled from the church for life; so is her husband if he consents to the operation."

Commenting on Pentecostalism, Hollenweger (1972, 347) said: ". . . very rarely. . . legalism is overcome. This has happened in the Christian Congregational Church of Brazil, which explicitly rejects Pentecostal legalism . . ." He further recounted the repudiation of marriage and funeral ceremonies by some in reaction to luxuriousness of Roman Catholic festivals" (ibid.). Even though the reaction against the festivities is understandable, legalism crops up in the very prohibition of these celebrations.

Few Historical Hang-ups

While Western church historians trace Pentecostalism back through the Arminian and holiness movements to the Reformation, GR movements usually recognize no such linkage. The Calvinist-Arminian tension is not generally a concern. Except for those in contact with U.S. Pentecostals, many know nothing about the dispensational perspective, even while their messages may stress the imminence of Christ's return. There may be a general fear of theological liberalism, but in some cases Evangelical observers fear that GR churches' naiveté in this regard makes them vulnerable to liberal influences (Hoff, 1994).

Liberation theology, with its substitution of collective and social salvation for an emphasis on personal salvation, has little appeal to the GR movements. But social concern may often arise out of simple Christian instincts to help one's neighbor rather than out of developed theological reasons for doing so. Unlike classical U.S. Pentecostals, GR movements often may not insist on speaking in tongues as the primary evidence of the filling of the Holy Spirit. Chilean Pentecostals, coming out of a Methodist tradition, look very much unlike their U.S. Pentecostal counter-parts. They maintain an episcopal church government and practice infant baptism, as examples.

A Deeper Question

More fundamental than many of the above issues is the greater sense of another reality than what is sensed by most North American or European Christians. Western Biblical theologies acknowledge the miraculous, but most Christians in developed countries do not incorporate this into their daily life.

Evangelicals everywhere differentiate themselves from the theological liberals by insistence on the supernatural--in the inspiration of Scriptures, in the Virgin birth, the miracles and resurrection of Christ. But they do not expect as much of the miraculous in their daily experience. "What do you think of first when you are sick?" is often a touchstone question. In peoples less affected by the rational fall-out of the Enlightenment, the answer is not medicine but prayer. We had to explain what a "Christian hospital" was to some people in Peru. To them it was a contradiction in terms.

Well-educated pastor Darío Silva, whose congregation we described in chapter 1 (the Church on the Rock in Santafé de Bogotá, Colombia), confessed that he is not impressed by rational attempts to prove the Bible, like Josh McDowell's *Evidence That Demands a Verdict*. He prefers to "leave the inexplicable to the action of the Holy Spirit in the heart of the believer" (1992, 72). The supernatural is sufficiently real to many Latins. It needs no explanation from the natural world.

A step further is a recognition of the reality of the spirit world, which is seldom acknowledged in many North American or European churches except when such as *A Mighty Fortress Is Our God* is sung ("And though this world with devils filled . . ."). In lands where black magic, witches' congresses, and even institutionalized Brazilian spiritism are facts of life, it makes sense for Latin American Evangelicals to take seriously Biblical passages about demons, the spirit world, and angels.

To many, the world of the spirit and the supernatural invade the visible world so that miracles are perceived everywhere. But the distinction between the spiritual world (good) and the visible world (bad) leads to the aforementioned accusation that such Christians subscribe to dualism. Christians, so concerned about spiritual things, are said to have no proper concern for the world around them and its problems. Criticism of this nature is losing some force now as GR movements, as well as other groups, are getting more socially and politically involved.

The logical step, after recognizing the existence of another reality with its good and evil beings, is exorcism. This is when Christians, more likely in "new generation" churches, become convinced that a demon-possessed person needs deliverance. A GR church in Costa Rica, *La Iglesia Libertad* (Freedom Church), which specializes in exorcism, was founded by Rita Cabezas, a Christian professional psychologist, who makes a serious attempt at distinguishing between ordinary psychological and physical disorders and true demon possession (Cabezas 1986, 134-135). Hers is not a careless spur-of-the-moment application of this practice (typical of many GR churches), but is performed after several sessions of spiritual orientation.

Spiritual warfare, interpreted as the practice of praying for the deliverance of a geographical area (e.g. a city or parts of it) from the oppression of territorial spirits as a prelude to an evangelistic effort, is not common. Some Argentinian evangelists, however, have made this a practice. A GR group in Mexico, *Mexicanos en Victoria* (Mexicans in Victory), claims to have identified the residual spirits of the pre-colonial pagan temples which they believe are the barrier to revival in that country. This revelation has been followed by prayer for the defeat of these spirits while circling the city in car caravans along its inner belt highway and in prayer meetings at the *Zócalo*, the large open plaza built over the former Aztec temples (Holland 1994).

Wilson Gomes, a Brazilian (in *Cadernos de CEAS*, no. 146, 47-63), has outlined how in the Universal Church of the Kingdom of God (IURD) of Brazil, current prosperity teaching is linked to views on demonology. The Christian's claim to his entitled prosperity is interposed by the devil, whose power over a person has to be removed not only through exorcism but also through a step of faith (or risk). This step is nothing less than an offering of some considerable sacrifice to God. As the widow of Zarephath (I Kings 17:7-16) risked her last ounce of flour and oil to feed Elijah, he rewarded her with a continuous flow of flour and oil. Of course, this teaching can lead to "abusive shearing of God's sheep" by unscrupulous pastors who identify such offerings to God with donations to the church. And, as Gomes (*ibid.*, 53) points out, this emphasis is increasingly further from New Testament concerns about sin, guilt, or personal responsibility.

The Bottom Line: One's World View

GR churches vary in their degrees of emphasis and involvement in practices derived from concepts about the reality of the spirit world. But, more than any differences over classic theological points, the fundamental contrast between Latin America's more traditional churches as well as churches in the developed world and the GR churches is a basic world view. It is a world view in which God intervenes, the miraculous is always possible, and the reality of the spiritual is often greater than the reality of that which is seen.

THIRTEEN

Facets of Church Life

Its Organization

A Spiritual Godfather: the Pastor's Role

Christian Lalive (1962) was the first to identify the pastor in a Chilean GR church as a benevolent *patrón*, a term originally describing the owner-boss of a large farm whose authority was the last word. But the boss was also a protector of those who worked for him. He advanced money to his workers, defended them in their legal problems, helped them make decisions and stood as godfather at family christenings. When displaced workers came to the city, they accepted the gospel, joined with a church, and recovered the *patrón* figure in their pastor.

This "godfather" image results from what has been called *charismatic caudillismo* (Deiros 1992, 169; Nida 1960, 11-12), in which the pastor's authority rests on his functional role, rather than his social and academic background. This central authority and rigidity reflect social and Roman Catholic structures (Suazo, 1991; Pecho, 1991).

In the lower socio-economic levels, people trust the pastor who may even hold all church properties in his name. They are "used to authority," said a Peruvian pastor. In some communities the people, poor though they be, are even proud of the way they can support their pastor in a more-than-comfortable lifestyle.

In more extreme cases, the pastor's personal physical touch acquires almost magical significance. "Most pentecostal pastors are closely involved in the daily lives of their congregation, authoritarian but warm and paternal," says Wattenburg (1990, 12). But in the most extreme case of pastor David Miranda of the God is Love Church, Wattenburg perceives him to be creating a "remote demigod" image for himself. The church's platform area far from the congregation is cordoned off with chains when he makes an appearance. In such scenes, the practice of the universal priesthood of believers is non-existent.

Centralized control can lead to the manipulation of individuals (Brazilian Said 1991; Guatemalan Suazo 1991; Puerto Rican García 1991) as well as related congregations. Often, offerings may still flow into the coffers of the central mother church. While this accumulation of wealth can certainly lead to abuses, it can provide enormous flexibility when the opportunity to buy a cinema building, a radio station or a new property arises. William Read (1965, 170) recognizes that strong mother churches can ". . . send evangelistic columns into all parts of the areas around about them . . . There comes, however, a saturation point in the growth of these Mother Churches. If they do not decentralize, they fossilize and lose their effectiveness as agents for evangelism and dynamic church growth."

But highly authoritarian control, with no space for alternative opinions, means that continuing dissent eventually results in divisions (Said 1991; Pardo 1992; Suazo 1991), the bane of GR movements. Chile, which has the highest number of believers in Latin American GR movements, is plagued with the highest number of divisions: 600 registered denominations and an estimated 2,500 non-registered denominations, some of which consist of only one or two congregations (Miller 1993, 21).

Many GR churches, however, pursue a middle course. "Theocratic and democratic," Marco Cárdenas (1992), leader in the Lamb of God Church in Quito, Ecuador, calls the government of his church. The slate for church officials is prepared by the leadership and confirmed by the congregation.

Rather than being entirely critical of the pastor's authority in GR churches, one successful Brazilian Baptist pastor spoke to us admiringly about the respected "man of God" image the GR pastor projected. Something gets lost, he felt, in some churches where the pastor is treated simply as an employee of the congregation.

One major exception to the general rule is the Christian Congregation of Brazil which has no pastors. Reed Nelson (1989, 39-51) studied this church from an organizational point of view and finds it runs "with enviable efficiency" under its system of elders. But it is no less authoritarian. "Constant informal visits among members create interdependence and monitor behavior . . . divergence from the church's norms carries a high social cost. . . . Prohibition of television, radio . . . insulate the member from dissonant influences" (*ibid.*).

Keep It Simple: Church Planning and Administration

Peruvian GR pastor, Samuel Nieva (1993), speaks of the proliferation of GR churches in the poor areas of Lima in places where one would least expect them. "They don't start thinking of all the problems, that they will need benches, a pulpit . . . they just start to build. Money may be raised through *'polladas'* (chicken dinners), clothing sales and other devices."

The director of a new GR ministry in Mexico, a psychologist with experience in working with North American organizations, rejects outright Western concepts of goal-setting and planning, not because of a lack of training or experience in administration, but because he feels they are incompatible with the culture (Cruz 1992).

"They [GR churches] don't complicate life," says evangelist Alberto Barrientos (1993), "but eventually they need [organizational] structures." One area most often suggested where GR pastors need help is in church administration.

But flexibility is one of the GR churches' virtues, and uncomplicated organizations are flexible. Inflexible budgets and programs would be their loss. Christ for the City director in Colombia, Ramón Carmona, points out (1992) that it is precisely this flexibility that allows GR churches to participate fully in city-wide evangelistic efforts, while those tied to traditional denominations find it difficult to break out of their denominationally imposed programs.

Many small independent churches also need legal help to meet government organizational requirements. The Peruvian Evangelical Council has been providing this service. The Vision of the Future movement in Argentina, on the other hand, an example of a large GR organization, showed us its documentation: clearly defined objectives, studies of growth rates and organizational charts.

While some churches seem content to remain small, many movements think big. Marco Cárdenas, leader of a GR church in Quito, Ecuador (1992), says, "I don't believe in any church that after 20 or 30 years, given the explosion in Latin America, has only 150, 200, 300 or 400 members." And in our descriptions of many movements, it is clear they have ambitions to conquer the world, establishing churches in the U.S. and in other continents.

The Weekly Church Calendar

Reclaimed movie houses or storefront chapels provide no space for the kind of activities offered by a large U.S. church. Furthermore, new people coming out of a Catholic tradition may not expect that church should consist of more than worship services, and leaders of many GR churches are little aware of other possibilities.

The Universal Church of the Kingdom of God in Santiago, Chile, posts the following weekly schedule of activities/topics:

Sundays and Wednesdays	the Holy Spirit
Mondays and Saturdays	Prosperity
Tuesdays	Divine healing
Thursdays	the Family
Fridays	Deliverance (Exorcism)

In addition to nightly meetings, Friday nights are reserved for all-night prayer vigils in Costa Rica's Rose of Sharon Church. But the calendar of churches like Santafé de Bogotá's middle-class Church on the Rock are more like its counterparts in the U.S.

Critics look at the *culto-centrismo* (meeting centeredness) of GR churches and wonder whether Christian education, social service and other activities take place. Sometimes these activities take other forms.

Whereas in the U.S. the church calendar may be filled with women's teas and youth basketball, what is considered to be the serious business of releasing demons, healing the sick, and praying for the unsaved is the order of the day in Latin America's GR churches. Besides, worship is exciting and interesting. There is a spirit of expectancy. Who wants to miss out on what God is doing? Also, for many lower-class people, home is not a pleasant place. Being with friends at church is a much better option than spending an evening in their own house.

Its Worship

Some Generalizations

1.   There is more emphasis on *experiencing* God than learning about Him. Traditional services are often knowledge-oriented ("It was a good sermon"); GR pentecostal services tend to be sense-oriented ("We felt God's presence"). Willems (1964 as cited by Escobar 1992, 14) emphasizes the participatory nature of liturgy and congregational life that does not depend on literacy or education, but disposition to be touched by the power of the Spirit.

2.   There is a *cycle of praise-confession-repentance-God's peace* that faintly echoes many ancient liturgies. The invitation at the close is not just for those professing to accept Christ for the first time, but for all those who are in need. In many cases, this may result in nearly the whole congregation coming to the altar. Who does not need forgiveness, physical and spiritual healing, and release from burdens? The completed cycle may be emotionally draining but it is cathartic as well.

3.   There is a sense that *God is at work now in the life of the church,* as evidenced by the testimonies, sermon illustrations and the service itself. Traditional churches may emphasize God's work in the past and the future, without the electrifying sense that He is doing things in the present.

4.   The service is *highly participatory.* Singing is not enough. More expression can be released as one claps, sways, shakes a tambourine or even dances with the song. Everyone with a guitar or other instrument may be encouraged to join the musicians. Testimonies and the antiphonal *"gloria a Dios"* responses to the pastor by the congregation make everyone a participant.

Music

Newer and older generational GR churches differ more in music than in any other detail. Older churches have sacralized their hymnal while newer ones constantly generate new music. Older churches limit themselves to the use of traditional band or orchestral instruments, and sometimes mandolins or guitars. Newer ones use electronics and drum sets.

The music of Marcos Witt, a Mexican-American songwriter, is heard in most of the churches of the new generation throughout the continent (see Julia Santibáñez Castañón's article "A New Sound from Mexico" in *Latin America Evangelist,* January-March, 1994, 6-11). But every country has its gospel music groups popularizing their original music on audio cassettes and on local Christian radio. Formerly Christians only learned new songs when a new hymnbook was published. Now waves of new choruses come and go, reflecting current themes and moods. One critic calls it "disposable" music.

Churches of the newer generation often project the text of the choruses on a screen or a wall with an overhead projector, thus people's hands are free to clap. This custom is taking over even in traditional churches, although many do not allow clapping. Some churches have adopted the practice of having a few girls and women up front dancing gracefully with tambourines to help the congregation keep up with the rhythm. Choirs are almost non-existent, though churches use "worship teams," standing in front with a microphone for each person, to lead in the singing.

New music heard on the media and adopted by the churches, is only one of the forms that is defined in the Christian media and influences all Evangelical churches. ". . . a cultural weave that orients the practices of [the churches'] leaders . . . carrying a specific definition of what evangelical churches should be. Thus they not only unite, but they also contribute to the definition of evangelical churches" (Wynarczk 1994, 38).

The production of Latin America's Evangelical idiom originates in ". . . epicenters close to pentecostalism. . ." (*ibid.*) and influences all churches, whether they like the rhythms and the lyrics or not.

The sermon

In addition to the already-mentioned antiphonal and participatory nature of pentecostal preaching as the pastor elicits "amens" and other expressions from the congregation, the narrative style predominates. It is ". . . a more appropriate communication vehicle than the classic conceptual exposition taught in [traditional] theological seminaries. This narrative style is what characterizes popular pentecostal preaching, for example, and the preaching in black churches in the U.S" (Escobar 1992, 3).

In churches where the spontaneous expression of the Holy Spirit through the preacher is highly valued, sermon preparation may actually be discouraged. This is true not only in the Christian Congregation, but wherever "the content . . . is drawn from the daily problems of the lower class with only minimal doctrinal elaboration . . . the principal resource of the speaker is the ability to interpret short passages in a creative and relevant manner" (Reed Nelson 1989, 39-51).

The Use of Scriptures, the Lord's Supper, Baptism, Prayer, and Testimony

The reading of the **Scriptures** was an important element of worship in Latin America's traditional Evangelical churches, calling for the congregation to stand in attention. But the loss of this moment of respectful attention in most GR churches does not mean less dedication to the Bible as the foundation of faith and walk.

People carry Bibles to church, and the pastor's texts are often carefully followed by the worshipers in their own Bibles, where the congregation is literate. The interpretation and application of many texts are taken literally. The Bible may at times carry subtle magical attributes--an open Bible in the home may be seen as shedding some blessing. There may be imbalances in the emphases given to certain teachings. But whatever the view, the Bible for the GR churches is foundational.

The **Eucharist** is clearly not the center of the worship experience as it is in Roman Catholicism. Its infrequent and austerely simple celebration in GR and Evangelical churches in general, can be understood as reaction to the Roman Catholic heretical belief and ornate practice of the sacrament.

Baptism, except notably in the case of the Methodist Pentecostal churches in Chile which baptize infants, is administered to adults by immersion upon their conversion. Baptisms by the Roman Catholic Church are not recognized as valid.

In the Waves of Love Church in Buenos Aires, which meets in a former cinema, a projection booth equipped with a large plastic-enclosed area containing water, serves as a baptismal font. In Brazilian churches, there are baptisms in the ocean and nearby lakes. Perhaps the greatest departure from evangelical tradition in Latin America is the practice among some GR churches of baptizing people the very day of their profession of faith in Christ. Such is the case of the *Relámpagos* (lightning) movement in Nicaragua. In Brazil, any visitor attending a Christian Congregation's baptismal service may be baptized on the spot. In churches of this kind, orientation and discipleship into the church's fellowship and practices follow, rather than precede, baptism.

Prayer seldom takes the form of the pastor bringing the GR congregation's collective praise or petition to God. Departing from the usually more collective spirit of pentecostal activities, prayer time in a service becomes a space for the individual to relate to God with his personal expression of praise or concern. Hundreds and even thousands of individuals praying aloud all at once, often with a musical background, becomes a "concert" in which many worshipers find an atmosphere conducive to talk to God.

The individual is also the focus in another respect--the personal attention given to prayer for the sick. This includes those suffering from a crisis, whether in physical or emotional health, or needing deliverance from demons. Pentecostal services may often end with a call to the altar and a majority of the congregation may go forward to pray or to be prayed for. In this context, there may be charismatic manifestations of tongues or words of prophecy.

Testimony is an essential element of worship in GR services. Whether it be the individual who testifies that his prayer has been answered or whether a miracle is described in a sermon, the current experiences of believers are reported. This is a satisfying completion of the cycle: there is prayer, but there is also the report of God's answer. To enter an assembly of people who are reporting on what God is currently doing in their lives can be electrifying.

Its Christian Education and Pastoral Training

Sunday schools are not necessarily normative. Sometimes they are replaced by programs that may be equally effective. The Waves of Love Church in Buenos Aires has its three-stage Ezra

Bible Institute which all new believers must attend. In the same city the Vision of the Future movement has its three-level program. Special services revolving around a theme (e.g. the family) may often fill the need.

But in many churches an adequate Christian education program, especially for children, is lacking (see Hoff 1991). In one large Chilean church an adult class simply consisted of eliciting everybody's comments on the assigned text. People had little guidance. Many comments simply turned into personal testimonies regarding irrelevant matters.

Some churches of the older generation still insist pastoral training is unnecessary or even wrong. There is something to be said for experience as a criterion for ordination rather than the diet of academic studies. Peter Wagner (1973, 108-109) describes the Methodist Pentecostal ladder to ministry which consists of serving successively at the following levels:
1. Street preacher
2. Sunday school teacher
3. "Preacher" (to lead a service)
4. Service at a new preaching point
5. Service as a "Christian worker"
6. "Pastor-deacon" (to found a new church)
7. Pastor. This level is attained when the church he has founded is large enough to support him and he can quit his secular occupation.

In effect, pastoral training takes the shape of an informal apprenticeship system. In explaining the background of this apprenticeship approach, Nida (*op.cit.*, 5) says: It ". . . was not worked out by special design. It was actually the only system the people have known, for this is precisely the manner in which many local persons ultimately became Roman Catholic priests, first as choir boys, then as catechists, sacristans, and finally they were

ordained. . . . In the process, they did solve two nagging problems:
(1) how to support a ministry (the ministers supported themselves
until they were capable of attracting a church which had sufficient
funds to support them) and (2) the more precarious difficulty of
selecting capable persons." It ". . . involved a kind of spiritual
'survival of the fittest,' which resulted in the development of
leadership, rather than 'followership'--the normal result of
paternalistic supervision." See another early description of the
process in Chile (Wagner 1976, 430-437).

René Padilla (1994, 89) states: "In sharp contrast with Roman
Catholicism, which is clerical and hierarchical, the Evangelical
movement in Latin America is truly participative. Regardless of
their social position, their economic situation, or their academic
preparation, people are given the opportunity to serve God and
neighbor. By doing so, they are given *a new sense of dignity and
are encouraged to develop their personal capabilities"* [italics
ours].

Having had a successful ministry at each level and success in
planting a church amounts to a lot of accumulated experience.
Generally this means that one cannot become a pastor much
before age 50. At the time of Lalive's study (1962), 82% of
Chilean Pentecostal pastors were over age 40 and 56% had not
finished primary school. The Methodist Pentecostals still prohibit
their pastors from taking formal theological studies. Paul Hoff
(1993, 23) says that many pastors of this stripe make a threefold
attack in each sermon on "the world, the flesh, and the Bible
school."

Fortunately, this is an extreme case. Many GR churches have
simple Bible schools on their premises for the training of their
leadership. For some pastors, their theological education consists
of an accumulation of seminars and short courses that they have
taken.

The process of many Chilean churches described by Nida and Wagner is accelerated in many of the GR movements of the newer generation, where leaders do not have to wait until 40 or 50 to become full-fledged pastors. A requisite for graduation from some Bible schools or for ordination in some movements is that a candidate have successfully planted a new church. Young men in their twenties who have done so are already pastors.

Paul Hoff's concern for the Chilean GR pastors led him to establish a Bible institute that is training about 800 leaders.

Black West Indian English-speaking pastors in Panama started an interdenominational evening program, the Manna Bible Institute, which has since expanded to serve a mix of Latins, Indians, Chinese, North Americans and black West Indians. It is a simple evening program offered at the facilities of the Crossroads Bible Church in the former Canal Zone.

A more highly organized GR school is the Caracas Evangelical Seminary which met for many years in the Las Acacias Pentecostal Church before acquiring its own building.

Many churches and schools are using the curriculum and materials developed by the Facultad Latinoamericana de Estudios Teológicos (FLET).

In several countries there are Evangelical weekly or monthly newspapers, which often contain articles that contribute to the enrichment of the Christian's life and knowledge. Some are published with the help of missionaries. Others are GR enterprises. News about events in the Evangelical world predominates, with occasional commentaries about secular events. Perhaps the largest enterprise is *El Puente* (The Bridge), an Argentine GR Evangelical monthly with a circulation of 40,000. The same group publishes a children's magazine, *El Puentecito*, and a Reader's Digest-type magazine, *Los elegidos* (The Chosen).

There is a great need for regional publishing houses--Christian literature written and published by Latin Americans. The great bulk of Christian books (most of them straight translations), videos and films are financed, produced and distributed by publishing houses based in the United States or controlled by foreign sources. As in the case of theological development, Christian literature must come from the mind and soul of Latin Americans.

A sobering thought and foretaste of what is in store is the growing possibility of governments in several countries requiring pastors of churches to have degrees. Says Paul Hoff of the situation in Chile, "It is only a matter of time before the government will demand that every evangelical pastor have Bible school studies. We hear that the Argentine government will soon be taking steps in that direction" (1993).

In almost every respect, GR churches do not fit the shape of many Western churches with regard to their organization, their carefully defined theologies, their formalized worship, or their programs of training. Hollenweger (1990, 165) stated it well: "For them the medium of communication is, just as it is in biblical times, not the definition but the description, not the statement but the story, not the doctrine but the testimony, not the book but the parable, not the systematic theology but the song, not the articulation of concepts but the celebration of banquets."

FOURTEEN

Dimensions of Outreach

Evangelistic Outreach

Large evangelistic campaigns and the use of mass media are widely recognized as effective instruments for evangelism by the GR churches. The following are the basic factors involved in their witness: mobilization, personal empowerment, promise of a miracle, methods and peoples, the electronic church, and ministries in the prisons and the military.

Mobilization

Without generally being aware of it, GR churches apply the theorem advanced by Kenneth Strachan of the Latin America Mission and tested in the Evangelism-in-Depth program in many countries in the 1960s and 1970s--that movements grow in proportion to the ability of the Church to mobilize all members in the propagation of its beliefs (Strachan 1968, 108). It is interesting to note that the Christian Congregation of Brazil utilizes no mass media, no literature, no campaigns, and no street preaching. Yet it is growing. Its members are talking to their friends about their faith.

As a matter of fact, evangelism is a vital part of the life of a GR church (Anabalón 1994). "It is a movement that mobilizes people for mission" (Escobar 1994, 132). "It is a religion of the plaza" (Marzal 1988, 415).

Mobilization extends beyond the every-believer-a-witness level. In many churches believers are mobilized to go to *campos blancos* ("whitened fields"--referring to unevangelized areas) to hold street meetings, or begin meetings in the *campo blanco* that eventually becomes a daughter congregation. Mobilization in such evangelistic activities itself becomes a leadership training program. A large number of mobilized volunteers becomes a surplus of leadership available for the new opportunities that arise on every side--another *campo blanco,* or an opening to hold services in a jail.

It is also well to recognize that mobilization of the entire congregation in outreach is ". . . derived from one of the fundamental tenets of the Protestant Reformation of the sixteenth century: the priesthood of all believers. . . It is probable that the influence of Protestantism on the history of England and, later on, of the United States, would have been considerably reduced had it not been for the rediscovery of the priesthood of all believers in Methodism in the eighteenth century . . . The lay ministry is one of the characteristics that show that the Protestantism which has taken root in Latin America is related to the revivalist Protestantism of the eighteenth century" (*ibid.*, 89).

Mobilization of Christians for witness has a long tradition. The GR church is in most cases unaware of it. It simply ". . . mobilizes all members in a propagation of its beliefs" (Strachan, *op. cit.*).

Personal Empowerment

In a previous study commenting on the *evangélicos* in Latin America, we said: "The mobilization concept is an undeniable formula for growth. But if it is accepted cerebrally--no one can deny that it is logical--it is not enough. People can be trained to witness and be exhorted to do so, but the ordinary person . . . is nervous and embarrassed. . . Most churches will give lip service to mobilization, but nothing happens. The . . . [GR] churches are often the ones in which mobilization really takes place. Theirs is a theology which empowers believers. People know that God will answer prayer about the person to whom they expect to witness, and they know that the Holy Spirit will give the witnessing Christian the words to say and take away their timidity" (Berg and Pretiz 1992, 119-120).

In other words, they are motivated spiritually--both as to God's Spirit moving them in their inner being to reach out, and to their real concern for the spiritual needs of others.

David Howard writes from his missionary experience (1973, 43-44) in Colombia about a man named Lupercio Taba who was preaching when ". . . a man appeared at a side window of the church, aimed a pistol at Lupercio and ordered him to stop preaching. The congregation, seeing the danger, dove to the floor and hid under the pews." Unmoved, Lupercio continued his sermon and the shots passed close to him without touching his body. "Such a reaction is not natural, to put it mildly. It could only have been a special filling of the Holy Spirit which enabled him to face the danger of death. . ."

Whether such courage to witness by people in many GR churches is derived from the experiences that Pentecostals describe as the baptism of the Holy Spirit, or whether it is a deep and quiet reliance on Him as others describe it, the kind of fearless witness that takes place in Latin America can only be explained by the spiritual power that believers have learned to appropriate.

In commenting on the central focus of this work, Roger Greenway (1995) comments: "What you say is true. The 'spontaneous combustion' you describe is particularly evident in the GR churches. Yet it is not exclusively theirs. It is shared by a wide assortment of churches, some using one methodology and some another. To my mind, this is clear evidence that Brazil is experiencing a mighty movement of the Holy Spirit at this time. Old barriers are coming down, and a new evangelical unity is being forged by spiritual zeal and commitment to mission."

Promise of a Miracle

In addition to the above elements, a third factor is an integral part of the GR churches' evangelistic outreach. Desperate people with no relief from their illness, from their demonic oppression, and from their poverty and the pressure of life's problems, will run to a church that offers an answer. When the word gets around that a healing really took place, as in the earthly ministry of our Savior, there is no need for additional publicity.

Eugene Nida (1960, 8-9) observed: "The emphasis upon divine healing is sometimes regarded by outsiders as a dangerous fad, but when one realizes that in Latin America there is such a preoccupation with psychosomatic disease, especially the 'evil eye' and the *susto* (fright or shock), it is no wonder that the gospel has a relevance which seems rather unwarranted to us who look in from the outside. Moreover, even in Roman Catholicism much of the focus of attention upon the saints is related to healing, and it is not strange that the same concern should carry over into these Protestant communities."

In speaking of healing, Roman Catholic Manuel Marzal (1988, 411-412) states that in his church, healing is expressed in use of sacramental means such as holy water and relics. These take place at certain specified places (e.g. Lourdes) and represent a marginal part of total Roman Catholic liturgy. But among Pentecostals (and other GR churches) it becomes a central element.

Viv Grigg in his article, "Squatters: The Most Responsive Unreached Bloc?" (in *Urban Mission*, May 1988), has this to say about urban Brazilian churches.

> "There are more churches in São Paulo and Rio [de Janeiro] than in other cities of Latin America or Asia--5,294 in São Paulo. There is a greater movement among the poor. Many *favelas* have three or four churches. . . (48)
>
> "These churches have what poor people need. Simple patterns of noisy, emotionally healing worship, strong authoritarian leadership, and many legalistic rules. They are very dependent on the leading of the Spirit of God. They tend to lack in good Bible teaching, and reject book learning, partly because of the rapid growth which precludes extensive training of pastors and deacons. . . . *I have not found in any city a church formed among the poor that was not the result of healings, deliverance, and signs and wonders*" (49) [italics ours].

Pablo Deiros (1992, 174-175) selects as one of the notable characteristics of *Protestantismo Popular* (Protestantism of the Masses, i.e. GR movements) in Latin America: *evangelismo de poder* (power evangelism). According to this concept of evangelization, the preaching of the gospel is not sufficient to give testimony of the presence of the kingdom of God. It is believed that along with the preaching, "signs and wonders" are a necessary part as authenticating the power of the gospel unto salvation.

Furthermore, preaching is understood as not simply communicating the message of God, but as a direct confrontation with the power of Satan and his demons. The object of the Christian testimony is not so much that the person will simply arrive at a knowledge of the truth, but rather, that there will be liberation from the clutches of Satan and all of its consequences.

While we have been discussing the intervention of the supernatural primarily from the point of view of the individual and the local church, it will be well also to mention its impact in the vibrant urban mass evangelistic efforts. There is no better example of this than what has been occurring during the past two decades in Argentina and to which reference has been made earlier.

Peter Wagner (1991, 131-137) describes the spiritual power that has been demonstrated in evangelism particularly in huge Buenos Aires. Citing Annacondia, Giménez, Cabrera and others, he concludes that they have skillfully contextualized their message and methodology to communicate with and meet the needs of the lower classes. With this he couples power evangelism and spiritual warfare. Powerful intercessory prayer is underscored as the chief weapon of spiritual warfare.

Under the subtitle, "What is the secret?", Wagner replies (*ibid.*, 134-135):

> "Annacondia has a great deal in common with traditional crusade evangelists. He preaches a simple gospel message, gives an invitation for people to come forward and receive Christ as their Lord and Savior, uses trained counselors to lead them to Christ and give them literature, takes their names and addresses, and invites them to attend a local church.
>
> "Like Billy Graham and Luis Palau, Annacondia secures a broad base of interdenominational support from pastors and Christian leaders. Like Dwight Moody and Billy Sunday, he has had no formal academic theological training. Like Reinhard Bonnke and   T.L.

Osborne, he features miracles, healings, and deliverance from evil spirits in his meetings. He is not the only one who preaches in the open air, conducts three-hour services, or has on-the-spot intercessors praying for the ministry.

"If I am not mistaken, the major difference is Carlos Annacondia's intentional, premeditated, high-energy approach to spiritual warfare. A permanent fixture of Annacondia's crusades is what has to be one of the most sophisticated and massive deliverance ministries anywhere. . . I have never observed a crusade evangelist who is as publicly aggressive in confronting evil spirits as Annacondia."

In concluding this section, we remind ourselves that in the Synoptic Gospels, the Lord gives "authority" to those He sends out. There is no mention that they are given the "power" in and of itself. Ministering done in the power of the Spirit must rest on the authority of the Scripture.

Likewise, it is important to take into account the full import of empowerment as authority to do God's will, such as:

-- The Holy Spirit's gifts that empower the Lord's laity to do His work;

-- The power to overcome alcoholism, other drugs, and all kinds of other *vicios* (vices);

-- The power to withstand the sins of the spirit, as well as the sins of the flesh.

-- The power to suffer for Christ whether by illness, in life's circumstances, or in witnessing for Christ;

-- The power to be Christian spouses, parents, or single persons.

-- The power to reach out in creative ways to impact the arts, politics, socio-economic structures, and society in general with the gospel of Jesus Christ.

Methods and Peoples

Those studying evangelistic strategies often focus on methods and approaches to certain people groups. More important than the methods, however, is mobilization and the spiritual dynamics that we have described. But the consideration of methods is also important.

A survey we conducted in Chile indicated that while the poor are interested in visiting an Evangelical church if invited, they do not respond to the idea of attending a Bible study in someone's home. Living rooms are small and furniture barely accommodates the family, so why go to someone's home and embarrass him? But among the middle class, attending a home Bible study was a welcome idea--by contrast, to go to one of those noisy churches in a poor neighborhood was not.

Most GR movements are among the poor, so home Bible studies are not often the usual evangelistic approach at this level. However, Vision of the Future in Argentina, which does reach into the middle class, promotes home study cells, calling these the "side door" into the church while the campaign kind of activities are the "front door."

Street preaching still goes on in a very marked way in Chile where it has become so much part of the culture. As a matter of fact, a statue depicting a street preacher has been erected in Santiago. But this method is attracting fewer bystanders. Church evangelistic campaigns, tent meetings or stadium gatherings are popular. Organized visitation is not very common among GR churches, even as it appears to be diminishing among *evangélicos* in general.

It is interesting to note that in his *¿Por qué se van los Católicos?* (Why are the Catholics Leaving?) to join the "sects," Peruvian priest J. L. Pérez Guadalupe (1992, 53) demonstrates unusual understanding of us. In comparing the evangelistic methodology of the *evangélicos* with other "sects," he notes: "They do not go from house to house." It is just the opposite, according to Pérez, with Jehovah's Witnesses and Mormons. About them, he says: "They go systematically from house to house." It is exactly this persistent house-to-house visitation by these groups that has made it an unpopular method for the *evangélicos* in many places.

The Electronic Church

In the media, Latin American *evangélicos* prefer ministries that verbally proclaim the gospel. GR groups are no exception. Missionary broadcast stations such as HCJB of Quito, Ecuador, led the way, but now the broadcast activities of GR churches and groups have been multiplying.

The larger and newer generation GR movements, however, are enamored with the mass media. Not only is broadcast time purchased, but radio and TV stations are being bought by churches or GR organizations. Mexico has not allowed religious broadcasts, and the doors in a few countries such as Venezuela have been closed, but elsewhere local GR Christians have taken to the air waves.

Some Brazilians have been the most enthusiastic purchasers of radio and TV time and sometimes even of the stations themselves. In addition to radio time on 573 stations, the "God is Love" movement in Brazil owns several stations of its own (Assman

1988, 100-101). Rio de Janeiro has twelve evangelical stations; Managua, Nicaragua, six.

Roman Catholic leaders such as Hugo Assman have plenty of material to criticize, especially regarding programs like that of Brazilian evangelist R.R. Soares of the International Church of the Grace of God (*ibid.*, 78-83). Assman published a transcript of a TV program in which a rose placed on top of the TV set of the viewers of Soares' program becomes "anointed," and which can then be taken to a sick friend. The evil spirit of illness, Soares asserts, will be absorbed by the rose, which then must be burned.

Although there are programs that are bizarre and others that certainly are confusing to the non-Christian viewer, many carry sound teaching and are well produced. An increasing number of programs interact with the listeners/viewers, answering their questions or praying for those who call in requests.

All the GR churches of the newer generation described in chapters five and six have radio and/or TV ministries.

Ministries in the Prisons and the Military

Some of the most active in preaching and visiting in Latin American prisons are the GR churches. In Chile, GR groups have established Evangelical "churches" in the various branches of the armed forces, all part of what is called the "Evangelical Military Church." In 1984, 14% of all Chile's military personnel attended these "churches" (Schuffenger 1986, 15).

Missions Outreach

To Peru Via Costa Rica and Beyond

Many years ago Pedro Paredes was sent from his home in the Peruvian Amazon region to a seminary in Costa Rica by the mission group that had led him to Christ. After graduation he was involved in a local Costa Rican church ministry which he later left to enter secular occupations. Although successful in business, he reports that he suffered a health crisis and experienced a vision of Christ as an immensely tall figure.

God restored his health and called him back to Peru, but told him that first he should plant five churches in Costa Rica which would serve as his support base. He established the MIVIA Amazon River Mission and has taken teams of workers from Central America to Peruvian jungle Indians, establishing schools and churches.

Christians in Peru itself have their own GR mission society, AMEN, to plant churches in remote areas of the country. AMEN missionaries have gone to European capitals to establish hispanic churches there.

Many Chilean Methodist Pentecostals migrated permanently to areas of Argentina, Bolivia and Peru to plant churches. But cultural differences between Latin American countries pose some problems to GR missionary efforts. The Chileans are too "foreign" culturally. Peruvians expect pastors to have theological training, which these Chileans scorn. So the Chilean-style churches are not growing in Peru.

Some of Brazil's GR denominations--the God is Love Church and the Universal Church of the Kingdom of God--are spreading into Peru, Argentina and Uruguay, but Evangelicals in these lands consider them sects.

This expansion by GR denominations into other countries goes on everywhere. Mexican groups plant churches in Central America, for example. But these are simply extensions of denominations into other peoples of the same social class, language and culture. Only recently has there been a surge of enthusiasm for cross-cultural missions with Brazilians leading the way.

A Missionary Challenge

Although the valuable work needs an up-date, Larry Pate in his *From Every People* (1989), a handbook of two-thirds-world missions with directory, histories, and analysis, focuses on Latin American churches' mission outreach on pages 31-42.

Luis Bush (1993) describes a 1993 missions congress in Brazil where 1,100 participated, coming from all 26 states of the country. There are 67 Brazilian mission agencies, 43 of which have targeted areas outside the nation's borders.

What was considered the task of foreign missionaries from the north is now being picked up by Christians in the developing nations. In fact, some missiologists (e.g. Mcintosh 1986) consider Western mission structures too complicated and expensive to get the job of world evangelization done. They are of the opinion that in the coming years, missionaries of these newer churches will be primary agents to witness to the unreached, both within their own countries and to those outside their borders.

Another, Samuel Escobar, in an address given at CLADE III in 1992 and entitled *"Las nuevas fronteras de la misión"* ("The New Frontiers of Mission"), challenges Latin American missionaries not to think so much in geographical terms. "The Gospel has crossed nearly every geographical border," he says. The frontiers to be crossed now are cultural. Efforts should be made to reach across to evangelize unreached Latin American social classes and ethnic groups.

Societal Outreach

The Mangueira Samba School, preparing Brazilians for participation in the riotous carnival celebrations, finds its enrollment diminishing because too many people are accepting Christ (Kamm 1991, A12). Personal reformation, whether renouncing the extravagant and sensual samba carnival dances or abstinence from liquor, leads to more orderly lives and personal progress, as mentioned in chapter nine. Likewise we reviewed the social contribution network that the local church provides--finding jobs and other forms of mutual aid. Critics of the GR movements, however, are not satisfied. They point to the lack of more pervasive effects of the gospel in society.

But some GR churches go beyond the above to help other people in their *barrios*. Those that do may not consider it noteworthy nor do they have the Scriptural underpinnings to support their activity or talk about it. But pressing the question, we find that a church like Brazil for Christ distributes tons of food and the Calacoaya Cultural Center in Mexico has classes in English and in computer science for the neighborhood. The Otomi Indian GR movement of Mexico took the initiative to see that roads were opened into their areas. Such cases of leadership in community development are not so common.

Institutional work likewise is not so developed, but day schools (generally related to local churches), drug rehab centers, homes for single mothers and daycare centers are the most typical.

For example, we saw the Nueva Vida drug rehab center, located in Guatire, Venezuela, east of Caracas, as such a GR project. It includes a large woodworking shop to give the residents vocational training. Manufacturing doors for an adjacent government housing project was the first contract to help support the ministry.

In Caracas itself, another ministry is reaching abandoned children. In a warm, affirming ambience, there is a network of ten homes--in each of which Christian houseparents raise ten or twelve children. Each house is located in a neighborhood where the children also go to school. Volunteers from local churches come regularly to teach special subjects as well as to do laundry and perform other tasks.

The vision for this project came to Elda de Lizcano--formerly a government psychologist rehabilitating juvenile delinquents. Feeling it would make more sense to work with street children before they were sucked into serious trouble, she founded ABANSA, a Christian program to help needy children. Mrs. Lizcano's son-in-law is a pediatrician, so the children receive medical attention. The volunteer help from many churches keeps the costs down.

In the above cases, the programs are interdenominational, belonging to, as it were, and supported by the entire Evangelical community. In other cases, institutions may belong to a single GR church or denomination.

An example is the Argentine "The Waves of Love" movement's plan for an apartment complex to house 1,400 poor families from among its followers, and a mutual aid society with a network of associated medical and dental clinics, and with ambulance and funeral services (*Amanecer* 1992, 36-38).

In countries where public education is poor, or where Evangelical children are subject to discrimination, churches often start a primary school on their property. While many schools founded by traditional denominational missions tend to become elitist--beyond the reach financially of the most needy--schools in

GR churches are generally more accessible to the poor families right in their *barrios*. In some countries the growth of small Christian schools has been phenomenal. According to "Peru para Cristo," a DAWN survey of Peru (1993, 73), an estimated one hundred operate in Lima, and another hundred in the rest of the country.

Medical work has not been, in general, a field of service for GR churches. However, Costa Rican Christians have founded a medical center, the Jerusalem Clinic in San José. This hospital is in addition to another Christian hospital in the city, the Clínica Bíblica, which had the advantage of being founded over sixty years ago by foreign missionaries.

In **politics**, with the return in Latin America to democratic governments in the 1980s after a period of military regimes, the growing number of Evangelicals have become aware of their political muscle and have even launched political parties. There are or have been such parties in Venezuela, Costa Rica, Argentina, and Colombia.

Voters often cast their ballots in favor of Evangelicals in countries where corruption encouraged even non-Evangelicals to vote for honest-looking people. Candidates like Peru's Alberto Fujimori courted the Evangelical bloc. However, voters were often disappointed at the lack of political experience of Evangelical officials, and Fujimori, after gaining the Presidency, turned his back on the Christians who helped vote him into office.

A Costa Rican GR pastor, Rafael Matamoros, entered the Presidential race in 1994 under the evangelical National Christian Alliance party banner. He drew only a handful of votes and confessed later, "I am no politician; what I did was preach" (*Maranatha*, 1994). In Guatemala Evangelical General Ríos Montt's administration was marked by continued violence, and

Elías Serrano had to abandon the presidency due to alleged corruption.

In Brazil the *bancada evangelica* (a bloc of Evangelical deputies in congress) was object of a study by Paul Freston (1991, 21-36). As Evangelicals began entering the political arena, this group of 14 during the 1983-1986 period grew to 33 (of a total of 505) in 1987-1990. Of these, eighteen were Pentecostal, a few from GR churches.

How do they line up politically? Freston (*ibid.*) quotes a study which counted the times deputies supported bills that favored the dispossessed, and constructs a score. In general the Evangelical bloc came out with a score slightly less favorable to the causes of the poor than the average. This would support those who identify Evangelicals with the political right and the status quo. When the Pentecostals are separated out from other *evangélicos*, they come out with a better-than-average score of voting in favor of the poor, faithfully reflecting their low-income constituencies. However, deputies from historic churches come out looking politically very conservative.

Observers do not necessarily assign an ideological tag to the Pentecostal deputies. "We should take care not to attribute to them a rationality of political action which they do not have," says Freston (*ibid.*). Issues important to Evangelical politicians are religious freedom, and matters relating to sexual and family morality. Those more cynical saw in the performance of the Evangelical bloc only the favors the deputies gained in exchange for votes, playing both sides ideologically and earning the charges of scandal in the public press. Only a handful were re-elected.

More clearly committed ideologically are some Chilean GR movements like the National Wesleyan Church. A condition of membership is to belong to a trade union and be active in a party of the left (Hollenweger 1972, 470). This contrasts with the already-mentioned association of many GR church leaders in Chile with Pinochet and the political right.

Another approach is that of the Chilean *teocráticos*. Officially the *Revolution for Christ* movement, their goal is to create a state where God's moral laws are operative. This GR movement began by campaigning against a pornographic tabloid newspaper and engaging in such antics as depositing garbage on the doorsteps of topless nightclubs and on the car of an alleged homosexual entertainer. "We use communist methods," they say. The leader, Christian Casanova, was a member of the radical MIR party before his conversion, and his followers are mainly university students. They have a handsome headquarters, suggesting money from abroad. But most Evangelicals were turned off by their tactics and they have recently become less visible (Hoff 1994).

Latin American Evangelicals are just beginning to consider their political responsibility. Lack of experience shows. "It is still too early to evaluate the long-range effects of this new phenomenon" (R. Padilla 1994, 83).

This is not to say that some *evangélicos* have not made significant contributions, but these have often been better educated people from traditional church backgrounds. Presbyterian Jaime Ortiz of Medellín, for example, played a significant role in rewriting Colombia's constitution. But GR groups will play an increasingly important role in Latin America's political scene, whether by supporting some party or candidate or launching their own banner.

René Padilla (*op. cit.*, 82-95) has written a masterful chapter entitled, "New Actors on the Political Scene in Latin America." He sees Evangelical entry into politics as a response to the socio-economic and political crises of the region. The effectiveness of this response is based on:

(1) The *evangélicos'* ability to mobilize the masses, not only for evangelism, but also to generate enthusiasm for a political cause. (Because of Evangelical support, Peru's Fujimori, with a campaign chest of only $12,000, won a Presidential election.)

(2) The leadership experience acquired by *evangélicos* in their churches where lay participation is emphasized.

(3) Spiritual motivation, which seeks the political freedoms for the gospel to be preached.

While the article speaks of the wider stream of Latin American Evangelicals, the political force that is generated by the above factors is particularly applicable to the GR flow of the Evangelical stream. These same factors of mobilization, leadership development and spiritual motivation are the driving forces that lead GR movements to reach out in evangelism, missions, and work towards social change.

FIFTEEN

Where Do We Go from Here?

What does this overview of the fast-growing GR churches in Latin America show us?

We can ask ourselves whether there are ways to relate to them in a manner that will encourage and help them. But more important, can we relate in ways that will encourage and help us?

One purpose of this book is to help build bridges between traditional mission movements with their related churches in North and Latin America, and Latin American GR movements.

The earliest examples of GR churches are found in the Scriptures. Groups of believers formed without the express initiative of the mother church in Jerusalem or the apostles. Such were the believers in Samaria (Acts 8:4-25) and the church in Antioch (Acts 11:19-30). In the case of Samaria, Philip was a deacon from Jerusalem and the Antioch church was started by laymen who traveled after the persecution of Stephen.

Remarkable similarities to today's GR churches are embedded in these Biblical accounts.

-- These groups in Samaria (Acts 8:6) and Antioch (11:21,24) were noted for their great numerical growth.

-- They faced frontline spiritual darkness with supernatural demonstrations of God's power--casting out evil spirits, healing paralytics and cripples in Samaria (8:6-7), and at Antioch, predicting a great famine (11:28).

-- They were subject to error, as in the case of Simon the sorcerer's unspiritual grasping for power (8:9-19).

247

-- The Antioch church, composed largely of Gentiles, was more contextualized in reaching out to Gentiles than the church in Jerusalem (cf. Peter's Jewish awkwardness in approaching Cornelius in Acts 11:1-17). Furthermore, by instigating the Jerusalem Council (15:1-35), Antioch's concern for the Gentiles led to a sharper definition of the gospel on the part of the total Church.

Other elements in these accounts give us additional clues for shaping our views toward GR churches, several of which merit closer examination.

1. We are one body in Christ

The Jerusalem church sought to learn about Samaria and Antioch. They sent representatives (Acts 8:14; 11:1,2,18) and established relationships with the new believers. We, too, must relate to those who are loyal to the Word of God and recognize Jesus Christ as Savior and Lord.

We who are "Anglos" or Westerners sometimes have difficulty understanding GR styles, worship, and even their doctrinal emphases. Despite our occasional bewilderment over the great diversity in the Church of God, we must recognize the clear New Testament teaching on the unity of the body of Christ (John 17:20-25; 1 Corinthians 12:12-26 and Ephesians 4:1-16).

This may call for a review of our convictions about the oneness of the Church. It extends beyond our local church, our denomination, or the churches planted by Western missions and our particular mission society. This view will affect our handling of the data (i.e. "counting noses") regarding the number of Christians in a given country, area, or city. It will affect our visiting the "field." Why not seek out other churches, rather than restricting ourselves to mission-related congregations?

It may be uncomfortable and require extra energy and time to relate to these churches. There also exists the tension of having to set boundaries--is this particular group really Christian or not? It is easier and less stressful, of course, to stay within one's own familiar territory and not face these issues. But we must come to terms with other members of the body of Christ.

There are various levels in which we can relate to these fellow members of God's Church. Certainly we can begin **on a personal level**. Honduran Belsazar Núñez (1992) stresses the importance of personal contact with Christian leaders whether or not an organizational connection is possible. Eugene Nida (1960, 12-13) also emphasized deep personal friendships with these leaders--in addition to acquiring a thorough acquaintance with the movements, sharing this information with missionaries, and eventually working on joint projects.

One thing is certain. Our sincerity and genuine interest in approaching and developing friendships with GR brothers and sisters is of greatest importance. Very quickly they will ascertain whether our interest in them "is for real" or not.

Our proud human organizations--the missionaries', the traditional pastors', and the GR leaders'--may temporarily hinder us from doing anything more than simply getting to know some of the leaders personally and, we hope, to "hang out" with them. But it is more than worth the effort!

On a local level, numerous opportunities arise from time to time to open doors between traditional churches and GR churches in the same city or rural area. True, often we fail to invite GR pastors and leaders to such events as united evangelistic campaigns, interdenominational workshops, and pastors' retreats. On the other hand, there are a growing number of positive examples.

In San José, Costa Rica, two hundred or so pastors, mostly from independent churches, meet every Tuesday morning in the downtown Bible Temple to pray and study together. It is a time of sharing problems, seeking counsel, and praying for each other and the impact of the gospel on their city. While a national Evangelical alliance deals primarily with interdenominational affairs and the representation of Evangelical causes before the government, the Tuesday morning meeting is where the parts of the body relate to each other personally and spiritually.

On a national and international level, we have already referred to the poor representation of GR movements' leaders on the invitation lists to Evangelical alliances and councils, pastors' fraternities, congresses, and other large events. There are notable exceptions to this, for which we give thanks. But by and large, there is little GR participation--due primarily to our apathy, disinterest or aversion.

Peruvian journalist and GR pastor Samuel Nieva (1993) describes a situation where GR movements turn out to be the most cooperative.

> "These groups are cooperating enthusiastically in the prayer movement of Christ for the City. In fact, the greatest participation is by these groups, rather than the 'standoffish' major denominations. These [GR] groups cannot become members of CONEP (national Evangelical council) because many have not been legally incorporated and/or do not meet the minimal number requirement. So, CONEP's membership is composed of major denominations. It has recently become engaged in human rights issues, church growth statistics, helping missionaries with visas, but has not given enough attention to these autochthonous groups."

2. We must learn together

In Acts 8 and 11, we are told that Jerusalem sent teachers to the new churches. But Antioch also influenced Jerusalem. By raising the question of the relationship between Jewish law and Gentile believers, it sparked the Jerusalem Council.

During the Amsterdam '86 International Conference for Itinerant Preachers, we conversed with members of the Mexican delegation regarding the obvious secularization of Holland, once a bastion of the reformed faith. The Mexicans were horrified at rampant scenes of immorality, prostitution, drug dependency and pornography. "How can we keep this from happening in such enormous proportions in Latin America?" they asked.

Church history often describes churches evolving from small sects into institutionalized middle-class denominations in an increasingly secularized society while losing both their evangelistic zeal and contact with the poor. Mexican Christians wanted to know if this could be avoided. Unfortunately, North American churches have not been all that successful in resolving the problem. If the secularization of society and the institutionalization of the Church are not to be inevitable in Latin America, the solutions have to be found as Christians in both continents work them out and share their conclusions.

Learning from the Grass-Roots

We begin to learn together by listening.

Fifty years ago Dietrich Bonhoeffer in his *Life Together* (1954, edition translated from the German) penned these words:

"The first service that one owes to others in the fellowship consists in listening to them. Just as love to God begins with listening to His Word, so

the beginning of love for the brethren is learning to
listen to them. It is God's love for us that He not
only gives us His Word but also lends us His ear.
So it is His work that we do for our brother when
we learn to listen to him. Christians, especially
ministers, so often think they must always
contribute something when they are in the
company of others, that this is the one service they
have to render. They forget that listening can be a
greater service than speaking."

(See also Vinoth Ramachandra's article "The Honor of
Listening: Indispensable for Mission" in *Evangelical Missions
Quarterly*, October 1994, 404-409.)

GR churches have much to teach us in certain areas.
Christians in the North can learn much about spirituality from
those unaffected as much by the humanistic influences of the
Enlightenment. There is among them a sense of closeness to
God. Rather than discovery of a new doctrine, theirs is a daily
discovery of a new, intense experience with God--a walk and life
of faith and prayer. Religious expression is simple, but decisive.
The forces of Satan and his demons are real to them, but so is the
power of the Spirit called upon to combat them. Such recognition
of the demonic, exorcism, prayer for the sick and other ministries
are increasingly being recovered in the West.

There is a growing recognition that many renewal movements
in the Church seldom begin at institutional headquarters nor
among the more religiously sophisticated, but rather on the social
and religious peripheries. Paul Pierson (1994) of Fuller
Theological Seminary describes the Church scene as a series of
concentric circles. Movements on the periphery--the GR kind of
churches--". . . tend to be more in contact with the secular world
and evangelize more actively and effectively." As such movements

become more institutionalized, they move towards the center of the circle. The center, in his view, includes historically the mainline Protestant denominations, the next circle the newer Evangelical movements, the third, the classic Pentecostals, and the fourth, the newer autochthonous churches sprouting up in all parts of the world.

Leslie Newbigin in *Toward the 21st Century in Christian Mission* (editors Phillips and Coote 1993, 2, 3) states, "At the heart of the Enlightenment lies the basic principle that the true explanation of all things is accessible through the use of human reason. Conscience was set free from the shackles of tradition and superstition. Human reason is basically the same everywhere. It simply needs to be liberated, and thus advances the whole human race as one 'family of man.'" This is done, according to Enlightenment focus, through education--"The school was to be the great agent of enlightenment, and it is a token of the degree to which missionaries accepted the ideas of the time that they gave schools such an important place in their work" (*ibid.*).

From an anthropological perspective, Charles Kraft in *Christianity With Power* (1989) entitles his fourth chapter "Enlightenment Christianity is Powerless." Some of the symptoms of Enlightenment Christianity that he mentions are:

-- A pervasive rationalism. We pray for guidance and then mostly reason it out.

-- Centering our church meetings on a lecture. True worship takes time and is more than intellectual exercise. It touches people at the emotional level.

-- Downplaying the value of experience.

-- Our tendency is to think of God's Word *only* as something written. Throughout the Bible, however, the phrase "the word of God" usually refers to God speaking to us rather than referring only to the written record of His words and deeds.

--   An approach to evangelism and missions that is primarily
a matter of knowledge and technique.   Developing our
understanding and our strategies and using our reasoning powers
are perfectly valid. But we need to discover how to keep from
running ahead of God in the use of such insights. Can we learn to
seek and wait for God to show us His will *before* and not *after* we
work out the strategy?

Missiologists, too, will learn from GR churches. Obviously,
those interested in church growth can find much to learn in GR
movements. Escobar (1994, 26) says: "Popular Protestant
churches are not growing because they have applied some
technique learned in a missiological school in North America. It
is the other way around. Missiological schools are trying to detect
in their growth some principles that might be helpful to other
Christians. . ."

Wilbert Shenk in his *The Contribution of the Study of New
Religious Movements to Missiology* (1990, 191) comments:
"Thus, long before the term contextualization came into vogue in
missiological circles, these new religious movements were living
laboratories of that which had to come about if the churches in the
non-Western world were to take root and survive. Because these
movements had arisen outside the control of Western influences,
they exhibited a contextualized religious response to what they
had heard in the Christian message from the outset."

Theologians are beginning to look at theologies emerging from
the Two-thirds World.   Harvard Divinity School is requiring
Spanish for its students so they can read the writings of Latin
American theologians firsthand. However, too much emphasis has
been given to the Liberation Theologies without listening to other
voices from the South. Unfortunately, many of the other thinkers
in Latin America are less inclined to devote time to putting their
insights into writing. They are too busy bringing in the harvest.

William Dyrness in *Learning About Theology From the Third World* (1990) and *Emerging Voices in Global Christian Theology* (1994) has encouraged the examination of the theologies being developed outside of the West.

A mine of insights concerning the development of worship forms, preaching styles and pastoral approaches in the Latin American GR churches is also available for others to examine and perhaps adopt.

Sharing with the Grass Roots

Even while we appreciate the more supernatural assumptions of Latin American GR Christianity, we have to recognize the advance of Western civilization into the region. Scientifically-oriented persons, especially youth, need to see that reason also is a gift from God and that the Christian faith has a rational basis. "To divest Christianity of its historicity and rationality deprives faith of much of its power as well as its attraction with regard to people with an intellectual or rational disposition," said one Latin American (Moreno 1994, A3-6).

Biblical supernaturalism underlies much of GR Christian thinking. At the same time, there is often a lack of basic Biblical teaching and doctrine. Guillermo Cook concludes *New Face of the Church in Latin America* (1994, 276) by saying, "If the Church in Latin America is truly to show 'a new face' as it turns to a new millenium . . . it must discover the Bible. . . The 'new reformation' that Latin America cries for will begin, as all reformations throughout history have done, from the grass-roots churches . . . that open themselves up to the action of the Holy Spirit . . . that let themselves be freed up by the Word of God in order to act as responsible agents of radical change for persons and society."

How can these churches be stimulated to study and teach the Scriptures? Where the church structures may be impermeable, personal friendship with GR leaders may be a quiet and more effective way of communication. Gilberto Nieves (1992) loaned books and cultivated a friendship with a GR leader in Venezuela.

The more informal kinds of programs can be effective. Kenneth Scott, a missionary who served for many years in Peru under the Regions Beyond Missionary Union, relates his experience with GR groups. His article, "New Religious Movements in Peru," in the *Latin America Evangelist* (January-March 1987, 15), says:

"In recent months I've had the privilege of preaching in the Christian Crusade [for the Nations--a Peruvian GR movement] on the Book of Revelation and also on church government and organization. Whereas other evangelical speakers have been rejected, they accept me. The reason, I think, was that I didn't try to change them, although I didn't agree with everything.

"Each religious movement has a right to self-determination, and paternalism is the last thing we should introduce into the area of church life.

". . . As we study each group over a period of time, and as we find how it stands on such issues as the person of Christ, the role of the Bible, the sacraments and church discipline, we should begin reaching conclusions.

"If a new movement is Christian, then our fellowship with it becomes an obvious responsibility. But if the group is not Christian,then our response must surely be to evangelize it."

Mennonites in West Africa invested their missionary efforts, not in planting Mennonite churches, but in making themselves available to the African Independent churches. The story of these efforts is documented in two books, both edited by David Shenk: *Ministry of Missions to African Independent Churches* (1987) and *Ministry in Partnership with African Independent Churches* (1991).

Likewise, until the revolution in Liberia forced missionaries of the Christian Reformed Church to terminate their activities, they too believed that a teaching ministry with the independent churches of the Bassa people was more appropriate than planting their own churches (Owens 1992).

Pastors of GR churches may well hesitate to participate in formal programs. However, the workshops and seminars conducted by the International Institute for In-Depth Evangelization in Central America and by Overseas Crusades in Brazil, and the pastors' retreats sponsored by World Vision, attract GR pastors as well as those of more traditional backgrounds.

Less formal is the teaching absorbed in the already-mentioned pastors' fraternities or associations. Every contact that GR leaders have with other pastors who have a solid Biblical foundation is one more element that may keep them from error and lead them into even more fruitful ministry.

More formal programs exist. But Bible institutes or seminaries must make it comfortable for the GR pastor who may be a layman with few hours for formal study. The schedule, the location, and the attitude with which they are received are important. The Evangelical Seminary of Caracas is a GR seminary which is reaching many GR leaders. Missionaries on the faculty are making a significant contribution. The Pentecostal Bible Institute in Chile caters primarily to leaders of the GR churches.

Books, radio programs, and tapes have their place. GR leaders may feel uncomfortable enrolling in a school, but they will buy an inexpensive book. More books by Latin American authors are still desperately needed, written with the style and idiom appropriate for GR leaders.

Even more is learned by observing models of ministry. Are any more churches needed in a city where there is a GR church in every *barrio*? Yes, if the new church can demonstrate how to reach some difficult segment of society not currently reached by the GR church--the drug addict, the university student, the Jewish merchant, or the professional.

3. We must evangelize together

The Antioch church is known for being the first to send missionaries intentionally. The Paul-Barnabas team was a mix of missionaries--Barnabas from the mother church in Jerusalem, and Paul, whose Christian formation was mostly in Antioch.

The motivation, zeal and methodologies of the GR churches in evangelism and missions make it imperative for us to take them into account in our strategies for world evangelization. Wherever possible, they should be invited to participate in united efforts.

In Caracas, Venezuela, six churches formed a "coalition," a mix of two large GR Pentecostal churches, a charismatic Presbyterian church, a traditional Presbyterian congregation, a Mennonite church and a Church of the Brethren congregation. The purpose of the coalition was to help each other plant churches in unreached neighborhoods with the assistance of the Latin America Mission's Christ for the City program.

But the coalition proved to be more than that. A visitation team from one church helped another in canvassing a neighborhood to start a new congregation. Musical groups and pastors were exchanged for special occasions. A new Mennonite missionary in one church said, "This coalition is the only way we could have had the constant input from the experience of the pastor of the largest church in the city." Since then, the coalition has included a larger number of churches and developed plans for a cooperative approach to evangelize even more of the city.

The united evangelistic efforts of Christ for the City programs in Colombia and Peru involve GR churches. In fact, these churches, not bound by denominational priorities, are among the most open to cooperation.

As GR churches look to sending missionaries cross-culturally, their candidates need training. One fruitful missionary career for North Americans is that of preparing these Latin Americans. Two schools currently involved in this ministry include IMDELA (the Missiological Institute of the Americas) in Costa Rica and CEMAA's Orlando Costas School of Missiology program in Lima, Peru.

Already mentioned has been the need to involve the participation of GR movements in the congresses and gatherings for national, regional or world evangelism. How much of our planning, goal setting and reporting actually involves these movements?

4. We must serve the world together

Following Barnabas' and Saul's year-long teaching ministry in the church of Antioch, we are told of the arrival of some prophets from Jerusalem. One of them, Agabus, predicted a severe famine, enveloping the entire Roman world. Christians in Antioch saw that the Jerusalem church was going to suffer. The response of this GR church to the need seemed to be spontaneous, a most natural expression of love towards the mother church. Antioch pioneered in organizing a relief program (Acts 11:25-30).

Caio Fabio, president of AEVB, the association of Brazilian Evangelicals, reflects the concern of many that GR churches are still not acting responsibly in society: "The Latin-American-style revival . . . vibrates with miracles, but does not practice justice and truth . . . it teaches its believers to raise their hands to heaven, but not to extend them to their neighbor . . . this kind of revival leads to great church growth, but it doesn't change our continent at all" (*El Puente* 1992 issue).

Yet GR churches, most often born and developed in situations of poverty, are in the most advantageous position to teach the rest of the world how to minister to the poor. The story of the GR peoples is one of survival. Living in poverty and plagued by social injustices, the GR churches teach those of us in the West in singular fashion how to live through ever-present tough situations. Again, they face things together as the community of God.

In Lima where the government often does nothing about repairing streets or other public works in poor *barrios*, GR Christians pitch in and follow patterns of ancient Indian culture where a whole community will take a day or two to work on a project. These community projects (called *minkas* in Peru or *mingas* in Ecuador) reflect the holistic concept of local people solving community problems without dependence on central government. It is the same aggressive spirit reflected in the multiplication of local GR churches--where one does not wait for a denomination to begin a work. *"Cueste lo que cueste"* (whatever the price), they face tough situations and take on this responsibility with Christ's help.

Some GR movements are ahead of the rest of the Church in their concern for the poor. But others need to be encouraged to broaden their vision in this regard. World Vision has done much in this area, conducting seminars on ministry that combine evangelism with attention to people's material needs. In addition, World Vision helps local churches, many of them GR, in projects that will raise the standard of living in poor communities.

There are staggering needs in Latin America--among the street children, the shantytown dwellers, the abused women, the dispossessed Indians, the politically oppressed and many other groups. The task of demonstrating Christian love by offering even a small cup of water to the needy millions seems impossible. But the Christians in the GR churches, if motivated to share out of their poverty, can make a difference, even in a small measure.

Of course, macro solutions lie in the realm of politics and economics. We have mentioned some of the disappointing Evangelical forays into Latin American politics. The Latin American Theological Fraternity as well as other groups, conduct seminars and other events to equip a generation of Evangelicals who will be able to take their places in secular leadership.

In relief and development, just as in politics, there have been mistakes and failures. A program to distribute outside relief through the GR churches after an earthquake in Chile "distorted" the Church, according to Bishop Francisco Anabalón. The churches were not prepared to think in terms of sharing relief with the surrounding community. Outside aid can create opportunists among Christians, foment dependency and produce temptations for corruption. Taking Christian responsibility for neighbors is never going to be easy.

Building bridges with the GR churches will take energy and motivation. But even more, it will require a commitment to the unity of the body of Christ and love for Christian brothers and sisters of diverse backgrounds.

5. We will rejoice together

When Barnabas arrived in Antioch and saw what God had done, he was "glad." His attitude towards an unofficially founded church was one of encouragement. It was significant that Jerusalem had sent Barnabas, the "encourager." This is the kind of pastor or missionary needed today to build bridges with GR churches.

The rise of GR churches should be an occasion for thanksgiving to God. These movements, with their particular doctrinal slants and differing practices, may be difficult for some of us to accept. And to add insult to injury, sometimes believers from traditional churches have been siphoned off into GR movements. It is also hard to admit that in many respects national brethren are more effective than missionaries. Nevertheless, we are called upon to praise God--as the Apostle Paul did-- for every work where Christ is preached.   Certainly their services are expressions of praise and thanksgiving to God in the Spirit with manifestations of joy, hope, and a will to live.

It is clear that GR churches are a goal of missions. We want the gospel to penetrate so deeply and thoroughly that national believers begin planting their own churches. Even when this occurs without being a part of a foreign missionary effort--all praise be to God.

When U.S. forces invaded Panama in December of 1989 to topple strong man Manuel Noriega, one of the last holdouts of Panamanian resistance and target of U.S. missle attacks was San Miguelito, a squatter settlement of 250,000 people on a hill outside Panama City. On one of the twisted walkways among the houses is found the *Gran Campaña de Amor* (The Great Campaign of Love) church, pastored by Willy Castillo. The loud *salsa* music from a neighboring home is turned off when the evening service begins--out of respect.

Respect, because the church makes available the equipment for its neighbors to make cement blocks, enabling them to replace their tin shacks with more substantial construction. The church has also donated tanks for the community's rubbish collection, has a first aid brigade, and a feeding program for children.

The night of our visit several hundred people sang lustily to an off-key guitar. The message on the Water of Life was simple, drawing three people to the front at the first invitation to make a profession of faith. Then a general invitation followed, focusing on people with concerns for prayer. Half of the congregation came forward.

Castillo was an atheistic agricultural engineer who challenged God to reveal Himself. One night a light illuminated his room and he heard a voice say, "I love you." Subsequent visions led him to establish the church in an area where "they were waiting for me with machetes."

The pastor's theological preparation takes place with a handful of other pastors who study materials of the FLET program in an extension program of Panama's Manna Bible Institute. He relates to other churches through CONEPA--Panama's Evangelical fraternity. His outreach to the community is reinforced with a videocassette library.

Violent San Miguelito is probably no place for foreign missionaries. But the growing reality of ministries arising in such places through spiritual spontaneous combustion places new priorities on missions. Programs of theological extension, production of appropriate evangelistic materials, and the development of networks within which the Willy Castillos can both learn and share with others their experience in outreach--this is the kind of fuel that fans the flame being ignited throughout Latin America.

Let us develop a prayerful appreciation for our GR brothers and sisters in Latin America,

-- as we praise God for their work of faith particularly among the poor of their lands,

-- as we experience a greater sense of unity of the body of Christ, and

-- as we accept our cultural differences and appreciate our different ways of relating to our Heavenly Father and to one another.

"Now that you have purified yourselves by obeying the truth so that you have sincere love for your brothers, love one another deeply, from the heart. For you have been born again, not of perishable seed, but of imperishable, through the living and enduring word of God."

1 Peter 1:22-23 (NIV)

GLOSSARY

**Terms Employed in Missiological Literature
That Often Refer to
"Grass-Roots" (GR) Churches**

AUTOCHTHONOUS (Au-TOK-toh-nus). This term would normally be our preference to describe these churches. In a context of botany, the word can refer to that which is part of the ecosystem. For example, orchids are "autochthonous" in Costa Rica--but exotic in Chicago. In discussing culture, autochthonous can refer to elements of a culture that are not imported.

In the Spanish language, the corresponding word (*autóctono*) is well known, perhaps because there is a long history of Latin Americans using it in their aspiration to preserve their autochthonous cultures in the face of overwhelming foreign influences. In some circles, the word is even limited to elements of culture that are Indian. But to speak of autochthonous churches in Latin America is usually understood as meaning those founded by Latin Americans. However, we find English-language audiences stumbling over this term and so, we reluctantly dismiss it for our purposes.

INDIGENOUS. This term might seem to be most logical. For years missions have been attempting to indigenize churches. When a mission gives a church its autonomy, it is said that the church is "indigenized." But such a church, with perhaps a long history of missionary influence, is a far cry from the congregation that begins on it own--when, for example, a person reads the Bible

265

and holds a meeting in a home that eventually becomes a church, one which by virtue of its customs, worship style and practice enjoys a more perfect fit with the culture. In fact, a congregation rooted in the local culture is what we are looking for.

It is also self-contradictory to say we can "indigenize" a church. A mission in reality is transplanting a church into native soil. It did not spring up there. To "indigenize" a missionary-founded church is akin to declaring every resident of New York "a native New Yorker," regardless of origin. Strictly speaking, we cannot "indigenize" any more than we can declare someone "native" who was not born there. Since the term has been applied to churches which have been "indigenized," it is not adequate to describe the kind of churches being considered.

Furthermore, for those who live in Latin America, because everything *indígena* refers to Indian matters, it is awkward applying it to non-Indian Christian groups.

INDEPENDENT.   Current   terminology   regarding   the corresponding African churches refers to them most often as "African Independent Churches." But *independence* refers only to relationships, not origins nor the degree to which the church is identified with the culture. Independent churches exist in Latin America that are not much more than independent franchises of U.S.-style churches. And many of the churches covered in this study are linked with others in denominations.

NATIVISTIC. This is a term more often used with reference to movements in Africa or Oceania. Like *indigenous* in Latin America, it may be pejorative for some. The image may be that of the bizarre, possibly involving ancestor worship or other non-Christian elements.

NEW RELIGIOUS MOVEMENTS. This phrase is favored in sociological, anthropological and religious studies of the new religions. But it is too broad for our purposes. It includes quasi- and non-Christian cults. We preferred to limit our discussion of Latin American movements basically to those within the Christian sphere.

SECOND GENERATION CHURCHES. This expression employed by the DAWN (Discipling a Whole Nation) movement (Montgomery 1983), refers to what we described. But the picture that this phrase conveys may be that of churches founded by second generation Christians within the same movement; for example, churches founded by Baptist Christians in a country following a "first generation" of churches, planted by Baptist missionaries. To avoid possible misunderstanding we hesitate to employ this term in a definitive manner.

SECTS. This word bears a longer history. Sociologists may use it quite antiseptically. That is, it refers to any congregation outside the established Church or the main stream of Christianity-- either organizationally or theologically. But despite its use in an unbiased way, it has a pejorative connotation. Latin American Protestants resent the current Roman Catholic references to most non-Catholics as members of "sects."

General Terms

AUTOCHTHONOUS. See discussion of this term in section above.

BARRIO. A neighborhood or section of a city or town in Spanish-speaking countries. Also in the U.S., especially in the Southwest, a Spanish-speaking quarter or neighborhood in a city or town.

B.E.C. (BASIC ECCLESIAL COMMUNITIES). See text, page 16.

CAUDILLISMO. A style of governing of a *caudillo*--a dictator-type leader who guides and commands his people.

CHARISMATIC.   Constituting charisma which is an extraordinary power or a spiritual gift given to a Christian by the Holy Spirit for the good of the Church and its work (Rom. 12:6-8; 1 Cor. 12:4-11, 28-30; Eph. 4:7-12). These are Christians who emphasize the gifts of the Spirit, but unlike traditional Pentecostals, they may not consider any one gift (e.g. speaking in tongues) as evidence of the filling of the Holy Spirit. They often remain in their respective non-charismatic churches and denominations, not always separating to form their own groups.

CONTEXTUAL/CONTEXTUALIZATION/CONTEXTUAL-IZED. Expression of Christianity in the culture of the people who have adopted it.

CULT. A system of religious beliefs and rituals, involving formal religious veneration, whose adherents are regarded as unorthodox or spurious.

ECUMENICAL MOVEMENT. The movement is an effort by the non-Roman Catholic historic churches to relate more closely to the World Council of Churches and other regional and local councils.

FETISHISM. Belief in the magical power of certain objects.

FOLK RELIGION. Beliefs and practices arising out of the customs of a people, as opposed to more formally developed religious systems.

GRASS-ROOTS CHURCHES. See text, page 12.

HACIENDA. Large estates that constitute the chief economic and social unit that functions in the rural areas of most Latin American countries, called *fazendas* in Brazil.

HISTORIC DENOMINATIONS OR GROUPS. Denominations with some historic roots in the Protestant Reformation of the 16th century.

INDEPENDENT. See discussion of the term in first section of this Glossary.

INDIGENOUS. See discussion of the term in first section of this Glossary as well as Alan Tippett's definition on page 189 of text.

LATIN AMERICA. See text, page 15.

LIBERATION THEOLOGY OR THEOLOGIES. A theological phenomenon in Latin America, tracing its beginnings to the late 1960s in the Roman Catholic Church, later also influencing some Protestants. According to its proponents, it attempts to analyze

Christian activity (praxis) through sociological (often marxist) analysis, leading to efforts to liberate the socially oppressed.

MACHISMO. A cultural characteristic stressing male pride, virility, and aggressiveness in political, social, religious, and personal situations with respect to women. It is related to Spanish pride and personal sense of honor.

NATIVISTIC. See discussion of term in first section of this Glossary.

NEW DENOMINATIONS. See text, page 39.

NEW RELIGIOUS MOVEMENTS (NRMS). See discussion of term in first section of this Glossary.

NOMINALISM. In general usage, a theory that no universal essences in reality exist. For the more restricted use of the term in this work, identification with the church or religious movement without active participation in it.

PENTECOSTAL CHURCHES. Evangelical Protestants characterized principally by emphasizing the baptism of the Spirit as an experience after conversion, demonstrated primarily by speaking in tongues.

PIETISM. A movement among Protestants beginning in the 17th and 18th centuries in Germany. There is a decided emphasis on the individual Christian's good works and holy life.

POPULAR RELIGION AND POPULAR RELIGIOSITY.
See text, chapter 9, beginning on page 147.

PROTESTANTE. Spanish for "Protestant."

SACRALIZATION. Attaching sacred or holy attributes to an
object or practice, often when such attributes are not warranted.

SECOND GENERATION CHURCHES. See discussion in the
first section of this Glossary.

SECTS. See discussion of the term in the first section of the
Glossary.

SYNCRETISM. See text, page 1.

WORLDVIEW. A comprehensive concept of the meaning of life
and the world from a specific standpoint.

BIBLIOGRAPHY

Acevedo, Carlos Alvear. "La Iglesia Mexicana en el período 1900 - 1992." *Historia general de la Iglesia en América Latina,* Vol. 5, CEHILA. Mexico: Ediciones Paulinas, 1984.

Aeschelman, Gordon. *Global Trends.* Downers Grove, IL: InterVarsity Press, 1990.

Alcancemos las etnias de México. Toluca, Mexico: Operación Samaria, 1993.

Allen, Roland. *The Spontaneous Expansion of the Church.* Grand Rapids: Eerdmans, 1963 (reprinting).

Alvarado, Alexis. Interview, April 1994, Costa Rica.

Alvarez, Carmelo. Interview, March 1992, Costa Rica.

Amanecer (Buenos Aires, Argentina) October 1992.

Anabalón, Bishop Francisco. Interview, May 1994, Chile.

Anderson, Gerald H. "A Moratorium on Missionaries?" *Mission Trends No. 1,* eds. Gerald H. Anderson and Thomas F. Stransky, New York: Paulist Press, and Grand Rapids: Eerdmans, 1974, 133-141.

Anderson, Gerald, and Stransky, Thomas, eds. *Mission Trends No. 1.* New York: Paulist Press, and Grand Rapids: Eerdmans, 1974.

_____. *Mission Trends No. 2: Evangelization.* New York: Paulist Press, and Grand Rapids: Eerdmans, 1975.

_____. *Mission Trends No. 3: Third World Theologies.* New York: Paulist Press, and Grand Rapids: Eerdmans, 1976.

Assman, Hugo. *La iglesia electrónica.* San José, Costa Rica: Editorial DEI, 1988.

Ayerra, P.J. *Los protestantes en Venezuela.* Caracas, Venezuela: Ediciones Tripode,1980.

Azevedo, Dermi. "Católicos rezam com fé. Em outras igrejas." *Jornal da Tarde.* São Paulo, February 13, 1991.

Bamat, Thomas. "Will Latin America Become Protestant?" *Maryknoll,* July 1992, 10-21.

Barbosa, Roberto. "The Gospel with Bread: an Interview with Brazilian Pentecostalist Manoel de Mello." *Mission Trends No. 2,* eds. Anderson, Gerald, and Stransky, Thomas, 1975, 145-154.

Barrett, David. *Schism and Renewal in Africa: an Analysis of 6000 Contemporary Religious Movements*. Nairobi: Oxford University Press, 1968.

_____. "The Status of Global Mission." *International Bulletin of Missionary Research*. 1994, 24-25.

_____, ed. *World Christian Encyclopedia*. New York: Oxford University Press, 1982.

Barrientos, Alberto. Interview, June 1993, Costa Rica.

Bastian, Jean Pierre. *Breve historia de la Iglesia en América Latina*. Mexico: CUPSA, 1986.

_____. *Los Disidentes: sociedades protestantes y revolución en México, 1872-1911*. Mexico: Fondo de Cultura Económica, El Colegio de México, 1989.

_____. *Protestantismo y sociedad en México*. Mexico: CUPSA, 1983.

_____. "Protestantism in Latin America." *The Church in Latin America 1492 - 1992*, ed. Dussell, Enrique. Maryknoll, NY: Orbis, 1992.

Bavinck, J. H. *An Introduction to the Science of Missions*. Philadelphia: Presbyterian and Reformed Publishing Co, 1960.

Berg, Clayton L., Jr. and Pretiz, Paul E. *The Gospel People of Latin America*. Monrovia, CA and Miami, FL: MARC/LAM, 1992.

Bergsma, Paul. *Religiosidad Popular*. Unpublished, undated paper.

Beyerhaus, Peter. "The 3 Self Formula -- Is It Built on Biblical Foundations?" *Readings in Dynamic Indigeneity*, eds. Charles Kraft and Tom Wisley. Pasadena: William Carey Library, 1979, 15-30.

Bieske, Sigifredo W. *El explosivo crecimiento de la Iglesia evangélica en Costa Rica*. Costa Rica: By the author, undated.

Bittencourt Filho, José. "Matriz religiosa brasileira -- notas ecuménicas." *Tempo e Presença*. Rio de Janeiro, July - August, 1992.

Bollati, Miguel. Interview, June 1994, Argentina.

Bonhoffer, Dietrich. *Life Together*. New York: Harper & Brothers, 1954.

Bottam, Elenilce. "Evangélicos e umbandistas em 'guerra santa.'" *O Globo*, Rio de Janeiro, October 23, 1988, 24.

Boudeijnse, Barbara, Droogers, André, and Kamsteeg, Frans, eds. *Algo más que el opio -- una lectura antropológica del pentecostalismo latinoamericano y caribeño*. San José, Costa Rica: DEI, 1991.

Buhlman, Walbert. *The Third Church: an Analysis of the Present and Future*. Maryknoll, NY: Orbis, 1977.

Burgess, Stanley, and Gary B. McGee, eds. *Dictionary of Pentecostal and Charismatic Movements*. Grand Rapids: Zondervan, 1990.

Bush, Luis. "Brazil, a Sleeping Giant Awakens." *Mission Frontiers Bulletin*. Pasadena. January-February 1994, pp. 34-37.

_____. *The Challenge of Latin America*. Address given in Redwood City, CA., October 11, 1989.

_____. *Funding Third World Missions*. Wheaton, IL: World Evangelical Fellowship Missions Commission, 1990.

Cabezas, Rita. *Desenmascarado*. San José, Costa Rica: Published by the author, 1986.

Cabrera, Omar. Interview, June 1994, Argentina.

Cárdenas, Marco. Interview, August 1992, Ecuador.

Carmona, Ramón. Interview, September 1992, Colombia.

Casteñón S., Julio. "A New Sound from Mexico." *Latin America Evangelist*, January-March 1994, 6-11.

CEHILA. *Historia general de la Iglesia na América Latina, Vol. V.* Mexico: Ediciones Paulinas, 1984.

CLADE II. América Latina y la evangelización en los años 80. Place of publication unidentified,1979.

Comblin, José. "Brazil: Base Communities in the Northeast." *New Face of the Church in Latin America.* ed., Cook, Guillermo. Maryknoll, NY: Orbis, 1944, 202-225.

Cook, Guillermo, ed. *New Face of the Church in Latin America.* Maryknoll, NY: Orbis, 1994.

Cox, Harvey. *Religion in the Secular City.* New York: Simon & Shuster, 1984.

_____. *The Seduction of the Spirit: the Use and Misuse of People's Religion.* New York: Simon & Shuster, 1973.

"Crecimiento en San Salvador." *Noticiero MILAMEX,* January 31, 1989, 4.

Cruz, Saúl. *Misión Urbana.* Paper presented at CLADE III in Quito, Ecuador, August 1992.

da Gama Leite, Tácito, Filho. *Heresias, seitas e denominacões: O fenômeno dos movimentos religiosos.* Rio de Janeiro: Junta de Educação Religiosa e Publicações da Convenção Batista Brasileira (JUERP), 1993.

_____. *Seitas neopentecostais.* Rio de Janeiro: JUERP, 1990.

Dávila, Sérgio. "A perua de Deus." *Revista da Folha,* São Paulo, May 22, 1994, 12 - 15

Dayton, Donald. "'Evangelical:' More Puzzling than you Think." *Occasional Papers No. 29.* Collegeville, MN, May 1988.

_____. "Yet Another Layer of the Onion, or Opening the Ecumenical Door to Let the Riffraff in." *Ecumenical Review*, January 1988, 88-101.

DAWN. See "*Despertar '93: el Desarrollo de la Iglesia evangélica 1982 - 1992 y los desafíos para el año 2000*. San Salvador: Confraternidad Evangélica Salvadoreña, 1993.

de la Torre, René and Fortuna, Patricia. "La construcción de una identidad nacional en la Luz del Mundo." *Cristianismo y Sociedad, No. 109*, 33-35.

Deiros, Pablo. *Historia del cristianismo en la América Latina*. Buenos Aires: Fraternidad Teológica Latinoamericana, 1992.

_____. Interview, May 1994, Argentina.

De León, Víctor. Quoted in Villafañe, Eldin. *The Liberating Spirit*. Lanham, MD:University Press of America, 1992.

de Mello, Paul Lutero. Interview, June 1994, Brazil.

Despertar '93: el Desarrollo de la Iglesia evangélica 1982 - 1992 y los desafíos para el año 2000. San Salvador: Confraternidad Evangélica Salvadoreña, 1993.

Directorio de iglesias evangélicas de Caracas.   Coalición de Iglesias Evangélicas de Caracas, y Amanecer, 1993.

Directorio de iglesias, organizaciones y ministerios del movimiento protestante: Guatemala. San José, Costa Rica: IINDEF, and Guatemala: SEPAL, 1981.

Directorio evangélico de Cali. Medellín, Colombia: Cristo para la Ciudad, 1992.

Directorio evangélico de Barranquilla. Medellín, Colombia: Cristo para la Ciudad, 1991.

Directorio evangélico de Cartagena. Medellín, Colombia: Cristo para la Ciudad, 1990.

Domínguez, Roberto. *Pioneros de Pentecostés*. (Two volumes).   Miami: Literatura Evangélica, 1971.

Douglas, J.D. *Let the Earth Hear His Voice*. International Congress on World Evangelization, Lausanne, Switzerland. Minneapolis: World Wide, undated.

Dussell, Enrique. *A History of the Church in Latin America, Colonialism to Liberation*. Grand Rapids: Eerdmans, 1981.

_____, ed. *The Church in Latin America, 1492 - 1992*. Maryknoll, NY: Orbis, 1992.

Dyrness, William. *Emerging Voices in Global Christian Theology*. Grand Rapids: Zondervan, 1994.

_____. *Learning Theology from the Third World*.   Grand Rapids: Zondervan, 1990.

El Puente (bulletin), Buenos Aires, 1992

Escobar, J. Samuel. "Las nuevas fronteras de la misión." Paper presented at CLADE III, Quito, Ecuador, 1992.

_____. "The Church in Latin America after Five Hundred Years: an Evangelical Missiological Perspective." *New Face of the Church in Latin America*. ed. Cook, Guillermo. Maryknoll, NY: Orbis, 1994, 25-37

_____. "Conflict of Interpretations of Popular Protestantism." *New Face of the Church in Latin America*. ed. Cook, Guillermo. Maryknoll, NY: Orbis, 1994, 99-111.

_____. "Los Evangélicos: Nueva Leyenda Negra." Pamphlet, 1991.

Esta Semana. San José, Costa Rica, November 3-10, 1992.

Estudios de casos de crecimiento de la Iglesia Evangélica en la Gran Ciudad de México. Mexico: VELA and PROCADES/ IDEA, 1989.

Fabio, Caio. "Avivamiento 'a la latinoamericana.'" *El Puente*. Buenos Aires, November 1992.

Fernandes, Rubem César. *Censo institucional evangélico CIN 1992*. Rio de Janeiro: ISER, 1992.

Festinger, Leon, Riecken, Henry W. and Schachter, Stanley. *When Prophecy Fails*. New York: Harper & Row, 1956.

Flores, Héctor. "Centro Cultural Calacoaya." *Estudio de casos del crecimiento de la Iglesia Evangélica en la Gran Ciudad de México*. Mexico: VELA and PROCADES/IDEA, 1989.

Foerester, Rolf. *Pentecostalismo entre los indigenas del cono sur*, undated mimeographed document.

Fontaine, Arturo and Beyer, Harald. "Retrato del movimiento evangélico a la luz de las encuestas de opinión pública." *Estudios Públicos, No. 44*, Santiago, Chile, primavera, 1991.

Francescon, Louis. "Behold, his soul which is lifted up is not upright in him: but the just shall live by his faith," Tract with personal account of the beginnings of the Italian Assemblies and the Congregação Cristã, undated.

Freston, Paul. "Brasil: en busca de un proyecto evangélico corporativo." *De la marginación al compromiso: Los evangélicos y la política en América Latina*, compiler Padilla, C. René. Buenos Aires: Fraternidad Teológica Latinoameri-cana, 1991, pp. 21-36.

Frigerio, Alejandro (compiler). *El pentecostalismo en la Argentina*. Buenos Aires: Centro Editor de América Latina, 1994.

Fuller, W. Harold. *Church-Mission Dynamics*. Pasadena: William Carey Library, 1980.

García, Israel. Interview, July 1991, Costa Rica.

Gaxiola, Maclovio. *Historia de la Iglesia Apostólica de la Fe en Cristo Jesús.* Mexico: Librería Latinoamericana, 1964.

Gaxiola, Manuel. *The Serpent and the Dove.* Pasadena: William Carey Library, 1970.

Giménez, Héctor. Interview, May 1994, Argentina.

Glasser, Arthur, Hiebert, Paul, Wagner, C. Peter, and Winter, Ralph. *Crucial Dimensions in World Evangelization.* Pasadena: William Carey Library, 1976.

Gomes, Wilson. "Demônios do fim so século: curas, ofertas, exorcismos na Igreja Universal do Reino de Deus." *Cadernos de CEAS*, No. 146, 47-63.

González, Justo L. *The Development of Christianity in the Latin Caribbean.* Grand Rapids: Eerdmans, 1969.

Greenway, Roger. *Apostles to the City.* Grand Rapids: Baker, 1978.

_____. Letter to the authors, 1995.

Grigg, Viv. "Squatters: the Most Responsive Unreached Bloc." *Urban Mission*, May, 1989, 41-50.

Grellert, Manfred, Myers, Bryant L. and McAlpine, Thomas H., eds. *Al servicio del Reino.* San José, Costa Rica: Visión Mundial, 1992.

Gros, Jeffrey. Review of *El Protestantismo fundamentalista: una experiencia ambigua para América Latina,* by Florenciano Galindo. In *Missiology*, October 1993, 492.

Guevara, José David. "¡Ni un paso atrás!" *La Nación*, Sección *Viva*, Costa Rica, November 8, 1992, 1-2.

Hatch, R. Allen. "The Bogotá Consultation -- Beyond Interdependence." *Latin America Pulse*, May 1981.

Hesselgrave, David J. and Rommen, Edward. *Contextualization: Meanings, Methods and Models.* Grand Rapids: Baker Book House, 1989.

Hiebert, Paul G. *Anthropological Insights for Missionaries.* Grand Rapids: Baker, 1985.

_____. "Critical Contextualization." *International Bulletin of Missionary Research*, July 1987, 104-112.

_____. "Popular Religions." *Towards the Twenty-first Century in Christian Mission*, eds. Phillips, James M. and Coote, Robert T., eds., 1993, 253-266.

História das Assembleias de Deus no Brasil. No author or publisher listed. Rio de Janeiro, 1960.

Hodges, Melvin L. *The Indigenous Church.* Springfield, MO: Gospel Publishing House, 1953.

Hoff, Paul B. "Chile's Pentecostals Face Problems Due to Isolation." *Evangelical Missions Quarterly*, July 1991, pp. 244-249.

_____. "Las crisis del pentecostalismo chileno." *Alternativa*, Puerto Rico, no. 16, 1993, pp. 22-25.

_____. Interview, Santiago, 1994, Chile.

Holland, Clifton H. *Directory of Hispanic Protestant Churches in Southern California*. Pasadena: Hispanic Association of Theological Education, 1986.

_____. Interview, September 1994, Costa Rica.

Hollenweger, Walter J. *Pentecost between Black and White*. Belfast: Christian Journals, 1974.

_____. *The Pentecostals: the Charismatic Movement in the Churches*. Minneapolis: Augsburg, 1972.

_____. "The Theological Challenge of Indigenous Churches." *Exploring New Religious Movements*. eds. Walls, A.F. and Shenk, Wilbert. Elkhart, IN: Mission Focus, 1990, 163-167.

Horrell, Scott. Interview, June 1994, Brazil.

Hortal, Jesus. *Nacionalismo Religioso no Brasil? A Igreja Católica Apostólica Brasileira (ICAB) e suas Ramnificações*, undated. Paper amplifying material in "As Igrejas Brasileiras" in *Cadernos do ISER, No. 23*, Rio de Janeiro.

Howard, David M. *By the Power of the Holy Spirit*. Downers Grove, IL: InterVarsity Press, 1973.

"Igreja Universal del Reino de Dios." *Folha Universal*, June 5, 1994.

Itioka, Neuza. *Os Deuses da Umbanda*. São Paulo: ABU Editora, 1987.

"Jesus na veia." *Veja*. São Paulo, June 8, 1994, 56-58.

Johnson, Paul. *Modern Times*. New York: Harper & Row, 1983.

_____. *A History of Christianity*. New York: Penguin Books, 1976.

Johnstone, Patrick. *Operation World*. Grand Rapids: Zondervan, 1993. The 1978 edition, from which there is a quotation, was published by STL

Kamm, Thomas. "Evangelical, Stressing 'Cures' for Masses' Misery, Make Inroads in Roman Catholic Latin America." *Wall Street Journal*, Oct. 16, 1991, A12.

Kasdorf, Hans. "Indigenous Church Principles: Survey of Origin and Development." *Readings in Dynamic Indigeneity*. eds. Kraft, Charles, and Wisley, Tom. Pasadena: William Carey Library, 1979, 71-86.

Kessler, John B. *A Study of the Older Protestant Missions and Churches in Peru and Chile*. Goes (The Netherlands): Oosterbaan & le Cointre N.V., 1967.

_____. *A Summary of the Costa Rican Evangelical Crises* (English edition). Pasadena: IDEA/Church Growth Studies Program, 1990.

_____. *Historia de la evangelización en el Perú.* Lima, Peru: El Inca, undated.

_____. Conversation, Costa Rica, 1994, October.

Kivitz, Ed René. Interview, June 1994, Brazil.

Kraft, Charles, and Wisley, Thomas, eds. *Readings in Dynamic Indigeneity.* Pasadena: William Carey Library, 1979.

Kraft, Charles. *Christianity in Culture.* Maryknoll, NY: Orbis, 1973.

_____. *Christianity with Power.* Ann Arbor: Servant Publishers, 1989.

_____. "Dynamic Equivalence Theologizing." *Readings in Dynamic Indigeneity.* eds. Kraft, Charles and Wisley, Tom. Pasadena: William Carey Library, 1979, 258-285.

_____. "Measuring Indigeneity." *Readings in Dynamic Indigeneity.* eds. Kraft, Charles and Wisley, Tom. Pasadena: William Carey Library, 1979, 118-152.

Kraft, Larry. Interview, June 1994, Brazil.

La hora de Dios para Guatemala. Guatemala: SEPAL, 1984.

La iglesia evangélica en números: resultados estadísticos del censo de iglesias de Lima y Callao. Lima, Peru: PROMIES, 1993.

Lalive, Christian. *Refugio de las masas.* Santiago de Chile: Editorial del Pacífico. (English edition: *Haven of the Masses.* London: Lutterworth), 1968.

Landim, Leilah, ed. *Sinais dos tempos: Igrejas e seitas no Brasil.* Rio de Janeiro: ISER, 1989.

Landrey, J. Paul. Letter of February 4, 1994.

Maranatha. San José, Costa Rica, No. 114, 1991, 17.

"Los Mitas están en Costa Rica." *Maranatha,* year 9, No. 116, San José, Costa Rica. An article based on research by Mario Marín.

Marcom, John, Jr. "The Fire Down South." *Forbes.* Oct. 15, 1990, 56-71.

Mariz, Cecilia. "Religion and Poverty in Brazil." *New Face in Latin America,* ed. Cook, Guillermo. Maryknoll, NY: Orbis, 1994, 75-81.

Martin, David. *Tongues of Fire: the Explosion of Protestantism in Latin America.* Cambridge, MA: Basil Blackwell, 1990.

Martínez, Abelino and Samandú, Luis. "Acerca del desafío pentecostal en Centroamérica." *Protestantismo y procesos sociales en Centroamérica.* Samandú, Luis, compilador. San José, Costa Rica: EDUCA, 1990, 39-65.

Marzal, Manuel. *Los caminos religiosos de los inmigrantes en la Gran Lima.* Lima, Peru: Pontificia Universidad Católica del Perú, Fondo Editorial, 1988.

Maust, John. *Cities of Change.* Miami: LAM, 1984.

McGavran, Donald. *Church Growth in Mexico.* Grand Rapids: Eerdmans, 1963.

McIntosh, Estuardo. *Introducción a la misiología latinoameri-cana.* Lima, Peru: PUSEL, 1986.

Merino, Pedro. Interview, August 1992, Ecuador.

México hoy y mañana. Directorio evangélico de la gran ciudad de México. Mexico: VELA and IMDELA, 1987.

Noticiero MILAMEX. Mexico City, January 31, 1993, 3.

Miller, David. "Protestants Work toward Reconciliation in Chile." *News Network International News Service*, July 12, 1993, 20-25.

_____, ed. *Coming of Age: Protestantism in Contem-porary Latin America.* Lanham, MD: University Press of America, 1994.

Montgomery, James. "Los Hechos de Crecimiento." *La hora de Dios para Guatemala.* Guatemala: SEPAL, 1983, 73-134.

Moore, Donald T. "Puerto Rico para Cristo." *Sondeos, No. 43*, 1969, 3/37-4/40.

Moreno, Pedro. "Una crítica a los evangélicos latinoamericanos." *Boletín CEV, No. VI*, Caracas, 1994, A1-A6.

Moya, Ronald. "El controversial mundo del pastor Zacarías." *La Nación*, Costa Rica, Aug. 9, 1992, 6A-7A.

Moya, Ronald, and Rodríguez, Armando. "Apedreado templo en Puntarenas." *La Nación*, Costa Rica, July 18, 1991, 10a

Muñoz, Alvaro. Interview, 1992, Costa Rica.

"Muy linda celebración davídica." *Maranatha*, year 9, San José, Costa Rica, 17.

Nasbitt, John, and Aburdene, Patricia. *Megatrends 2000.* New York: William Morrow, 1990

Neil, Stephen. *The Story of the Christian Church in India and Pakistan.* Grand Rapids: Eerdmans, 1970.

Nelson, Marlin I. *Readings in Third World Missions.* Pasadena: William Carey Library, 1978.

Nelson, Reed E. "Five Principles of Indigenous Church Organization." *Missiology*, January, 1989. 39-51.

Nelson, Wilton M. *Diccionario de la Historia de la Iglesia.* Miami: Editorial Caribe, 1989.

_____. *History of Protestantism in Costa Rica.* Eugene, OR: Institute of Church Growth, 1963.

Newbigin, Leslie. Preface of *Toward the 21st Century in Christian Mission*, eds. Phillips, James M. and Coote, Robert T., Grand Rapids: Eerdmans, 1993, 1-6.

Nida, Eugene A. "African Influence in the Religious Life of Latin America." *Practical Anthropology*, July - August, 1960.

_____. *The Indigenous Church in Latin America*. New York: CCLA, 1960.

Niebuhr, H. Richard. *Christ and Culture*. New York: Harper & Row, 1951.

Nieva, Samuel. Interview, August 1993, Costa Rica.

Nieves, Gilberto. Interview, August 1992, Ecuador.

"No soy político, lo que hice fue predicar." *Maranatha, No. 145*, 1994, 8.

Núñez, Belsazar. Interview, August 1992, Costa Rica.

Núñez, Emilio A. and Taylor, William D. *Crisis in Latin America, an Evangelical Perspective*. Chicago: Moody Press, 1989.

Operación Samaria, 1993, 56-57.

Owen, Joseph. Interview, July 1993, Costa Rica.

Padilla, C. René. "New Actors on the Political Scene in Latin America." *New Face of the Church in Latin America*. ed. Cook, Guillermo. Maryknoll, NY: Orbis, 1994, 82-95.

_____. "¿Prosperidad o fidelidad?" *Orientación Cristiana* (a supplement of *Iglesia y Misión*), October-December, 1993, 1, 8.

_____. Interview, July 1986, Argentina.

_____, ed. *De la marginación al compromiso*. Buenos Aires: Fraternidad Teológica Latinoamericana, 1991.

Padilla, Washington. *La Iglesia y los dioses modernos: Historia del protestantismo en Ecuador*. Quito, Ecuador: Corporación Editorial Nacional, 1989.

Pagura, Bishop Federico, Interview, March 1992, Costa Rica.

Pardo, Héctor. Interview, September 1992, Colombia.

Paredes, Rubén (Tito). *El Evangelio en platos de barro*. Lima, Peru: Ediciones Presencia, 1989.

_____. "Popular Religiosity: a Protestant Perspective." *Missiology*, April 1992, 205-220.

Pate, Larry. *From Every People*. Monrovia, CA: MARC, 1989.

Pecho, Pablo. Interview, May 1991, Costa Rica.

Pérez, José Luis. *¿Por qué se van los católicos?* Lima, Peru: Conferencia Episcopal Peruana, 1992.

Perú para Cristo. Lima, Peru: I Congreso Nacional Evangelístico Misionero, 1993.

Perfil del estado del Cristianismo en Colombia. Bogotá: SEPAL, 1980.

Phillips, James M. and Coote, Robert T., eds. *Toward the 21st Century in Christian Mission.* Grand Rapids: Eerdmans, 1993.

Piepkorn, Arthur. *Profiles in Belief: the Religious Bodies of the U.S. and Canada.* New York: Harper & Row, 1979.

Pierson, Paul E. Letter to the authors, 1994.

Pinto, Silas. *As Igrejas da gran São Paulo.* Published by the author. São Paulo, Brazil, 1985.

Pittman, Richard S. and Grimes, Joseph E., eds. *Ethnologue.* Dallas: Summer Institute of Linguistics, 1988.

Pretiz, Paul E. "Gospel Radio's Increasing Impact in Latin America." *Latin America Evangelist,* May-June, 1977, 2 - 3.

Prien, Hans-Jürgen. *La historia del Cristianismo en América Latina.* Salamanca: Ediciones Sígueme, 1985.

PROCADES (Proyecto Centroamericano de Estudios Socio-Religiosos). San José, Costa Rica, 1981.

Prokopchuk, Alberto. Interview, June 1994, Argentina.

Puebla: III Conferencia General del Episcopado Latinoame-ricano. Bogotá: CELAM. Second edition, 1979.

Puente bulletin, Quito, Ecuador, 1980.

Ramachandra, Vinoth. "The Honor of Listening: Indispensable for Mission." *Evangelical Missions Quarterly,* October 1994, 404-409.

Ramos, Marcos Antonio. *Protestantism and Revolution in Cuba.* Miami: University of Miami, 1989.

_____. *Panorama del protestantismo en Cuba.* San José, Costa Rica: Editorial Caribe, 1986.

Read, William R. *New Patterns of Church Growth in Brazil.* Grand Rapids: Eerdmans, 1965.

Rengifo, Rolando. "Centro de Fe, Esperanza y Amor." *Estudios de casos de crecimiento de la Iglesia evangélica en la Gran Ciudad de México.* Mexico: VELA and IDEA/PROLADES, 1989.

Renshaw, Parke. "A New Religion for Brazilians." *Practical Anthropology.* July-August 1966, 126 - 138.

Ribeiro, Claudio. "El poder en el nombre de Jesús." *Signos de Vida.* Lima, Peru, 1992, 10-14.

Ríos, Asdrúbal. *De los pequeños principios a las grandes realizaciones.* Maracaibo, Venezuela: Editorial Libertador, 1976.

Robertson, Rolando, ed. *Sociology of Religion*. Baltimore: Penguin Books, 1969.

Rooy, Sidney. Interview, July 1994, Costa Rica.

Ruiz Luz, Sérgio. "Crente pra frente: quem são os evangélicos que pregam Jesus e rock' n' roll na TV." *Veja*, São Paulo, April 13, 1994, 18-21.

"Ruibal y el tema de la salud." *Maranatha*, year 11, No. 138, San José, Costa Rica, 12.

Said, Dalton. Interview, June 1991, Costa Rica.

Samandú, Luis F. *Protestantismo y Procesos Sociales en Centroamérica*. San José, Costa Rica: EDUCA, 1990.

Saracco, Norberto. *Directorio y censo de iglesias evangélicas de la Ciudad de Buenos Aires*. Buenos Aires: Directorio Evangélico, 1993.

Schuffenger, Humberto L. "La función de la religión en el gobierno militar y en las fuerzas armadas y del orden en Chile." *Misión*, March 1986, 13-20.

Schultze, Quentin. "Orality and Power in Latin American Protestantism." *Coming of Age: Protestantism in Contemporary Latin America*. ed., Daniel R. Miller, ed. Lanham, MD: University Press of America, 1994, 65-85.

Scott, David Kenneth. "New Religious Movements in Peru." *Latin America Evangelist*, January-March 1987, 14-15.

_____. *Los Israelitas del Nuevo Pacto Universal: una historia*. Lima, Peru: PUSEL, 1990a.

_____. *Los Israelitas del Nuevo Pacto Universal: símbolos y tradiciones*. Lima, Peru: PUSEL, 1990b.

Scott, Lindy. *Salt of the Earth: a Socio-political History of Mexico City Evangelical Protestants (1964-1991)*. Mexico: Editorial Kyrios, 1991.

Shaull, Richard. Undated copy of an address given in Nicaragua.

Shenk, David A., ed. *Ministry in Partnership with African Independent Churches*. Elkhart. IN: Mennonite Board of Missions, 1991.

_____,ed. *Ministry of Missions to African Independent Churches*. Elkhart, IN: Mennonite Board of Missions, 1987.

Shenk, Wilbert R. "The Contribution of the Study of New Religious Movements to Missiology." Exploring New Religious Movements. Elkhart, IN: Mission Focus, 1990, 180-197.

Sheridan, Mary Beth. "Vaticano examina causas de deserción de católicos." *El Nuevo Heraldo*, Miami, April 6, 1991, 6a.

Silva-Silva, Darío. *El Hombre que escapó del infierno*. Bogotá, Colombia: Published by the author, 1991.

_____. Interview, September 1992, Colombia.

Smalley, William A. "Cultural Implications of an Indigenous Church." *Readings in Dynamic Indigeneity*. eds, Kraft, Charles, and Wisley, Tom. Pasadena: William Carey Library, 1979, 31-51.

Snyder, Howard A. *The Problem of Wineskins*. Downers Grove, IL: InterVarsity Press, 1975.

Stackhouse, Max. "Pietists and Contextualists: the Indian Situation." *Christian Century*, January 20, 1993, 56 - 58.

Steuernagel, Valdir R., compiler. *La misión de la iglesia: una vista panorámica*. San José, Costa Rica: Visión Mundial, 1992.

Stoll, David. *Is Latin America Turning Protestant?* Berkeley, CA: UCLA Press, 1990.

Strachan, R. Kenneth. *The Inescapable Calling*. Grand Rapids: Eerdmans, 1968.

Suazo, Miguel. Interview, August 1992, Guatemala.

Talavera, Arturo Fontaine and Beyer, Harald. "Retrato del movimiento evangélico a la luz de las encuestas de opinión pública." *Estudios Públicos*. Spring, 1991.

Tippett, Alan. "Indigenous Principles in Mission Today." *Readings in Dynamic Indigeneity*. eds, Kraft, Charles, and Wisley, Tom. Pasadena: William Carey Library, 1979, 52-70.

Turner, Harold W. "Religious Movements in Primal (or Tribal) Societies." *Mission Focus*. September 1981, 45-55.

Trextler, Edgar. *The New Face of Missions*. St. Louis: Concordia, 1973.

Vaccaro, Gabriel. *Aportes del pentecostalismo al movimiento ecuménico*. Quito, Ecuador: CLAI, 1991.

Valverde, Jaime. *Las sectas en Costa Rica -- pentecostalismo y conflicto social*. San José, Costa Rica: DEI, 1990.

Vaughn, John N. *The World's 20 Largest Churches*. Grand Rapids: Baker, 1984.

Vera, Oscar, ed. *Directorio evangélico de Medellín*. Medellín, Colombia: Cristo para la Ciudad, 1993.

Vergara, Ignacio. *El protestantismo en Chile*. Santiago, Chile: Editorial del Pacífico, 1962.

Verkuyl, J. *Contemporary Missiology, an Introduction*. Grand Rapids: Eerdmans, 1978.

Villafañe, Eldin. *The Liberating Spirit: towards a Hispanic Pentecostal Social Ethic*. Lanham, MD: University Press of America, 1992.

Wagner, C. Peter. *Cuidado, alli vienen los pentecostales*. Miami: Editorial Vida, 1973.

_____. *On the Crest of the Wave*. Ventura, CA: Regal Books, 1983.

_____. "Spiritual Power in Urban Evangelism: Dynamic Lessons from Argentina." *Evangelical Missions Quarterly*, April 1991, 130-137.

_____. *The Third Wave of the Spirit, Encountering the Power of Signs and Wonders*. Ann Arbor, MI: Vine Books, 1988.

_____. "Those Amazing Post-Denominational Churches." *Ministries Today*, July-August 1994, 49-53.

_____. "Training in the Streets of Chile." *Crucial Dimensions in World Evangelization*. Glasser, Hiebert, Wagner, Winter. Pasadena: William Carey Library, 1976, 430-437.

Walls, A.F. and Shenk, Wilbert. *Exploring New Religious Movements*. Elkhart, IN: Mission Focus, 1990.

Wattenburg, Daniel. "Protestants Create an Altered State." *Insight on the News*, July 16, 1990, 9-17

Weber, Max. *The Protestant Ethic and the Spirit of Capitalism*. New York: Scribners, 1958.

Wesley, Luis. Interview. June 1994, Brazil.

Westmeier, Karl-Wilhelm. "Themes of Pentecostal Expansion in Latin America." *International Bulletin of Missionary Research*, April 1993, 72-78.

Willems, Emilio. *Followers of the New Faith: Culture Change and the Rise of Protestantism in Brazil and Chile*. Nashville: Vanderbilt University Press, 1967.

_____. "Religious Pluralism and Class Structure: Brazil and Chile." *Sociology of Religion*, ed. Roland Robertson, 1969, 195-217.

Wilson, Bryan. *Religion in Secular Society*. Harmonsworth, UK: Penguin Books, 1969.

Wilson, Everett. Interview, 1993, Costa Rica.

Winn, Peter. *Americas, the Changing Face of Latin America and the Caribbean*. New York: Pantheon Books, 1992.

Winter, Ralph. *The 25 Unbelievable Years, 1945 to 1969*. Pasadena: William Carey Library, 1970.

Wong, James, Larson, Peter, and Pentecost, Edward. "Missions from the Third World." *Crucial Dimensions in World Evangelization*. Glasser, Hiebert, Wagner, Winter. Pasadena: William Carey Library, 1976, 345-396.

Wynarczyk, Hilario and Semán, Pablo. "Campo evangélico y pentecostalismo en la Argentina." *El Pentecostalismo en la Argentina.* compiler, Alejandro Frigerio. Buenos Aires: Centro Editor de América Latina, 1994, 29-43.

Yamamori, Tetsunao, and Taber, Charles, eds. *Christopaganism or Indigenous.* Pasadena: William Carey Library, 1975.

Zapata, Virgilio. *Historia de la Iglesia evangélica en Guatemala.* Guatemala: CAISA, 1982.

INDEX

Vargas Sein, Teófilo, 135
Vásquez, Javier, 84
Vatican Council II, 32, 51, 62, 170-
        171, 179
Vega, Gonzalo, 98
Venezuela, 37, 46, 52, 56, 57, 89,
        135, 153, 180, 237, 241,
        243, 256, 258
Venn, Henry, 190-191
Vida Nova Church, 114
Vingren, Gunnar, 79-80, 85
Vision of the Future Church, 50, 92-
        94, 142, 201, 236
von Zinzendorf, Nicolaus, 188
Wagner, Peter, 202-203, 225, 234
Warneck, Gustav, 191
Waves of Love and Peace Church,
        96-97, 142, 223-224, 242
Wesley, John, 188
Wesley, Luis, 115
Wesleyan Church (Brazil), 49, 60
Witt, Marcos, 24
World Council of Churches, 103,
        199-200
World Evangelical Fellowship, 197,
        199-201
World Vision, 93, 257, 261
YNOL, 55
Zapata, Virgilio, 41
Zionist Church, 133